PARENTS AND EDUCATORS PRAISE THE CORE KNOWLEDGE SERIES

"Though I have twenty-five years' teaching experience, this is my first year as a **Core Knowledge** teacher. Now, for the first time in a long time, I am excited about teaching again. As for my students, I seriously believe that many of them would eliminate summer vacation to get on with the business of learning!"

—*Joan Falbey, teacher, Three Oaks Elementary School, Fort Myers, Florida*

"Thank you for writing such wonderful books! My children and I have thoroughly enjoyed them. Your books have been a great source and a guide to us. I have a degree in elementary education and I think this is the best curriculum I have encountered."

—*Barbara de la Aguilera, parent, Miami, Florida*

"For three years, we have been using elements of the **Core Knowledge** program, and I have watched as it invigorated our students. These books should be in every classroom in America."

—*Richard E. Smith, principal, Northside Elementary School, Palestine, Texas*

"Hirsch made it quite clear (in *Cultural Literacy*) that respect for cultural diversity is important but is best achieved when young people have adequate background knowledge of mainstream culture. In order for a truly democratic and economically sound society to be maintained, young people must have access to the best knowledge available so that they can understand the issues, express their viewpoints, and act accordingly."

—*James P. Comer, M.D., professor, Child Study Center,*
Yale University (in Parents *magazine)*

The
CORE KNOWLEDGE
Series

Resource Books for
Kindergarten Through Grade Six

Bantam Books Trade Paperbacks

New York

Core Knowledge®

What Your Second Grader Needs to Know

Fundamentals of a Good Second-Grade Education

(Revised Edition)

Edited by E. D. Hirsch, Jr.

2014 Bantam Books Trade Paperback Edition

Copyright © 1991, 1998, 2014 by The Core Knowledge Foundation

Published in the United States by Bantam Books, an imprint of Random House, a division of Random House LLC, a Penguin Random House Company, New York.

BANTAM BOOKS and the HOUSE colophon are registered trademarks of Random House LLC.

CORE KNOWLEDGE is a trademark of the Core Knowledge Foundation.

Originally published in hardcover in the United States in 1991. A revised hardcover edition was published in 1998 by Doubleday, an imprint of the Knopf Doubleday Publishing Group, a division of Random House LLC, and subsequently in trade paperback in 1999 by Delta Books, an imprint of Random House, a division of Random House LLC.

Library of Congress Cataloging-in-Publication Data
Hirsch, E. D. (Eric Donald).
What your second grader needs to know : fundamentals of a good second-grade education / E.D. Hirsch, Jr. — Revised and updated.
pages cm
Includes index.
ISBN 978-0-553-39240-1 (paperback) — ISBN 978-0-553-39241-8 (ebook)
1. Second grade (Education)—Curricula—United States.   2. Curriculum planning—United States.   I. Title.
LB15712nd .H57   2014
372.19—dc23
2014004299

Printed in the United States of America on acid-free paper

www.bantamdell.com

2 4 6 8 9 7 5 3 1

Book design by Diane Hobbing

Editor-in-Chief of the Core Knowledge Series: E. D. Hirsch, Jr.

Editor, revised edition: John Holdren

Project Manager and Art Editor: Alice Wiggins

Writers: Diane Darst (Visual Arts); Matt Davis (History and Geography, Visual Arts); Tricia Emlet (Visual Arts); John Hirsch (Mathematics); Susan Tyler Hitchcock (Science); John Holdren (Language and Literature, History and Geography, Visual Arts, Music, Mathematics, Science); Mary Beth Klee (History and Geography); Janet Smith (Music)

Artists and Photographers: AllyAnne Downs, Jonathan Fuqua, Julie Grant, Steve Henry, Hannah Holdren, Sara Holdren, Phillip Jones, Bob Kirchman, Gail McIntosh, Jeanne Nicholson Siler, Nic Siler

Art and Photo Research, Art and Text Permissions: Emma Earnst, Christina Erland, Liza Green, Erin Lynch, Julian Molitz, Jamie Talbot

Research Assistant: Brandi Jordan Johnson

Computer Assistance: Barbara Fortsch

Acknowledgments

This series has depended on the help, advice, and encouragement of some two thousand people. Some of those singled out here already know the depth of our gratitude; others may be surprised to find themselves thanked publicly for help they gave quietly and freely for the sake of the enterprise alone. To helpers named and unnamed we are deeply grateful.

Advisors on Multiculturalism: Minerva Allen, Barbara Carey, Frank de Varona, Mick Fedullo, Dorothy Fields, Elizabeth Fox-Genovese, Marcia Galli, Dan Garner, Henry Louis Gates, Cheryl Kulas, Joseph C. Miller, Gerry Raining Bird, Connie Rocha, Dorothy Small, Sharon Stewart-Peregoy, Sterling Stuckey, Marlene Walking Bear, Lucille Watahomigie, Ramona Wilson

Advisors on Elementary Education: Joseph Adelson, Isobel Beck, Paul Bell, Carl Bereiter, David Bjorklund, Constance Jones, Elizabeth LaFuze, J. P. Lutz, Sandra Scarr, Nancy Stein, Phyllis Wilkin

Advisors on Technical Subject Matter: Marilyn Jager Adams, Karima-Diane Alavi, Richard Anderson, Judith Birsh, Cheryl Cannard, Barbara Foorman, Paul Gagnon, David Geary, Andrew Gleason, Ted Hirsch, Henry Holt, Blair Jones, Connie Juel, Eric Karell, Morton Keller, Joseph Kett, Charles Kimball, Mary Beth Klee, Barbara Lachman, Karen Lang, Michael Lynch, Diane McGuinness, Sheelagh McGurn, Joseph C. Miller, Jean Osborn, Vikas Pershad, Margaret Reed, Donna Rehorn, Gilbert Roy, Nancy Royal, Mark Rush, Janet Smith, Ralph Smith, Keith Stanovich, Paula Stanovich, Nancy Strother, Nancy Summers, Marlene Thompson, James Trefil, Patricia Wattenmaker, Nancy Wayne, Christiana Whittington, Linda Williams, Lois Williams

Conferees, March 1990: Nola Bacci, Joan Baratz-Snowden, Thomasyne Beverley, Thomas Blackton, Angela Burkhalter, Monty Caldwell, Thomas M. Carroll, Laura Chapman, Carol Anne Collins, Lou Corsaro, Henry Cotton, Anne Coughlin, Arletta Dimberg, Debra P. Douglas, Patricia Edwards, Janet Elenbogen, Mick Fedullo, Michele Fomalont, Mamon Gibson, Jean Haines, Barbara Hayes, Stephen Herzog, Helen Kelley, Brenda King, John King, Elizabeth La-

Fuze, Diana Lam, Nancy Lambert, Doris Langaster, Richard LaPointe, Lloyd Leverton, Madeline Long, Allen Luster, Joseph McGeehan, Janet McLin, Gloria McPhee, Marcia Mallard, William J. Maloney, Judith Matz, John Morabito, Robert Morrill, Roberta Morse, Karen Nathan, Dawn Nichols, Valeta Paige, Mary Perrin, Joseph Piazza, Jeanne Price, Marilyn Rauth, Judith Raybern, Mary Reese, Richard Rice, Wallace Saval, John Saxon, Jan Schwab, Ted Sharp, Diana Smith, Richard Smith, Trevanian Smith, Carol Stevens, Nancy Summers, Michael Terry, Robert Todd, Elois Veltman, Sharon Walker, Mary Ann Ward, Charles Whitten, Penny Williams, Clarke Worthington, Jane York

Schools: Special thanks to Three Oaks Elementary for piloting the original *Core Knowledge Sequence* in 1990. And thanks to the schools that have offered their advice and suggestions for improving the *Core Knowledge Sequence,* including (in alphabetical order): Academy Charter School (CO); Coleman Elementary (TX); Coral Reef Elementary (FL); Coronado Village Elementary (TX); Crooksville Elementary (OH); Crossroads Academy (NH); Gesher Jewish Day School (VA); Hawthorne Elementary (TX); Highland Heights Elementary (IN); Joella Good Elementary (FL); Mohegan School–CS 67 (NY); The Morse School (MA); Nichols Hills Elementary (OK); North East Elementary (MD); Ridge View Elementary (WA); R. N. Harris Elementary (NC); Southside Elementary (FL); Thomas Johnson Elementary (MD); Three Oaks Elementary (FL); Vienna Elementary (MD); Washington Core Knowledge School (CO). And to the many other schools teaching Core Knowledge—too many to name here, and some of whom we have yet to discover—our heartfelt thanks for "sharing the knowledge"!

Benefactors: The Brown Foundation, The Challenge Foundation, Mrs. E. D. Hirsch, Sr., The Walton Family Foundation.

Our grateful acknowledgment to these persons does not imply that we have taken their (sometimes conflicting) advice in every case, or that each of them endorses all aspects of this project. Responsibility for final decisions must rest with the editors alone. Suggestions for improvements are very welcome, and we wish to thank in advance those who send advice for revising and improving this series.

This book is dedicated to the staff of the Core Knowledge Foundation.
They work tirelessly to fulfill the mission of
"Educational Excellence and Equity for All Children."

A Note to Teachers

We hope you will find this book useful, especially those of you who are teaching in the growing network of Core Knowledge schools. Throughout the book, we have addressed the suggested activities and explanations to "Parents," since you as teachers know your students and will have ideas about how to use the content of this book in relation to the lessons and activities you plan. If you are interested in the ideas of teachers in Core Knowledge schools, please write or call the Core Knowledge Foundation (801 East High Street, Charlottesville, VA 22902; 434-977-7550) for information on ordering collections of lessons created and shared by teachers in Core Knowledge schools. Many of these teacher-created lessons are available through the Core Knowledge website: www.coreknowledge.org.

Author's earnings from sales of the Core Knowledge Series go to the nonprofit Core Knowledge Foundation. E. D. Hirsch, Jr., receives no remuneration for editing the series nor any other remuneration from the Core Knowledge Foundation.

Contents

I. Language and Literature

II. History and Geography

III. Visual Arts

IV. Music

V. Mathematics

VI. Science

General Introduction to the Core Knowledge Series

Schools and Your Child

If Charles Dickens were alive today and observing the state of American schools, he might be tempted to comment anew that it is the best of times and the worst of times. Seldom has there been more attention and energy aimed at our nation's education system. Unacceptable inequities in achievement between income and ethnic groups, long viewed with alarm, are being addressed with unprecedented urgency and resources. Years of dismay over lackluster performance have created a sense of crisis, even fear, that if we do not set our educational house in order, American competitiveness, our economy, and even our way of life are at risk. The response has been an unprecedented era of educational dynamism and innovation. Seen through this lens, it might seem to be the best of times for American education.

Yet for all our admirable focus, urgency, and investment, we have surprisingly little to show for it. Reading test scores for American seventeen-year-olds, the ultimate report card for our schools, have hardly budged in forty years. That's two generations with no discernible progress. How can this be? We have tried testing every child and holding teachers accountable. We have built charter schools and filled classrooms with computers. We have even made it the law of the land that every child read at grade level, but to no avail. Surely it is the worst of times.

Do not blame teachers. They are among our most committed and generous-spirited citizens. We have not lacked urgency, idealism, or even resources. What we have lacked is a coherent plan for educating all children to proficiency.

The book you hold in your hands exemplifies an essential building block of that coherent plan.

Why Knowledge Matters in the Era of Google

American public education sprang from the nineteenth-century idea of the common school. We sent our children to learn reading and writing, but also a common curriculum of history, geography, math, and other subjects. Such schools also strived to create virtuous, civic-minded citizens for the new nation. As America matured and became more diverse, the concept of a common curriculum gradually melted away. Today we have all but abandoned the notion that there is a body of knowledge that every child should learn in school, and the broad mission of education is to maximize each individual's potential. But there is good reason to believe that the idea of common schooling is more relevant and effective than ever before.

Ask yourself: Would I rather have my child go to school to gain knowledge of history, science, art, and music? Or should schools emphasize skills such as critical thinking and problem solving? The answer should ideally be both. Knowledge and skills are not two different things; they are two sides of the same coin. Thinking skills are what psychologists call "domain specific." In plain English, this means that you cannot think critically about a subject you know little about. If we want our children to be broadly competent readers, thinkers, and problem solvers, they must have a rich, broad store of background knowledge to call upon, enabling them to flex those mental muscles.

Unfortunately, too many of our schools have lost touch with this critical insight. It is commonly believed to be a fool's errand to think we can teach children all they need to know—far better simply to spark in children a lifelong love of learning. Indeed, many well-intentioned educators believe that the in-depth study of a few topics, practice with a variety of "thinking skills," and access to the Internet are all anyone needs today. Why clutter our minds with facts and trivia when you can just Google them? Today's classroom and curriculum, it is commonly argued, should be built around "twenty-first-century skills" such as media literacy and working cooperatively to solve "authentic" problems. These are the skills that will ensure a lifetime of learning, productivity, and engaged citizenship. The rest is mere trivia. Right?

On its surface, the idea that skills are more important than knowledge has a basic, commonsense appeal. Why should your child learn about the Civil War, the water cycle, or who painted *The Starry Night*? What child hasn't asked, "Why do we need to know this?" Unfortunately, this benign, even obvious-sounding idea contains a great paradox: it takes knowledge to gain knowledge. Those who repudiate a coherent, knowledge-rich curriculum on the grounds that you can always look things up have failed to learn an important lesson from cognitive science: deemphasizing factual knowledge actually prevents children from looking things up effectively. When you have just a little bit of information about a subject, you cannot readily evaluate the importance of new knowledge. When you know nothing, you're flying blind, like reading a book whose words you don't know. Thus, emphasizing procedural skill at the expense of factual knowledge hinders children from learning to learn. Yes, the Internet has placed a wealth of information at our fingertips. But to be able to use that information—to absorb it, to add to our knowledge—we must already possess a storehouse of knowledge. That is the paradox disclosed by cognitive research.

Common Knowledge, Not "One Size Fits All"

All children are different. Similar to the idea that skills are more important than knowledge, there is a warm, intuitive appeal to the idea that we should tailor schooling to allow every child to find what most excites and engages him, and let those interests drive his "child-centered" education. But again, this ignores some fundamental facts about how we learn.

Language and vocabulary—like critical thinking and problem solving—also depend a great deal on a broad base of shared knowledge. When a sportscaster describes a surprising performance by an underdog basketball team as "a Cinderella story," or when a writer compares an ill-fated couple to Romeo and Juliet, it is assumed that the audience will know and understand the reference. So much of our language is dependent on a shared body of knowledge. Yes, you must know the words. But you must also understand the context in order to understand and be understood. The word "shot," for example, means something different in a doctor's office, on a basketball court, or when a repairman says your dishwasher is beyond fixing. Fluency depends on context, and context is largely a function of shared background knowledge.

Yet it remains all too easy to deride a knowledge-rich curriculum as "mere facts" and "rote learning." The idea that all children should be taught a common body of knowledge to enable them to read, communicate, and work cooperatively with others does sound old-fashioned, but the overwhelming evidence argues that this is precisely the case. Learning builds on learning: children (and adults) gain new knowledge only by augmenting what they already know. It is essential to establish solid foundations of knowledge in the early grades, when children are most receptive, because for the vast majority of children, academic deficiencies from the first six grades can permanently impair the success of later learning. Poor performance of American students in middle and high school can be traced to shortcomings inherited from elementary schools that have not imparted to children the knowledge and skills they need for further learning.

All of the highest-achieving and most egalitarian elementary school systems in the world (such as those in Sweden, France, and Japan) teach their children a specific core of knowledge in each of the first six grades, thus enabling all children to enter each new grade with a secure foundation for further learning. U.S. schools, with their high student mobility rates, would especially benefit from a carefully sequenced core curriculum in the elementary and middle school years.

Commonly Shared Knowledge Makes Schooling More Effective

We know that the one-on-one tutorial is the most effective form of schooling, in part because a parent or teacher can provide tailor-made instruction for the individual child. But in a non-tutorial situation—in, for example, a typical classroom with twenty-five or more students—the instructor cannot effectively impart new knowledge to all the students unless each one shares the background knowledge upon which the lesson is being built.

Consider this scenario. In third grade, Ms. Franklin is about to begin a unit on early explorers—Columbus, Magellan, and others. In her class she has some students who were in Mr. Washington's second-grade class last year and some students who were in Ms. Johnson's second-grade class. She also has a few students who have moved in from other towns. As Ms. Franklin begins the unit on explorers, she asks the children to look at a globe and use their fingers to trace a route across the Atlantic Ocean from Europe to North America. The students who had Mr. Washington look blankly at her: they didn't learn that last year. The students who had Ms. Johnson, however, eagerly point to the proper places on the globe, while two of the students who came from other towns pipe up and say, "Columbus and Magellan again? We did that last year."

When all the students in a class share the relevant background knowledge, a classroom can begin to approach the effectiveness of a tutorial. Even when some children in a class do not have elements of the knowledge they were supposed to acquire in previous grades, the existence of a specifically defined core makes it possible for the teacher or parent to identify and fill the gaps, giving all students a chance to fulfill their potential in later grades.

Commonly Shared Knowledge Makes Schooling Fairer and More Democratic

When all the children who enter a grade can be assumed to share some of the same building blocks of knowledge, and when the teacher knows exactly what those building blocks are, then all the students are empowered to learn. In our current system, children from disadvantaged backgrounds too often suffer from unmerited low expectations that translate into watered-down curricula. But if we specify the core of knowledge that all children should share, then we can guarantee equal access to that knowledge and compensate for the academic advantages some students are offered at home. In a Core Knowledge school, all children enjoy the benefits of important, challenging knowledge that will provide the foundation for successful later learning.

Commonly Shared Knowledge Helps Create Cooperation and Solidarity in Our Schools and Nation

Diversity is a hallmark and strength of our nation. American classrooms are usually made up of students from a variety of cultural backgrounds, and those different cultures should be honored by all students. At the same time, education should create a school-based culture that is common and welcoming to all because it includes knowledge of many cultures and gives all students, no matter what their background, a common foundation for understanding our cultural diversity.

Commonly Shared Knowledge Creates the Conditions That Make Higher-Order Thinking Possible

"We don't just read about science. We do science," a teacher in New York City recently wrote. One of the greatest misconceptions in contemporary education is the idea that in order to best prepare students for college and careers, we should train them to "think like an expert." In other words, we should help them understand and practice what scientists, historians, and other highly skilled professionals do. But it is clear from cognitive science that in order to think like an expert, you must know what the expert knows. Unfortunately, there are no shortcuts to expertise. Deep knowledge and practice are essential. Yet our schools try to teach children to engage in learning by doing, under the assumption that skills trump knowledge. They do not. You cannot have one without the other.

All of our most cherished goals for education—reading with understanding, critical thinking, and problem solving—are what psychologists call "domain-specific" skills. Simply put, there is no such thing as an all-purpose critical thinker or problem solver. Such skills are a function of your background knowledge.

What Knowledge Needs to Be Taught?

One of the primary objections to a content-rich vision of education is that it offends our democratic sensibilities. The title of this book—*What Your Second Grader Needs to Know*—can easily be viewed as presumptuous: "Who are you to say what knowledge matters? Why do you get to decide what goes in my child's curriculum and what gets left out?" Deciding what we want our children to know can be a politically and emotionally charged minefield. No grade-by-grade sequence of knowledge or course of study will satisfy everyone. But it is educationally reckless to ignore what we know about the importance of a broad knowledge base. The effort may be difficult, but we are duty-bound to try.

The content in this and other volumes in the Core Knowledge series is based on the *Core Knowledge Sequence,* a document of specific grade-by-grade content guidelines in history, geography, mathematics, science, language arts, and fine arts. As the core of a school's curriculum, it offers a solid, coherent foundation of learning while allowing flexibility to meet local needs. The entire *Sequence,* from preschool to eighth grade, can be downloaded for free at the Core Knowledge Foundation's website (www.coreknowledge.org/download-the-sequence).

The Core Knowledge Foundation invested a considerable amount of time, energy, and resources in an attempt to find a consensus on the most enabling knowledge—the content that would best enable all children to read, write, listen, and speak with understanding.

Shortly after the establishment of the Core Knowledge Foundation in 1987, we analyzed the many reports issued by state departments of education and by professional organizations—such as the National Council of Teachers of Mathematics and the American Association for the Advancement of Science—that recommend general outcomes for elementary and secondary education. We also tabulated the knowledge and skills, through grade 6, specified in the successful educational systems of several other countries, including France, Japan, Sweden, and Germany.

In addition, we formed an advisory board on multiculturalism, which proposed a specific knowledge of diverse cultural traditions that all American children should share as part of their school-based common culture. We sent the resulting materials to three independent groups of teachers, scholars, and scientists across the country, asking them to create a master list of the knowledge children should have by the end of grade 6. About one hundred fifty education professionals (including college professors, scientists, and administrators) were involved in this initial step.

These items were amalgamated into a master plan, and further groups of teachers and specialists were asked to agree on a grade-by-grade sequence of the items. That sequence was then sent to some one hundred educators and specialists who participated in a national conference to develop a working agreement on an appropriate core of knowledge for the first six grades; kindergarten, grades 7 and 8, and preschool were subsequently added to the *Core Knowledge Sequence.*

This important meeting took place in March 1990. The conferees were elementary school teachers, curriculum specialists, scientists, science writers, officers of national organizations, representatives of ethnic groups, district superintendents, and school principals from across the country. A total of twenty-four working groups decided on revisions to the *Core Knowledge Sequence.* The resulting provisional sequence was further fine-tuned during a year of implementation at a pioneering school, Three Oaks Elementary, in Lee County, Florida.

In only a few years, many more schools—urban and rural, rich and poor, public and private—joined in the effort to teach Core Knowledge. Based largely on suggestions from these schools, the *Core Knowledge Sequence* was revised in 1995; separate guidelines were added for kindergarten, and a few topics in other grades were added, omitted, or moved from one grade to another, in order to create an even more coherent sequence for learning. Because the *Sequence* is intended to be a living document, it has been—and will continue to be—periodically updated and revised. In general, however, there is more stability than change in the *Sequence.*

The purpose of the *Core Knowledge Sequence* is not to impose a canon. It is an attempt to *report* on a canon—to identify the most valuable, empowering knowledge across subject areas, and to create a plan for imparting it from the first days of school.

Knowledge Still Matters

This book, as well as the work of the Core Knowledge Foundation and the efforts of Core Knowledge teachers in hundreds of schools nationwide, swims strongly against the anti-knowledge tide of mediocrity that threatens to drag down our schools, our children, and ultimately our nation.

A broad, rich store of background knowledge is not merely nice to have. Knowledge is the essential raw material of thinking. Cognitive scientist Daniel Willingham observes, "Knowledge is not only cumulative, it grows exponentially. Those with a rich base of factual knowledge find it easier to learn more—the rich get richer. In addition, factual knowledge enhances cognitive processes such as problem solving and reasoning. The richer the knowledge base, the more smoothly and effectively these cognitive processes—the very ones that teachers target—operate. So, the more knowledge students accumulate, the smarter they become."

If all of our children are to be fully educated and participate equally in civic life, then we must provide each of them with the shared body of knowledge that makes literacy and communication possible. This concept, so central to the new Common Core State Standards adopted by more than forty states, and to the Core Knowledge Foundation's goal of equity and excellence in education, manifests itself in the *Core Knowledge Sequence*—and in these popular grade-by-grade books. It is a pleasure to introduce this latest refinement of them to a new generation of readers.

E. D. Hirsch, Jr.
Charlottesville, Virginia

I
Language and Literature

Reading, Writing, and Your Second Grader: A Note to Parents

In the Core Knowledge books for kindergarten and first grade, we described some features of an effective reading and writing program in schools. A good program, we said, not only is rich in literature but also presents varied opportunities for a child to work and play with letters and sounds. An effective program presents important skills sequentially, with plenty of practice and review. It includes phonics and decoding (turning the written symbols into sounds) as well as practice at spelling, handwriting, punctuation, and grammar.

By the end of second grade, a reasonable goal is for children to become independent readers and writers. By this we don't mean that children should be able to read any book in the library or write a perfectly polished essay; rather, they should be able to read books appropriate to beginning readers, and write legibly.

Nothing is more important in a child's schooling than learning to read and write confidently by the end of first grade or more important than extending that ability by the end of second grade.

Based on authoritative advice from mainstream scientific research, the Core Knowledge Foundation has compiled a description of reading and writing goals that a school should work to achieve with *all* students in second grade. Those goals are included in the *Core Knowledge Sequence*, the curriculum guidelines upon which this book is based, and in the *Core Knowledge Language Arts Program* used in schools across the country. Parents who wish to have some benchmarks by which to gauge the adequacy and effectiveness of the reading and writing programs in their child's school should visit:
https://www.coreknowledge.org
for information on downloading or ordering a copy of the *Core Knowledge Sequence*.

In addition, as parents, you can do many things to help your children.

- Read aloud regularly and talk with your children about what they are reading
- Take your children to the library
- Help your children write thank-you notes and letters to relatives
- Play word games like Hangman or Scrabble Junior
- Check on homework
- Be encouraging and supportive of your children's efforts to learn more about language

Suggested Resources for Parents and Children

The resources recommended here are meant to supplement at home the more thorough and systematic instruction that should take place in the classroom.

Ready . . . Set . . . Read: The Beginning Reader's Treasury and *Ready . . . Set . . . Read—and Laugh! A Funny Treasury for Beginning Readers*, compiled by Joanna Cole and Stephanie Calmenson (Doubleday, 1990 and 1995). Two nicely illustrated collections containing stores, poems, riddles, and word games by well-known writers such as Arnold Lobel and Eve Merriam.

Spider. Colorful, attractive artwork illustrates each issue of this monthly magazine for children from six to nine years old, which features many stories, activities, and puzzles, with no advertising. Many libraries carry the magazine. For subscription information, go to the Cricket Magazine Group website (http://www.cricketmag.com).

Literature

Introduction

For your second grader, we offer a selection of poetry, stories, and myths. The poetry includes traditional rhymes as well as a few favorites by modern writers. We encourage you to read many more poems with your child, to delight in the play of language, and occasionally to encourage your child to memorize a favorite poem.

The stories presented here are mostly traditional tales that have stood the test of time. Some of the selections from other lands may not be familiar to American readers, but by including them here we hope to make them so. Parents and teachers may want to connect the folktales we include from China, Japan, and India with the introductions to those lands in the World History and Geography section of this book. We also offer a selection of Greek myths, which you can tie in with the discussion of ancient Greece in the World History and Geography section.

The stories here are meant to complement, not replace, stories with controlled vocabularies and syntax that children may be given in school as part of their instruction in reading. While some second graders may be able to read the stories in this book on their own, those who find the language too complex can readily understand and enjoy these stories when they are read aloud and talked about with an adult. You may also want to try some "shared reading," in which you read aloud parts of a story and your child reads aloud parts to you.

Many of these stories convey traditional values such as honesty, courage, generosity, and diligence. Those parents who hope that schooling will instill ethical values can feel somewhat reassured if their children are being taught good literature. Next to human role models who exemplify the desired virtues, good literature is one of the best means of instilling ethical values. Plato said that stories are the most important part of early education and advised parents and teachers to take great care in choosing the right stories: "Let them fashion the mind with such tales even more fondly than they mold the body."

We offer the stories in this book as a good starting point, and we encourage you and your child to explore further. Your local library has a treasury of good books, fiction and nonfiction. You might want to consult the lists of recommended works in such guides as:

Books That Build Character by William Kilpatrick et al. (Simon and Schuster/ Touchstone, 1994)

Books to Build On: A Grade-by-Grade Resource Guide for Parents and Teachers edited by John Holdren and E. D. Hirsch, Jr. (Dell, 1996)

The New York Times Parent's Guide to the Best Books for Children by Eden Ross Lipson (Harmony, revised and updated 2000)

Poetry

Bed in Summer

by Robert Louis Stevenson

In winter I get up at night
And dress by yellow candle-light.
In summer, quite the other way,
I have to go to bed by day.

I have to go to bed and see
The birds still hopping on the tree,
Or hear the grown-up people's feet
Still going past me in the street.

And does it not seem hard to you,
When all the sky is clear and blue,
And I should like so much to play,
To have to go to bed by day?

Buffalo Dusk

by Carl Sandburg

The buffaloes are gone.
And those who saw the buffaloes are gone.
Those who saw the buffaloes by thousands and how they pawed the prairie sod
    into dust with their hoofs, their great heads down pawing on in a great pag-
    eant of dusk,
Those who saw the buffaloes are gone.
And the buffaloes are gone.

Caterpillars
by Aileen Fisher

What do caterpillars do?
Nothing much but chew and chew.

What do caterpillars know?
Nothing much but how to grow.

They just eat what by and by
will make them be a butterfly,

But that is more than I can do
however much I chew and chew.

Make a Connection
Learn more about caterpillars
and butterflies on page 443.

Bee! I'm Expecting You!
by Emily Dickinson

Bee! I'm expecting you!
Was saying Yesterday
To Somebody you know
That you were due——

The Frogs got Home last Week——
Are settled, and at work——
Birds, mostly back——
The Clover warm and thick——

You'll get my Letter by
The seventeenth; Reply
Or better, be with me——
Yours, Fly.

Hurt No Living Thing

by Christina Rossetti

Hurt no living thing;
Ladybird, nor butterfly,
Nor moth with dusty wing,
Nor cricket chirping cheerily,
Nor grasshopper so light of leap,
Nor dancing gnat, nor beetle fat,
Nor harmless worms that creep.

Discovery

by Harry Behn

In a puddle left from last week's rain,
A friend of mine whose name is Joe
Caught a tadpole, and showed me where
Its froggy legs were beginning to grow.

Then we turned over a musty log,
With lichens on it in a row,
And found some fiddleheads of ferns
Uncoiling out of the moss below.

We hunted around, and saw the first
Jack-in-the-pulpits beginning to show,
And even discovered under a rock
Where spotted salamanders go.

I learned all this one morning from Joe,
But how much more there is to know!

Harriet Tubman

by Eloise Greenfield

Harriet Tubman didn't take no stuff
Wasn't scared of nothing neither
Didn't come in this world to be no slave
And wasn't going to stay one either

"Farewell!" she sang to her friends one night
She was mighty sad to leave 'em
But she ran away that dark, hot night
Ran looking for her freedom

She ran to the woods and she ran through the woods
With the slave catchers right behind her
And she kept on going till she got to the North
Where those mean men couldn't find her

Nineteen times she went back South
To get three hundred others
She ran for her freedom nineteen times
To save Black sisters and brothers

Harriet Tubman didn't take no stuff
Wasn't scared of nothing neither
Didn't come in this world to be no slave
And didn't stay one either

And didn't stay one either

> **Make a Connection**
> Read more about Harriet
> Tubman in the History and
> Geography section of this book.

Lincoln

by Nancy Byrd Turner

There was a boy of other days,
A quiet, awkward, earnest lad,
Who trudged long weary miles to get
A book on which his heart was set—
And then no candle had!

He was too poor to buy a lamp
But very wise in woodmen's ways.
He gathered seasoned bough and stem,
And crisping leaf, and kindled them
Into a ruddy blaze.

Then as he lay full length and read,
The firelight flickered on his face,
And etched his shadow on the gloom,
And made a picture in the room,
In that most humble place.

The hard years came, the hard years went,
But, gentle, brave, and strong of will,
He met them all. And when today
We see his pictured face, we say,
"There's light upon it still."

The Night Before Christmas

(Originally titled A Visit from St. Nicholas)

by Clement C. Moore

'Twas the night before Christmas,
When all through the house
Not a creature was stirring, not even a mouse.
The stockings were hung by the chimney with care,
In hopes that St. Nicholas soon would be there.
The children were nestled all snug in their beds,
While visions of sugarplums danced in their heads.
And mama in her kerchief, and I in my cap
Had just settled our brains for a long winter's nap,
When out on the lawn there arose such a clatter,
I sprang from my bed to see what was the matter.
Away to the window I flew like a flash,
Tore open the shutters and threw up the sash.
The moon on the breast of the new-fallen snow,
Gave the luster of midday to objects below.
When what to my wondering eyes should appear,
But a miniature sleigh and eight tiny reindeer
With a little old driver so lively and quick
I knew in a moment it must be St. Nick.
More rapid than eagles his coursers they came,
And he whistled, and shouted, and called them by name:
"Now, Dasher! Now, Dancer! Now, Prancer and Vixen!
On, Comet! On, Cupid! On, Donder and Blitzen!
To the top of the porch! To the top of the wall!
Now dash away! Dash away! Dash away all!"
As dry leaves that before the wild hurricane fly,
When they meet with an obstacle, mount to the sky,
So up to the housetop the coursers they flew,

With a sleigh full of toys and St. Nicholas, too.
And then, in a twinkling, I heard on the roof
The prancing and pawing of each little hoof.
As I drew in my head and was turning around,
Down the chimney St. Nicholas came with a bound!
He was dressed all in fur from his head to his foot,
And his clothes were all tarnished with ashes and soot;
A bundle of toys he had flung on his back,
And he looked like a peddler just opening his pack.
His eyes—how they twinkled, his dimples how merry!
His cheeks were like roses, his nose like a cherry!
His droll little mouth was drawn up in a bow,
And the beard on his chin was as white as the snow.
The stump of a pipe he held tight in his teeth,
And the smoke, it encircled his head like a wreath.
He had a broad face and a little round belly,
That shook when he laughed like a bowl full of jelly.
He was chubby and plump, a right jolly old elf,
And I laughed when I saw him in spite of myself!
A wink of his eye and a twist of his head
Soon gave me to know I had nothing to dread.
He spoke not a word, but went straight to his work,
And filled all the stockings; then turned with a jerk,
And laying his finger aside of his nose,
And giving a nod, up the chimney he rose!
He sprang to the sleigh, to his team gave a whistle,
And away they all flew like the down of a thistle.
But I heard him exclaim, 'ere he drove out of sight—
"Happy Christmas to all, and to all a good night!"

Something Told the Wild Geese

by Rachel Field

Something told the wild geese
It was time to go.
Though the fields lay golden
Something whispered, —"Snow."
Leaves were green and stirring,
Berries, luster-glossed,
But beneath warm feathers
Something cautioned, —"Frost."
All the sagging orchards
Steamed with amber spice,
But each wild breast stiffened
At remembered ice.
Something told the wild geese
It was time to fly,
Summer sun was on their wings,
Winter in their cry.

Rudolph Is Tired of the City

by Gwendolyn Brooks

These buildings are too close to me.
I'd like to PUSH away.
I'd like to live in the country,
And spread my arms all day.

I'd like to spread my breath out, too—
As farmers' sons and daughters do.

I'd tend the cows and chickens.
I'd do the other chores.
Then, all the hours left I'd go
A-SPREADING out-of-doors.

Smart

by Shel Silverstein

My dad gave me one dollar bill
'Cause I'm his smartest son,
And I swapped it for two shiny quarters
'Cause two is more than one!

And then I took the quarters
And traded them to Lou
For three dimes—I guess he don't know
That three is more than two!

Just then, along came old blind Bates
And just 'cause he can't see
He gave me four nickels for my three dimes,
And four is more than three!

And I took the nickels to Hiram Coombs
Down at the seed-feed store,
And the fool gave me five pennies for them,
And five is more than four!

And then I went and showed my dad,
And he got red in the cheeks
And closed his eyes and shook his head—
Too proud of me to speak!

Who Has Seen the Wind

by Christina Rossetti

Who has seen the wind?
Neither I nor you:
But when the leaves hang trembling,
The wind is passing through.

Who has seen the wind?
Neither you nor I:
But when the leaves bow down their heads,
The wind is passing by.

Windy Nights

by Robert Louis Stevenson

Whenever the moon and stars are set,
Whenever the wind is high,
All night long in the dark and wet,
A man goes riding by.
Late in the night when the fires are out,
Why does he gallop and gallop about?

Whenever the trees are crying aloud,
And ships are tossed at sea,
By, on the highway, low and loud,
By at the gallop goes he;
By at the gallop he goes, and then
By he comes back at the gallop again.

There Was an Old Man with a Beard

by Edward Lear

Edward Lear, an English artist and writer, was a master of the kind of humorous poem called a limerick. A limerick has five lines: the first two lines rhyme, then the next two lines rhyme, and the last line rhymes with the first two lines. The first line of a limerick often begins "There was a . . ." or "There once was a . . ." Limericks are fun to read aloud, and fun to make up; try it!

There was an Old Man with a beard,
Who said, "It is just as I feared!—
Two Owls and a Hen,
Four Larks and a Wren,
Have all built their nests in my beard!"

There Is a Young Lady, Whose Nose

by Edward Lear

There is a young lady, whose nose,
Continually prospers and grows;
When it grew out of sight,
She exclaimed in a fright,
"Oh! Farewell to the end of my nose!"

The Blind Men and the Elephant
by John Godfrey Saxe

It was six men of Hindustan,
To learning much inclined,
Who went to see the elephant
(Though all of them were blind);
That each by observation
Might satisfy his mind.

The first approached the elephant,
And happening to fall
Against his broad and sturdy side,
At once began to bawl,
"Bless me, it seems the elephant
Is very like a wall."

The second, feeling of his tusk,
Cried, "Ho! What have we here
So very round and smooth and sharp?
To me 'tis mighty clear
This wonder of an elephant
Is very like a spear."

The third approached the animal,
And happening to take
The squirming trunk within his hands,
Then boldly up and spake.
"I see," quoth he, "the elephant
Is very like a snake."

The fourth stretched out his eager hand
And felt about the knee,

"What most this mighty beast is like
Is mighty plain," quoth he;
"'Tis clear enough the elephant
Is very like a tree."

The fifth, who chanced to touch the ear
Said, "Even the blindest man
Can tell what this resembles most;
Deny the fact who can,
This marvel of an elephant
Is very like a fan."

The sixth no sooner had begun
About the beast to grope
Than, seizing on the swinging tail
That fell within his scope,
"I see," cried he, "the elephant
Is very like a rope."

And so these men of Hindustan
Disputed loud and long,
Each of his own opinion
Exceeding stiff and strong,
Though each was partly in
    the right,
And all were in the wrong!

Stories

The Fisherman and His Wife

Once there was a fisherman who lived with his wife in a little old run-down hut by the sea. Every day the fisherman went down to the sea to fish.

One day, as he sat looking into the clear, shining water, he felt a strong tug on his line. He pulled and pulled until, at last, out flopped a large golden fish. Then, all of a sudden, the fish spoke.

"Please let me go," said the fish. "I am not an ordinary fish. I am an enchanted prince. Put me back in the water and let me live!"

"Swim away!" said the fisherman. "I would not eat a fish that can talk!"

At the end of the day, the fisherman went back to his wife and the little old run-down hut.

"Did you catch anything today?" she asked.

"No," said the fisherman. "I did catch one fish, but he told me he was an enchanted prince and asked me to throw him back, so I did."

"You fool!" said the wife. "That was a magic fish! You should have asked him for something."

"Like what?" said the fisherman.

"Go back and ask him to use his magic to transform this dinky hut into a charming cottage."

The fisherman did not want to go, but he did not want to get into a fight with his wife, either. So he made his way back to the sea.

When he arrived, the water was no longer clear and shining. It was dull and greenish.

The fisherman called:

"Hear me, please, O magic fish. My wife has sent me with a wish."

The fish swam up to the surface and asked, "What does she want?"

"She says she wants to live in a charming cottage," said the fisherman.

"Go home," said the fish. "She has her cottage."

The fisherman went home. Sure enough, there was his wife, standing in the

doorway of a charming cottage. The cottage had a front yard, with a garden and some chickens and geese pecking at the ground. Inside there was a living room, a kitchen, a dining room, and a bedroom.

"Wonderful!" said the fisherman. "This is sure to make you very happy!"

The fisherman's wife *was* happy—for about a week.

Then she said, "Husband, I am sick and tired of this tiny little cottage. I want to live in a big stone castle. Go and ask the fish to give us a castle."

"But, wife," said the fisherman, "he has just given us this cottage. If I go back again so soon, he may be angry with me."

"Go and ask!" said the wife.

The fisherman shook his head and mumbled to himself, "It's not right." But he did as he was told.

When he reached the sea, the water had turned dark purple and gray. The fisherman called:

"Hear me, please, O magic fish. My wife has sent me with a wish."

When the fish swam up, the fisherman said, "My wife wishes to live in a big stone castle."

"Go home," said the fish. "You will find her in a castle."

When the fisherman got back, he could hardly believe his eyes. The charming cottage had been replaced by a large stone castle. A servant lowered a drawbridge for him. The fisherman went across the bridge and into the castle, where he found two servants sweeping a smooth marble floor. The walls were covered with lovely tapestries. Crystal chandeliers hung from the ceilings. His wife stood in the center of the room, next to a table piled high with delicious foods.

"Now, indeed, you will be content," said the fisherman to his wife. And she was—until the next morning.

When the sun rose, the fisherman's wife poked her husband in the ribs and said, "Husband, get up. Go to the fish at once and tell him that I wish to be queen of all the land."

"Heavens!" cried the fisherman. "I can't ask for that!"

"Go and ask him!" said his wife.

The dejected fisherman walked to the sea. The water was black. It bubbled and gave off a foul smell. The fisherman hesitated, and then called:

"Hear me, please, O magic fish. My wife has sent me with a wish."

The fish swam up and asked, "Now what does she want?"

With his head hung low, the fisherman said, "My wife wishes to be queen of all the land."

"Go home," said the fish. "She is already queen."

The fisherman went home and found that the castle had grown even larger. It had tall turrets on each corner and crimson flags flapping in the wind. Two sentries in suits of armor stood at the door.

The sentries escorted the fisherman inside, where he found his wife sitting on a high throne studded with diamonds. She wore a long silk dress and a golden crown. In her hand she held a scepter studded with sapphires and pearls. On one side of her stood barons, dukes, and duchesses. On the other side stood a line of ladies-in-waiting, each one shorter than the one before.

"So," said the fisherman, "now you are queen."

"Indeed," said his wife haughtily.

"Well, then," said the fisherman. "I suppose there is nothing more to wish for."

But that very evening, as the sun went down and the moon began to rise in the sky, the fisherman's wife sent for her husband.

"Husband!" she bellowed, "it displeases me that the sun and moon will not rise and set at my command. Go to the fish and tell him I must have the power to make the sun and the moon rise and set whenever I choose. See that it is done immediately!"

The fisherman walked back to the sea. He felt sick all over. At the seaside, thunder roared and lightning flashed. Huge dark waves crashed on the shore. The fisherman had to shout:

"Hear me, please, O magic fish. My wife has sent me with a wish."

The fish swam up and asked, "What does she want?"

The fisherman replied, "My wife wants the power to make the sun and the moon rise and set whenever she chooses."

This time, all the fish said was "Go home." And so the fisherman made his way home. There, he found his wife sitting in the old run-down hut. And there the two of them live to this very day.

Talk

(Retold by Harold Courlander and George Herzog)

"Talk" is a folktale from the Ashanti people (also called Asante), who live in West Africa, in what is now the country of Ghana. Many Ashanti are farmers, and the major crops include cacao (a main ingredient in chocolate) and, as you'll see in the story, yams. To better appreciate a detail near the end of this story, it may help to know about an Ashanti tradition: almost every Ashanti man and woman once owned a carved wooden stool. Besides being useful, the stool, according to tradition, embodied the owner's spirit.

Once, not far from the city of Accra on the Gulf of Guinea, a country man went out to his garden to dig up some yams to take to market. While he was digging, one of the yams said to him:

"Well, at last you're here. You never weeded me, but now you come around with your digging stick. Go away and leave me alone!"

The farmer turned around and looked at his cow in amazement. The cow was chewing on her cud and looked at him.

"Did you say something?" he asked.

The cow kept on chewing and said nothing, but the man's dog spoke up.

"It wasn't the cow who spoke to you," the dog said. "It was the yam. The yam says leave him alone."

The man became angry because his dog had never talked before, and he didn't like his tone besides. So he took his knife and cut a branch from a palm tree to whip his dog. Just then the palm tree said:

"Put that branch down!"

The man was getting very upset about the way things were going, and he started to throw the palm branch away, but the palm branch said:

"Man, put me down softly!"

He put the branch down gently on a stone, and the stone said:

"Hey, take that thing off me!"

This was enough and the frightened farmer started to run for his village. On the way he met a fisherman going the other way with a fish trap on his head.

"What's the hurry?" the fisherman asked.

"My yam said, 'Leave me alone!' Then the dog said, 'Listen to what the yam says!' When I went to whip the dog with a palm branch the tree said, 'Put that branch down!' Then the palm branch said, 'Do it softly!' Then the stone said, 'Take that thing off me!'"

"Is that all?" the man with the fish trap asked. "Is that so frightening?"

"Well," the man's fish trap said, "did he take it off the stone?"

"Wah!" the fisherman shouted. He threw the fish trap on the ground and began to run with the farmer, and on the trail they met a weaver with a bundle of cloth on his head.

"Where are you going in such a rush?" he asked them.

"My yam said, 'Leave me alone!'" the farmer said. "The dog said, 'Listen to what the yam says!' The tree said, 'Put that branch down!' The branch said, 'Do it softly!' And the stone said, 'Take that thing off me!'"

"And then," the fisherman continued, "the fish trap said, 'Did he take it off?'"

"That's nothing to get excited about," the weaver said, "no reason at all."

"Oh yes it is," his bundle of cloth said. "If it happened to you, you'd run too!"

"Wah!" the weaver shouted. He threw his bundle on the trail and started running with the other men.

They came panting to the ford in the river and found a man bathing.

"Are you chasing a gazelle?" he asked them.

The first man said breathlessly:

"My yam talked at me and it said, 'Leave me alone!' And my dog said, 'Listen to your yam!' And when I cut myself a branch the tree said, 'Put that branch down!' And the branch said, 'Do it softly!' And the stone said, 'Take that thing off me!'"

The fisherman panted, "And my trap said, 'Did he?'"

The weaver wheezed, "My cloth spoke too!"

"Is that why you're running?" the man in the river asked.

"Well, wouldn't you run if you were in their position?" the river said.

The man jumped out of the water and began to run with the others. They ran down the main street of the village to the house of the chief. The chief's servants brought his stool out, and he came and sat on it to listen to their complaints. The men began to recite their troubles.

"I went out to my garden to dig yams," the farmer said, waving his arms. "Then everything began to talk! My yam said, 'Leave me alone!' My dog said, 'Pay attention to your yam!' The tree said, 'Put that branch down!' The branch said, 'Do it softly!' And the stone said, 'Take it off me!'"

"And my fish trap said, 'Well, did he take it off?'" the fisherman said.

"And my cloth said, 'You'd run too!'" the weaver said.

"And the river said the same," the bather said hoarsely.

The chief listened to them patiently, but he couldn't refrain from scowling.

"Now this is really a wild story," he said at last. "You'd better all go back to your work before I punish you for disturbing the peace."

So the men went away, and the chief shook his head and mumbled to himself, "Nonsense like that upsets the community."

"Fantastic, isn't it?" his stool said. "Imagine, a talking yam!"

The Emperor's New Clothes

Once there was an emperor who loved fine clothes. He did not care for hunting. He did not care for plays or opera. He was no lover of gourmet food or fine wine. His only ambition was always to be well dressed. He had a different coat for every hour of the day. He loved to walk about and show off his fancy outfits.

One day two strangers arrived in town. They were swindlers, but they said they were master weavers from a faraway land. They told the emperor that they could weave the most beautiful cloth in the world. They said that their cloth was beautiful and magical. It was specially woven so that only the most intelligent people could see it. Those who were stupid and ignorant could stare at the cloth all day and not see a thing.

"Astonishing!" thought the emperor. "I will have these men make a suit for me. When it is done, I will figure out who can see it. Then I will be able to tell which of the men who serve me are intelligent and which are fools."

The emperor gave the swindlers a purse filled with gold coins and told them to begin weaving the magic cloth right away.

The swindlers set up two looms and pretended to be weaving their wonderful cloth. But they had nothing at all on their looms.

After a few days, the emperor grew curious to see the cloth. At first he thought he might check up on the weavers himself. But then he remembered what they had said: only intelligent people could see the cloth. He was confident that he was intelligent. There could be little doubt of that. But . . . what if he was not? What if he could not see the cloth? Just to be on the safe side, he decided to send his prime minister to have a look.

"He is very intelligent," said the king. "If he can't see the cloth, I dare say nobody can!"

The emperor called for the prime minister and sent him to check up on the weavers. The prime minister went to the room and peeked in. The two swindlers were working away at their looms.

"Prime Minister!" one of the swindlers called out. "You are welcome here! Come in! Come in! Come and see the cloth we have produced." The man waved his hand at the empty loom and said, "Isn't it gorgeous?"

The prime minister squinted and rubbed his head. He did not see any cloth at all, but he did not dare to admit it. That would mean he was a fool. So he pretended he could see the cloth.

"Yes!" said the prime minister. "It is gorgeous, indeed! I like it very much! Keep up the good work!"

The prime minister turned to leave, but the second swindler called out to him, "Wait! Don't go. You must not leave without touching the cloth! I think you will be impressed. We were just saying that it is the softest cloth we have ever created."

The prime minister hesitated for a moment. Then he said, "Of course! Of course!" and walked up to one of the looms. He reached out his hand and rubbed his fingers together in the area where he thought the cloth must be. He could not feel anything, but he said, "It is very soft, indeed! Why, I have never felt anything like it!"

"Thank you!" said the first swindler. "We are pleased with what we have done. And we are making very good progress, too. But we need a bit more money—for thread and other materials. Of course, you understand."

"Of course! Of course!" said the prime minister. He reached into his pocket and pulled out a bag of coins. Then he handed the coins to the swindlers.

The prime minister went back to the emperor and told him that the cloth was quite lovely, and as soft as anything he had ever felt. He said he was confident that the emperor would like it.

That was what the emperor had hoped to hear. The next day, he went to have a look for himself. After all, if his prime minister had seen the cloth, surely he could see it, too. But when he stepped into the room where the two men had set up their looms, he saw nothing on the looms.

"This is terrible!" he thought. "I don't see anything at all. What can this mean? If the prime minister saw the cloth, it must be there. Then why can't I see it? Am I stupid? Am I unfit to be emperor? That would be the most dreadful thing that could happen to me."

But out loud he said, "It is magnificent! Truly magnificent! Why, I have never seen cloth so lovely!"

"Shall we go ahead and make you a suit, then, Your Majesty?"

"Yes, yes. By all means!" said the emperor. "You can get my measurements from the royal tailor."

The two swindlers sat up late into the night pretending to work on the suit. They wove more invisible cloth. They cut the air with scissors and stitched the wind with threadless needles.

Other noblemen came to inspect the cloth, and all of them pretended to be able to see it, for they did not wish to appear stupid. Soon the whole court was talking about the wonderful cloth and the emperor's new suit.

At last the day came when the emperor was to wear his new clothes in public.

The two swindlers presented themselves in the emperor's dressing room at daybreak.

"Here is the jacket!" said the first swindler, holding up an empty hanger.

"And here are the pants!" said the other, holding one hand in the air. "What do you think of them?"

All of the emperor's men agreed that the new clothes were splendid. The emperor took off his clothes, and the two swindlers pretended to help him put on the make-believe garments.

"Slip your left leg in here, Your Majesty. That's it! Now your right leg. Good. Now I must tell you: these pants are not like regular pants. The fabric is so light and airy that it feels like you are wearing nothing at all, but that is why they are so special!"

When the emperor had put on all of the imaginary clothes, the two swindlers led him to his looking glass.

"How handsome you look, Your Majesty!" said one of the men. All of the courtiers nodded their heads in agreement.

The emperor marched out of the dressing room and made his way out of the palace, followed by many advisors and servants. He marched down the main street of town, with soldiers and bodyguards surrounding him on all sides.

The streets were lined with great crowds. Everyone had heard about the emperor's new clothes, made of magic fabric that only the wise could see.

"How lovely the emperor's new clothes are!" one man said.

"And how well they fit him!" added a woman.

None of them would admit that they could not see a thing.

Then, a young child stepped out of the crowd and cried out, "He hasn't got anything on!"

A hush fell over the crowd. For a few seconds, nobody said anything. Then everyone began to whisper, "The child is right. The emperor isn't wearing a thing!" Then people began to giggle and laugh as they cried out, "He hasn't got any clothes on!"

At last the emperor knew he had been tricked. He tried to march back to the palace as proudly as ever. But he was blushing from head to toe, as everyone could plainly see.

How Iktomi Lost His Eyes

(A story from the Assiniboine tribe)

Iktomi was walking through the wood one afternoon when he heard a strange noise; a bird was singing in his language, Assiniboine! Each time the bird sang the song, its eyes flew from its head and perched in the top of a tall tree, and when it sang another song, its eyes fluttered back again.

Iktomi wanted to learn this trick because he thought everyone would admire his power so much that he could be a great chief someday. He asked, "Little brother, would you please show me how to do that?"

After the bird taught Iktomi how to do the trick, he warned him, "You must use this trick no more than four times."

Iktomi tried it once to make sure it worked. Sure enough, his eyes flew up to the treetop and then fluttered down again. He was so excited that he tried it a second time and a third time. And when he ran into Brother Gopher, he did it again, just to show off. Gopher was very impressed. But Iktomi forgot that he had now used the trick four times.

When he returned to camp, he gathered everyone around to watch his powerful trick. Iktomi sang the bird's song, and up flew his eyes to a treetop. Iktomi was very proud, and the people gasped. He sang again, and waited for the people to praise him. But his eyes refused to come back. Iktomi pleaded with his eyes, and the people began to laugh.

Iktomi was frightened because he had not listened to the bird's warning, and he stumbled from the camp to find the bird. He couldn't see a thing! Suddenly, he heard a little field mouse ask, "Why are you crying?" When Iktomi explained, the little field mouse felt sorry for him. "Take one of my eyes," he said, "and then you won't be afraid." Iktomi thanked the little mouse, and set out again.

Soon, he ran into a buffalo calf. "Why are you blinded in one eye?" the calf asked. When Iktomi told him, the calf said, "Take one of my eyes, and then you can find the bird." And Iktomi took one of the calf's eyes and thanked it.

Blessed with the kindness and the sight of the animals, it wasn't long before Iktomi found the bird. "Please help me," he said. "I will never again be so vain or try to be more powerful than anyone else." With this promise, the bird taught him a new song, and when Iktomi sang it, his eyes flew down from the tree and returned to his head. Happy, Iktomi set out to give the animals their own eyes back.

Check your library for funny Iktomi stories by Paul Goble, including *Iktomi and the Berries, Iktomi and the Boulder,* and *Iktomi and the Buffalo Skull* (Orchard Books).

The Magic Paintbrush

(A folktale from China)

Once upon a time, long ago in the land of China, there lived a poor orphan named Ma Liang. He had no one to care for him or protect him. So, to make a living, he gathered bundles of firewood to sell. But what he really wanted to do, more than anything else in the world, was paint. Ma Liang was so poor, however, that he could not buy even a single paintbrush.

One day, as Ma Liang passed by the village school, he saw the children busily painting pictures. "Please, sir," said Ma Liang to the teacher, "I would like to paint, but I have no brush. Will you loan me one?"

"What!" cried the teacher. "You are only a little beggar boy. Go away!"

"I may be poor," said Ma Liang, "but I *will* learn to paint!"

The next time he went to gather firewood, Ma Liang used a twig to draw birds on the ground. When he came to a stream, he dipped his hands in the water and used his wet finger to draw a fish on the rocks. That night, he used a piece of burned wood to draw animals and flowers.

Every day Ma Liang found time to make more pictures. People began to notice. "How lifelike the boy's pictures look!" they said. "That bird he has drawn looks as though it's ready to fly away. You can almost hear it sing!"

Ma Liang enjoyed hearing the people's praise, but still he thought, "If only I had a paintbrush!"

One night, after Ma Liang had worked hard all day, he fell into a deep sleep. In a dream, he saw an old man with a long white beard and a kind face. The old man held something in his hand. "Take this," he said to Ma Liang. "It is a magic paintbrush. Use it with care."

When Ma Liang awoke, he found his fingers wrapped around a paintbrush. "Am I still dreaming?" he wondered. Quickly he got up and painted a bird. The picture flapped its wings and flew away!

He painted a deer. As soon as he had put the last spot on the animal's coat, it brushed its nose against Ma Liang, then ran into the woods.

"It *is* a magic brush!" said Ma Liang. He ran to where his poor friends lived. He painted toys for the children. He painted cows and tools for the farmers. He painted bowls full of food for the hungry.

No good thing can remain a secret forever. Soon, news of Ma Liang and the magic paintbrush reached the ears of the greedy emperor.

"Bring me that boy and his brush!" the emperor commanded. His soldiers found Ma Liang and brought him back to the palace.

With a scowl, the emperor looked at Ma Liang. "Paint me a dragon!" he yelled. Ma Liang began to paint. But instead of painting a lucky dragon, he painted a slimy toad that hopped right on the emperor's head!

"Stupid boy!" said the emperor. "You will regret that!" He grabbed the magic paintbrush and ordered his soldiers to throw Ma Liang in jail.

Then the emperor called for his royal painter. "Take this brush and paint me a mountain of gold," he commanded. But when the royal painter finished the picture, all the gold turned into rocks.

"So," said the emperor, "this brush will only work for the boy. Bring him to me!"

Ma Liang was brought to the emperor. "If you will paint for me," said the emperor, "I will give you gold and silver, fine clothes, a new house, and all the food and drink you want."

Ma Liang pretended to agree. "What do you want me to paint?" he asked.

"Paint me a tree that has gold coins for leaves!" said the emperor with greed in his eyes.

Ma Liang took the magic paintbrush and began to paint. He painted many blue waves, and soon the emperor saw an ocean before him.

"That is not what I told you to paint!" he barked.

But Ma Liang just kept painting. In the ocean he painted an island. And on that island he painted a tree with gold coins for leaves.

"Yes, yes, that's more like it," said the emperor. "Now quickly, paint me a boat so that I can get to the island."

Ma Liang painted a big sailboat. The emperor went on board with many of his highest officials. Ma Liang painted a few lines and a gentle breeze began to blow. The sailboat moved slowly toward the island.

"Faster! Faster!" shouted the emperor. Ma Liang painted a big curving stroke, and a strong wind began to blow. "That's enough wind!" shouted the emperor. But Ma Liang kept painting. He painted a storm, and the waves got higher and higher, tossing the sailboat like a little cork on the water. Then the waves broke the boat to pieces. The emperor and his officials were washed up on the shore of the island, with no way to get back to the palace.

And as for Ma Liang, people say that for many years, he went from village to village, using his magic paintbrush to help the poor wherever he went.

A Christmas Carol

(Based on the story by Charles Dickens)

Once there was a tight-fisted, grasping, greedy man named Ebenezer Scrooge. On a cold, bleak, biting Christmas eve, old Scrooge sat in his office. His poor clerk, Bob Cratchit, shivered in the next room, for Scrooge gave him only one coal for his fire.

Scrooge frowned at Bob Cratchit and growled, "I suppose you'll be wanting the whole day off tomorrow."

"Yes sir," the clerk replied meekly. "If it's convenient."

"It's not convenient," said Scrooge. "Be here even earlier the next morning!"

"Thank you sir," said Bob Cratchit. "And a merry Christmas to you, sir."

"Christmas! Bah, humbug!" grumbled Scrooge as he left the office. Through the frost and fog, he made his way home. As he approached his front door, he stopped and stared. Where he expected to see the door knocker, he saw a face! It was the face of his old business partner, Jacob Marley. But Marley had been dead for seven years. Scrooge blinked his eyes, and the face vanished.

"Bah, humbug!" said Scrooge as he walked in. He changed into his robe and slippers. He was about to fix his dinner when he heard a noise. It sounded like someone dragging heavy chains over the floor. Then, right through the closed door walked the ghost of Jacob Marley. Around his waist was wrapped a large chain.

"Hear me!" said the ghost. "I wear the chain I forged in life. I cared only about money. And you are making your own chain now, Ebenezer. You care too much for money, and too little for your fellow man. You must change, before it is too late! There is still a chance for you to escape my fate. You will be visited by three spirits." Then, with a fearful groan, the ghost vanished.

When the clock struck one, a pale hand drew back the curtain that hung around Scrooge's bed. It was the first spirit. It looked like a child but at the same time like an old man. "I am the Ghost of Christmas Past," said the spirit. Then the spirit took Scrooge's hand. Suddenly Scrooge found himself in an old school-room. All the children were gone home for the holidays—all but one. One neglected child sat at his desk. "Why, that's me," said Scrooge. And he sobbed as he recalled his sad, lonely childhood.

Scrooge had a dim sense of being back in his bed again. He heard the clock striking and saw a bright light. He got out of bed and saw a large, bearded man wearing a loose robe and a crown of holly. This jolly giant was seated on a great heap of roast turkeys, pies, apples, oranges, cakes, and puddings.

"Come in and know me better, man!" laughed the spirit. "I am the Ghost of Christmas Present. Touch my robe!"

When Scrooge touched the robe, he found himself moving through the busy city streets on a Christmas morning. He saw smiling faces and heard people wishing each other a merry Christmas. As the spirit took him from house to house, they could see people making their Christmas dinners. Then they came to the home of Bob Cratchit. The family was sitting down to a meager dinner, but

they seemed as happy as if they had a great feast before them. The happiest of all was the youngest child, a small, frail boy called Tiny Tim, who walked with a crutch.

Scrooge saw Bob Cratchit lift his glass and say, "A merry Christmas to us all, my dears!"

"And God bless us, every one," said Tiny Tim. Scrooge saw how Bob held his little son close by his side, as if he feared he might lose him.

"Spirit," said Scrooge, "tell me if Tiny Tim will live."

"I see an empty seat," said the spirit, "and a crutch without an owner. If things remain as they are, the child will die."

"Oh, no, kind Spirit!" said Scrooge. "Say he will be spared."

But the Ghost of Christmas Present was disappearing before Scrooge's eyes. And in his place, Scrooge saw a dark, hooded phantom. "Am I in the presence of the Ghost of Christmas Yet to Come?" asked Scrooge.

The spirit did not answer but pointed onward with its hand. Scrooge found himself in a dark house. On the bed, beneath a sheet, lay something cold, still, and lifeless. Scrooge heard people talking outside.

"When did he die?" asked a man.

"Last night," said another.

"It's likely to be a very cheap funeral," said a third, and they all laughed.

The silent spirit spread its dark robe like a wing, and suddenly Scrooge was at Bob Cratchit's house. It was quiet. Very quiet. The noisy Cratchit children now sat still as statues in a corner. Near the wall a crutch leaned against an empty chair. Then Scrooge heard Bob Cratchit's voice. "I am sure that we shall never forget poor Tiny Tim," he said. "Oh, my little, little child!"

Again the spirit waved its dark robe, and now Scrooge found himself in a graveyard choked with weeds. The spirit stood among the graves and pointed to one.

Scrooge crept toward the grave. And there he read upon the stone his own name, Ebenezer Scrooge.

"No, Spirit!" cried Scrooge. He clutched at the spirit's robe. "I am not the man I was. Please tell me I may yet change what you have shown me." The spirit

began to pull away, but Scrooge held on tight. "Good Spirit," he cried, "I will honor Christmas in my heart, and try to keep it all the year!"

Scrooge tried to grasp the spirit's hand, but suddenly the phantom was gone. Scrooge found himself sitting in his own bed with his arms around the bedpost.

Yes, the bed was his own, and the room was his own. Best of all, his life was still his own, and there was still time to make himself a better man. Scrooge ran to the window and called to a boy passing in the street, "What's today, my fine fellow?"

"It's Christmas day, of course!" said the boy.

"I haven't missed it!" said Scrooge. Then he said to the boy, "Do you know that big prize turkey they're selling in the store in the next street?"

"You mean the one as big as me?" said the boy.

"A remarkable boy!" cried Scrooge. "Yes, that's the one. Run to the store and tell them to take it to Bob Cratchit's house. If you're back in half an hour, I'll give you a nice reward."

Scrooge dressed quickly and hurried into the street. "Merry Christmas!" he cried to everyone he met. He patted children on the head, and found that everything gave him happiness.

The next morning, Scrooge arrived early at his office, before Bob Cratchit. When Bob entered, Scrooge tried very hard to put on his old voice and growled, "Well, what do you mean by coming in eighteen and a half minutes late?"

"I am very sorry, sir," said Bob Cratchit.

"I am not going to stand for that sort of thing any longer!" barked Scrooge. "And therefore," he said, as he leaped down from his stool, "I am going to raise your salary! A merry Christmas to you, Bob Cratchit!"

From then on, Scrooge helped Bob Cratchit's family, and he shared his wealth with other people in need. To Tiny Tim, who did *not* die, Scrooge became like a second father. He became as good a friend, as good a master, and as good a man as the good old city knew. And it was always said of him that he knew how to keep Christmas well. May that be truly said of all of us. And, as Tiny Tim observed, "God bless us, every one!"

"Before Breakfast" (from *Charlotte's Web*)

by E. B. White

Illustration copyright © renewed 1980 by the Estate of Garth Williams.
Used by permission of HarperCollins Publishers.

PARENTS: Here we present the first chapter of a book that has become a beloved classic since it was published in 1952. *Charlotte's Web* tells the story of a young girl named Fern, her pig, Wilbur, and Wilbur's dear friend, the wise spider named Charlotte. We hope you take this first chapter as an invitation to read aloud the whole book with your child. (The pictures here are by Garth Williams, from the original edition.)

"Where's Papa going with that ax?" said Fern to her mother as they were setting the table for breakfast.

"Out to the hoghouse," replied Mrs. Arable. "Some of the pigs were born last night."

"I don't see why he needs an ax," continued Fern, who was only eight.

"Well," said her mother, "one of the pigs is a runt. It's very small and weak, and it will never amount to anything. So your father has decided to do away with it."

"Do *away* with it?" shrieked Fern. "You mean *kill* it? Just because it's smaller than the others?"

Mrs. Arable put a pitcher of cream on the table. "Don't yell, Fern!" she said. "Your father is right. The pig would probably die anyway."

Fern pushed a chair out of the way and ran outdoors. The grass was wet and the earth smelled of springtime. Fern's sneakers were sopping by the time she caught up with her father.

"Please don't kill it!" she sobbed. "It's unfair."

Mr. Arable stopped walking.

"Fern," he said gently, "you will have to learn to control yourself."

"Control myself?" yelled Fern. "This is a matter of life and death, and you talk about *controlling* myself." Tears ran down her cheeks and she took hold of the ax and tried to pull it out of her father's hand.

"Fern," said Mr. Arable, "I know more about raising a litter of pigs than you do. A weakling makes trouble. Now run along!"

"But it's unfair," cried Fern. "The pig couldn't help being born small, could it? If *I* had been very small at birth, would you have killed *me*?"

Mr. Arable smiled. "Certainly not," he said, looking down at his daughter with love. "But this is different. A little girl is one thing, a little runty pig is another."

"I see no difference," replied Fern, still hanging on to the ax. "This is the most terrible case of injustice I ever heard of."

A queer look came over John Arable's face. He seemed almost ready to cry himself.

"All right," he said. "You go back to the house and I will bring the runt when I come in. I'll let you start it on a bottle, like a baby. Then you'll see what trouble a pig can be."

When Mr. Arable returned to the house half an hour later, he carried a carton under his arm. Fern was upstairs changing her sneakers. The kitchen table was set for breakfast, and the room smelled of coffee, bacon, damp plaster, and wood smoke from the stove.

"Put it on her chair!" said Mrs. Arable. Mr. Arable set the carton down at

Fern's place. Then he walked to the sink and washed his hands and dried them on the roller towel.

Fern came slowly down the stairs. Her eyes were red from crying. As she approached her chair, the carton wobbled, and there was a scratching noise. Fern looked at her father. Then she lifted the lid of the carton. There, inside, looking up at her, was the newborn pig. It was a white one. The morning light shone through its ears, turning them pink.

"He's yours," said Mr. Arable. "Saved from an untimely death. And may the good Lord forgive me for this foolishness."

Fern couldn't take her eyes off the tiny pig. "Oh," she whispered. "Oh, *look* at him! He's absolutely perfect."

She closed the carton carefully. First she kissed her father, then she kissed her mother. Then she opened the lid again, lifted the pig out, and held it against her cheek. At this moment her brother Avery came into the room. Avery was ten. He was heavily armed—an air rifle in one hand, a wooden dagger in the other.

"What's that?" he demanded. "What's Fern got?"

"She's got a guest for breakfast," said Mr. Arable. "Wash your hands and face, Avery!"

"Let's see it!" said Avery, setting his gun down. "You call that miserable thing a pig? That's a *fine* specimen of a pig—it's no bigger than a white rat."

"Wash up and eat your breakfast, Avery!" said his mother. "The school bus will be along in half an hour."

"Can I have a pig, too, Pop?" asked Avery.

"No, I only distribute pigs to early risers," said Mr. Arable. "Fern was up at daylight, trying to rid the world of injustice. As a result, she now has a pig. A small one, to be sure, but nevertheless a pig. It just shows what can happen if a person gets out of bed promptly. Let's eat!"

But Fern couldn't eat until her pig had had a drink of milk. Mrs. Arable found a baby's nursing bottle and a rubber nipple. She poured warm milk into the bottle, fitted the nipple over the top, and handed it to Fern. "Give him his breakfast!" she said.

A minute later, Fern was seated on the floor in the corner of the kitchen with her infant between her knees, teaching it to suck from the bottle. The pig, although tiny, had a good appetite and caught on quickly.

The school bus honked from the road.

"Run!" commanded Mrs. Arable, taking the pig from Fern and slipping a doughnut into her hand. Avery grabbed his gun and another doughnut.

The children ran out to the road and climbed into the bus. Fern took no notice of the others in the bus. She just sat and stared out of the window, thinking what a blissful world it was and how lucky she was to have entire charge of a pig. By the time the bus reached school, Fern had named her pet, selecting the most beautiful name she could think of.

"Its name is Wilbur," she whispered to herself.

She was still thinking about the pig when the teacher said: "Fern, what is the capital of Pennsylvania?"

"Wilbur," replied Fern, dreamily. The pupils giggled. Fern blushed.

How the Camel Got His Hump

by Rudyard Kipling

PARENTS: Like all of Kipling's humorous *Just So Stories*, this tale comes alive when read aloud.

In the beginning of years, when the world was so new and all, and the Animals were just beginning to work for Man, there was a Camel, and he lived in the middle of a Howling Desert because he did not want to work; and besides, he was a Howler himself. So he ate sticks and thorns and tamarisks and milkweed and prickles, most 'scruciating idle; and when anybody spoke to him he said "Humph!" Just "Humph!" and no more.

Presently the Horse came to him on Monday morning, with a saddle on his back and a bit in his mouth, and said, "Camel, O Camel, come out and trot like the rest of us."

"Humph!" said the Camel; and the Horse went away and told the Man.

Presently the Dog came to him, with a stick in his mouth, and said, "Camel, O Camel, come and fetch and carry like the rest of us."

"Humph!" said the Camel; and the Dog went away and told the Man.

Presently the Ox came to him with the yoke on his neck and said, "Camel, O Camel, come and plow like the rest of us."

"Humph!" said the Camel; and the Ox went away and told the Man.

At the end of the day the Man called the Horse and the Dog and the Ox together, and said, "Three, O Three, I'm very sorry for you (with the world so new-and-all); but that Humph-thing in the Desert can't work, or he would be here by now, so I am going to leave him alone, and you must work double-time to make up for it."

That made the Three very angry (with the world so new-and-all), and they held a palaver and an *indaba*, and a *punchayet*, and a powwow on the edge of the Desert; and the Camel came chewing milkweed *most* 'scruciating idle, and laughed at them. Then he said "Humph!" and went away again.

Presently there came along the Djinn [jin] in charge of All Deserts, rolling in a cloud of dust (Djinns always travel that way because it is Magic), and he stopped to palaver and powwow with the Three.

"Djinn of All Deserts," said the Horse, "is it right for any one to be idle, with the world so new-and-all?"

"Certainly not," said the Djinn.

"Well," said the Horse, "there's a thing in the middle of your Howling Desert (and he's a Howler himself) with a long neck and long legs, and he hasn't done a stroke of work since Monday morning. He won't trot."

"Whew!" said the Djinn, whistling, "that's my Camel, for all the gold in Arabia! What does he say about it?"

"He says 'Humph!'" said the Dog, "and he won't fetch and carry."

"Does he say anything else?"

"Only 'Humph!' and he won't plow," said the Ox.

"Very good," said the Djinn. "I'll 'humph' him if you will kindly wait a minute."

The Djinn rolled himself up in his dust cloak, and took a bearing across the desert, and found the Camel most 'scruciating idle, looking at his own reflection in a pool of water.

"My long and bubbling friend," said the Djinn, "what's this I hear of your doing no work, with the world so new-and-all?"

"Humph!" said the Camel.

The Djinn sat down, with his chin in his hand, and began to think a Great Magic, while the Camel looked at his own reflection in the pool of water.

"You've given the Three extra work ever since Monday morning, all on

account of your 'scruciating idleness," said the Djinn; and he went on thinking Magics, with his chin in his hand.

"Humph!" said the Camel.

"I shouldn't say that again if I were you," said the Djinn; "you might say it once too often."

And the Camel said "Humph!" again; but no sooner had he said it than he saw his back, that he was so proud of, being covered with a great big lolloping humph.

"Do you see that?" said the Djinn. "That's your own humph that you've brought upon yourself by not working. Today is Thursday, and you've done no work since Monday, when the work began. Now you are going to work."

"How can I," said the Camel, "with this humph on my back?"

"That's made a-purpose," said the Djinn, "all because you missed those three days. You will be able to work now for three days without eating, because you can live on your humph; and don't you ever say I never did anything for you. Come out of the Desert and go to the Three, and behave. Humph yourself!"

And the Camel humphed himself, humph and all, and went away to join the Three. And from that day to this the Camel always wears a humph (we call it "hump" now, not to hurt his feelings); but he has never yet caught up with the three days that he missed at the beginning of the world, and he has never yet learned how to behave.

El Pajaro Cu

(A folktale from Mexico)

When God made the world, He took great care in forming the birds. He made their bodies and then feathered them, creating Owl and Dove and Peacock, each different from the other. And then He ran out of feathers. The last bird, Pajaro Cu [PA-ha-row COO], received no feathers whatsoever. Pajaro Cu didn't seem to care. He went anywhere he wished, never caring that he was as naked as the palm of your hand.

But the other birds worried.

"What can we do for him?" asked Owl.

"Pity on the little thing," said Dove.

"He looks awful," said Peacock. "All of the other animals talk about him."

The birds agreed that something must be done.

Then Owl said, "If we each give him one of our feathers, he'll be completely covered, and we'll never feel the difference."

All of the birds thought this was a splendid idea. Parrot gave a green feather; Canary's was yellow; Guinea Bird offered silver; Crow gave black; Swan's was white; and Redbird gave a bright red feather. Just as Pajaro Cu was about to receive his new coat, Peacock suddenly screeched, "No! With these feathers, Pajaro Cu will be the most beautiful bird around, and before long, he will be strutting around with pride."

"But we can't leave him naked," said Dove. "He is a disgrace to the entire community of birds!"

Everyone, including Pajaro Cu, wondered what to do.

"I know," said Owl. "If you each give him your feather, I will watch over him and protect us from his vanity."

In no time at all, Pajaro Cu was the best-dressed bird around. Even Peacock was awed into silence. Lifting his glistening wings, Pajaro Cu flew straight to the pond, where he took one look at his marvelous self, and darted high up toward heaven.

Owl, old and heavy, tried to follow him, but his short wings weren't meant for such flying. Slowly, he spiraled back down to earth, where he found the others waiting in the branches.

Parrot said, "None of us has ever flown to heaven. This can only bring trouble. We're all going to pay for his vanity."

"It's Owl's fault," said Peacock. "I warned you all."

Whereupon they drove Owl from his tree and chased him. Owl found safety in a cave. Many days passed while he pondered: how can we lure Pajaro Cu from heaven? One day, he received a visitor.

"Oh, do come in, Roadrunner," cried Owl. "I am ever so glad to see you."

"I have brought you some dinner," Roadrunner said.

"Thank you. But whatever am I to do?" said Owl.

"You must stay here," Roadrunner warned. "Crow has sworn to kill you unless you get back his feather."

Owl said, "Then I will hunt by night, when Crow is asleep. And I will call for Pajaro Cu until he comes."

"And I will search for him on the road," said Roadrunner.

Even today they are looking. This is why the Roadrunner streaks from one place to another, searching the road for Pajaro Cu. And when you listen at night, you can hear Owl calling "Cu, Cu, Cu, Cu, Cu."

Beauty and the Beast

Once upon a time, in a faraway country, there lived a merchant. The merchant was very rich. Indeed, he had more money than he needed, until a great misfortune occurred. Two of his biggest cargo ships were lost in a great storm at sea. The merchant lost his fortune and was left with almost nothing. He was even forced to give up his lavish home in the city.

The merchant told his three daughters that they would have to move to a little cottage in the woods, far from town, and work hard and live simply. The two older daughters complained bitterly, for they had grown accustomed to a life of luxury. But the youngest daughter, who was called Beauty, always tried to make the best of things.

Several months later, the merchant heard that one of his ships, which he thought had been lost at sea, had in fact landed with a cargo of valuable goods to sell. As the merchant prepared to make the long trip to the city to claim his goods, he asked his daughters what he might bring them when he returned. The eldest daughter asked for a fancy gown. The second daughter asked for a diamond necklace. But Beauty replied, "Please bring me a rose, for I have not seen one since we came here, and I love them so much."

When the merchant finally reached his ship, he found that most of his goods had been stolen. He sold what remained and made just enough money to buy a dress for his eldest daughter and a necklace for his second daughter. Then he set off for home.

On the way home, snow began to fall. It covered the road and made it hard to see. The wind blew so hard, it almost knocked the merchant off his horse. He was worried that he might lose his way in the blizzard. The merchant decided that he should stop at the next house he came to and wait there until the storm passed.

Eventually he came upon a large palace with lights blazing. He knocked, but no one answered. He found that the door was unlocked, so he opened it and peered in.

"Hello!" he called out, but there was no answer. He stepped into the front hall and brushed the snow off his coat.

Curious, yet hesitant, the merchant slowly made his way into a large dining hall. He found a fire burning in the fireplace and a little table set with a sumptuous meal, just right for one person.

"Hello?" he called again. "Is anybody here?"

Again, there was no answer.

The merchant inspected the food.

"Is someone eating this food?" he asked. "Would you mind if I had a few bites? I have been riding in a bitter snowstorm, and . . . ," he continued.

When there was no reply, the merchant decided that he would have a few bites of food and then look for the owner of the palace.

After he had eaten, he set off to find the owner. He wandered through the rooms on the ground floor, but neither master nor servant appeared. At last he stepped outside into a beautiful garden.

The merchant was astonished to discover that the garden was in full bloom, even though it was the middle of winter and most of the countryside was covered in a thick blanket of snow. In the garden, birds chirped. Flowers bloomed. The air was sweet and balmy. The man explored the garden until he came upon a row of beautiful rosebushes. He remembered that Beauty had asked him to bring her a rose. He reached out to pluck a rose. But just as the stem broke, he heard a loud roar behind him.

"Who told you that you might gather roses in my garden?" said a low, gruff voice.

The startled merchant turned around and saw a fearsome creature, half man and half beast.

"What?" said the beast. "Is it not enough that I have given you dinner and a place to wait out the storm? You must also steal my roses?"

"Please forgive me," said the merchant, falling to his knees. "I tried to find you to thank you for the meal. I will pay you for it, if you like. As for the rose, I only wanted it for my youngest daughter, Beauty. Her only wish when I left her was that I return with a rose for her. Your gardens are so magnificent. I did not think you would miss a single rose."

"You are very ready with excuses and flattery!" the beast said. "But that will not save you from the punishment you deserve!"

"Oh, forgive me," said the merchant. "If not for my own sake, then for the sake of my daughters. If I do not return home, they will have no one left to support them."

There was a long pause. Then the beast spoke again.

"I will forgive you," he said, "on one condition. You must send one of your daughters to live with me. Go and see if any of them is brave enough and loves you enough to save you. If one of them will come, you may send her in your place. Otherwise, you must come yourself and face your punishment."

When the storm was over, the merchant returned home. He gave his daughters their presents: a gown for the eldest, a diamond necklace for the second, and a rose for Beauty.

The older sisters were delighted, but Beauty could sense that something was wrong.

"Father," she said, "why did you sigh so deeply when you gave me that beautiful rose?"

"In a few days I will tell you," said the merchant. "But for now, let's just enjoy being together again."

A few days later, the merchant told his daughters what had happened to him in the rose garden at the beast's castle. He told them how he had plucked the rose and been confronted by the beast. He explained that he had promised to return to the beast and accept his punishment.

"But do you have to go?" the girls asked.

He explained that the beast had said that the only way for him to avoid it would be if one of them was willing to go and live with the beast. "But I won't allow that!" added the merchant.

"I will go," Beauty said quietly.

"No, Beauty," said her father. "I am the one who took the rose. I shall go back to the beast. I would rather go myself than send you."

"No, Father," said Beauty. "I want to go."

Her father tried to change her mind, but Beauty was determined. A few days later, Beauty and her father returned to the castle. When she first saw the beast, Beauty could not help shuddering, but she tried to conceal her fear.

"Good evening, old man," said the beast. "Is this your daughter?"

"Yes," said the merchant. "This is my youngest daughter, Beauty." Beauty curtsied before the beast.

"Good evening, Beauty," said the beast. "Are you here to take your father's place and live here, with me, in the castle?"

"Yes, I am," said Beauty.

The following day, the beast gave Beauty's father a trunk filled with golden coins and sent him on his way. As Beauty watched her father ride away, she struggled to hold back the tears.

"Beauty," said the beast, "fear not. Things are not as bad as they may seem. You have given yourself for your father's sake, and your goodness will be rewarded. Listen to me and heed this advice: Do not be deceived by appearances. Trust your heart, not your eyes."

The next day, Beauty explored her new home. The beast had been right. Things were not as bad as she had feared. The palace was actually quite lovely. She found a huge library filled with books she had always wanted to read. She went for a walk in the lovely gardens, where songbirds chirped her favorite tunes. When it was time for dinner, Beauty was greeted by a staff of pleasant servants, who prepared a delicious meal.

"Good evening, Beauty," said the beast.

Beauty was still startled by the beast's appearance, but the more time she spent with him, the more she found that he treated her with kindness and courtesy. He pulled out her chair and sat next to her at dinner. He listened to her stories about her family and conversed with her while they dined. The dinner turned out to be less painful than Beauty had imagined. When it was over and it was time to say good night, though, the beast turned to Beauty and asked, "Do you love me, Beauty? Will you marry me?"

Beauty did not know what to say. She was afraid that the beast would be upset if she declined.

Seeing this, the beast said, "Say yes or no, without fear."

After a few moments, Beauty replied, "No, thank you," as gently as she could.

"Very well," said the beast. "Good night, then."

After that, every night was much the same. Beauty dined with the beast, and the beast treated her with great kindness. She even began to enjoy his conversation. Little by little Beauty got used to the way he looked. Despite his appearance, the beast was polite, and his elegant manners put Beauty's fears to rest. But when the meal was over and it was time to say good night, the beast always turned to her and asked, "Do you love me, Beauty? Will you marry me?"

Although she cared for him more and more with each passing day, Beauty always felt that, as hard as it was, the only answer she could give was "no, thank you."

One night, the beast noticed a sorrowful look on Beauty's face. "Beauty," he said, "I cannot bear to see you unhappy. What is the matter?"

"Oh," she said, wiping away a tear, "I am just sad because I miss my family." She paused. "Especially my father. He is getting older, and if his health is failing, I worry that he may need me. If only I could see him just to make sure that he is well."

"But, Beauty," said the beast, "if you leave me, I fear that I will never see you again and I will be alone forever."

"Dear Beast," said Beauty softly, "I do not want to leave you. I would be very sad if I could not see you again. But I long to see my father. If you will let me visit him for one month, I promise to come back and stay with you for the rest of my life."

"Very well," sighed the beast. "But remember your promise. And wear this locket as a constant reminder. When you want to come back, simply open the locket and say the words *I wish to go back to my beast.*"

When Beauty awoke the next morning, she was in her father's house—not the old country cottage, but a fine new house in the city that he had bought with the riches the beast had given him. Her father hugged her and wept for joy when he saw her.

Soon Beauty's sisters came to visit with their new husbands. They seemed to be happy, but Beauty could tell they were not. One sister had married a very handsome man who was so in love with his own face that he thought of nothing else. The other sister had married a clever man who entertained himself by making fun of other people.

Beauty enjoyed being with her father and doing whatever she could to help him. When the time came for her to return to the beast, she found that she could not bring herself to say goodbye to her father. Every day she told herself, "Today I will go back." But every night she put it off again.

Then one night, she dreamed that she was wandering in the garden behind the beast's castle when suddenly she heard someone groaning in agony. She followed the sounds and discovered the beast lying on the ground.

Beauty awoke with a start. "Oh, how could I do this to my poor Beast?" she cried. "It does not matter that he is not handsome. Why have I been refusing to marry him? I would be happier with him than my sisters will ever be with their husbands. The beast is honest and good, and that matters more than anything else."

She opened the locket hanging around her neck and said firmly, "I wish to go back to my beast." In an instant, she found herself at the palace. But where was the beast?

Beauty ran through the rooms of the castle, calling for the beast. There was no answer. Then she remembered her dream. She ran to the garden, and there she found the beast stretched out on the ground.

Beauty cried, "Oh, no, he is—" She could not bring herself to finish the sentence. "It is all my fault!" She fell to the ground and took him in her arms. The beast lay still as Beauty's tears fell upon his face. Then he slowly opened his eyes.

"Oh, Beast," Beauty sobbed, "how you frightened me! Thank goodness you are still alive. I never knew how much I loved you until now, when I feared it was too late."

In a faint voice the beast said, "Beauty, I was dying because I thought you had forgotten your promise. But you have come back. Can you really love such a dreadful creature as I am?"

"Yes!" said Beauty. "I do love you!"

Then once again the beast asked, "Beauty, will you marry me?"

"Yes," she answered. "Yes, Beast, I will marry you!"

As she said these words, a burst of light flashed around her.

Beauty gasped and covered her eyes to shield them from the bright light. When she opened her eyes again, she no longer saw the beast. But there, lying at her feet, was a handsome prince.

"What has happened to my beast?" she asked.

"I was the beast," said the prince. "A fairy put a spell on me and changed me into a beast until someone would agree to marry me. You are the only one who has been good enough to see past my appearance and into my heart."

Beauty gave the young prince her hand and helped him to his feet. They were married the very next day, with Beauty's whole family there to help celebrate. And they lived happily ever after.

The Tongue-Cut Sparrow

(A folktale from Japan)

Long, long ago in Japan, there lived an old man and his wife. The old man was good, kind, and hardworking, but his wife was cross, mean, and bad-tempered. They had no children, so the old man kept a tiny sparrow as a pet. Every day when he came home from working in the woods, he loved to pet the little bird, talk to her, and feed her food from his own plate. The sparrow's sweet singing brought happiness into the old man's life. But his wife did not like the sparrow. She complained that her husband paid too much attention to a silly bird.

One morning, the old man went away to cut wood, and his wife prepared to wash clothes. On this day, she had made some starch, which she set out in a wooden bowl.

Make a Connection

This is an old folktale from Japan. Learn about modern Japan on page 158.

While her back was turned, the sparrow hopped down on the edge of the bowl and pecked at some of the starch. When the old woman saw the sparrow, she got so mad that she grabbed a pair of scissors and cut off the sparrow's tongue. "Go away, you greedy thing!" she shrieked, and the poor bird flew away to the woods.

When the old man returned home and heard what had happened, he felt very sad for his pet. The next morning, he went to the woods to look for the sparrow. Everywhere he went he cried, "Oh sparrow, little sparrow! Where are you, my friend?"

The woods grew thick and dark, and the old man began to worry that he might never see the sparrow again. With little hope he called out, "Little sparrow, please come home!" And just then he heard the fluttering of the sparrow's wings. And, to his great surprise, he heard the sparrow speak.

"Old man," said the sparrow, "you have been very kind to me. Now I wish to show you kindness in return." She led the old man to a pretty little house with a bamboo garden and a tiny waterfall. "Come in and meet my family," said the sparrow.

The old man bowed, removed his shoes, and entered the sparrow's house. Inside, many sparrows were singing sweet songs. They served the old man a delicious meal, with rice cakes, sweet candies, and plenty of hot tea. Then they did a wonderful dance that brought joy to his heart.

"This has been a magical day for me," said the old man, "and I thank you for your kindness. But I see that the sun is setting. Forgive me, but I must return home before my wife starts to worry."

"Before you go," said the sparrow, "please accept a gift." She placed two baskets before the old man. One was big and heavy, while the other was small and light. "Please choose one of these," said the sparrow, "and do not open the basket until you reach home."

The old man was not greedy, so he chose the small basket. With many thanks and goodbyes, he left the sparrow's house and returned home.

When the old man arrived at this home, he told his wife all that had happened. Then they opened the small basket. It spilled over with jewels, gold and silver coins, and other treasures.

The old man was delighted, but his wife cried, "You fool! Why didn't you take the big basket?" Then, without another word, she hurried into the woods to find the sparrow's home.

When she at last arrived at the sparrow's house, she called out, "Sparrow! Let me in!" Of course the polite sparrow invited her into the house and served her some hot tea. She took one sip and then said, "Enough of this. I am ready to leave." The sparrow again brought out two baskets, one big and one small. "Please choose one," said the sparrow, "and do not open it until you return home." The old woman grabbed the big basket and ran out the door.

"Oof!" she cried. "This basket is so heavy!" She sat down to rest. She looked at the basket. "Why should I wait to get home?" she said. "One little peek won't hurt."

She opened the basket. Instead of gold and silver, it was filled with toads that leaped into her hair, snakes that slithered around her arms and legs, and wasps that stung her all over.

The old woman screamed and ran as fast as she could. When she reached home, she fell into the old man's arms. He took care of her, and when she got better, she said to him, "I was too greedy, and I am sorry that I hurt the sparrow."

From that day forward, the old woman helped the old man feed any birds that came to their house, and their home was always filled with sweet songs.

The Tiger, the Brahman, and the Jackal

Once upon a time, a tiger was caught in a cage. He clawed and gnawed at the bars of his cage, but he could not escape.

While the tiger was struggling to escape, a Hindu holy man passed by the cage.

The tiger called out to the holy man: "O pious Brahman, please help me! Let me out of this cage!"

Now, the Brahman was kind and gentle to everyone he met, and it was part of his religion to treat animals like brothers. But at the same time, he saw the danger of letting the tiger out.

"Why should I let you out?" asked the Brahman. "You might eat me."

"No, no!" said the tiger. "I promise I won't eat you. In fact, if you let me out, I will be forever grateful to you and serve you forever!"

The tiger began to sob and moan. The pious Brahman's heart softened and at last he took pity on the tiger and agreed to open the door of the cage.

As soon as he was out of the cage, the tiger pounced on the Brahman.

"What a silly man you are!" said the tiger. "What is to prevent me from eating you now?"

"Nothing," said the Brahman. "Nothing at all. But, Brother Tiger, consider what it is you are about to do. Isn't it unfair to eat me when I have done you a good turn by letting you out of the cage? Do you think it is just to eat me when you promised that you would not do so?"

"It is perfectly fair," said the tiger. "Ask anyone and they will tell you that this is the way of the world."

"Will they?" said the Brahman. "Suppose we ask the next three things we see? Will they agree that it is fair for you to eat me?"

There was an old buffalo standing farther down the road. The Brahman called out to him.

"Brother Buffalo, what do you think? Is it fair for Brother Tiger here to devour me when I have freed him from his cage? Before I let him out he promised not to eat me."

"I served my master well when I was young and strong," said the buffalo in a hoarse, tired voice. "I carried heavy loads and carried them far. But now that I am old and weak, how does he reward me for my years of service? He leaves me here by the side of the road, without food or water. I say, let the tiger eat the Brahman, for these men are an ungrateful bunch."

"Aha!" said the tiger. "You see that the buffalo's judgment is against you!"

"Indeed, it is," said the Brahman. "But let us hear a second opinion."

A few yards away, there was an ancient banyan tree that cast a shadow on the road.

"Brother Banyan," said the Brahman. "What do you think? Is it fair for this Tiger to eat me when I have freed him from his cage? Is it just for him to do this when he promised he would not?"

The banyan tree looked down and sighed.

"In the summer," said the banyan tree, "when it is hot, men take shelter from the sun in my shade. But when the sun goes down, they break off my branches and burn them in their fires. I say, let the tiger eat the Brahman, for these men are selfish and think only of themselves."

"You see that the banyan tree and the buffalo agree," the tiger said.

"Indeed, he does," said the Brahman. "But let us hear one more opinion."

The Brahman looked down the road and spotted a jackal slinking along the edge of the woods.

"Brother Jackal," he called out. "What do you think? Is it fair for Brother Tiger here to eat me when I have freed him from his cage?"

"I'm sorry," said the jackal. "I'm afraid I don't quite understand. Would you mind explaining exactly what happened?"

The Brahman explained the events. He told the whole story, from start to finish. When he was done, the jackal shook his head as if he still did not quite understand.

"It's very odd," he said. "I hear what you are saying, but I can't seem to understand it. It all seems to go in one ear and out the other. Perhaps, if I can see where these things happened, I will be able to understand what exactly took place. Then I can give you my opinion."

So the Brahman led the jackal back to the cage, with the tiger trailing along behind them, licking his chops in anticipation of a tasty meal.

"So this is the cage?" said the jackal.

"Yes," said the Brahman.

"Tell me again what happened."

The Brahman told the whole story over again, not missing a single detail.

"Oh, my poor brain!" cried the jackal, wringing its paws. "Let me see! How did it all begin? You were in the cage, and the tiger came walking by—"

"No!" interrupted the tiger. "What a fool you are! I was the one in the cage."

"Of course!" cried the jackal. "That is very helpful. So let's see: I was in the Brahman, and the cage came walking by—no, that's not it, either! Oh, my! I fear I shall never understand!"

"You are not listening to me!" roared the tiger. "It's so simple! Look here—I am the tiger."

"Yes, my lord!"

"And that is the Brahman."

"Yes, my lord!"

"And that is the cage."

"Yes, my lord!"

"And I was in the cage—do you understand?"

"Yes—no—please, my lord—"

"Well?" cried the tiger impatiently.

"Excuse me, my lord! But how did you get in?"

"How? Why, in the usual way, of course!"

"Oh, dear me! I am getting confused again! Please don't be angry, my lord, but what is the usual way?"

At this the tiger lost his patience. He ran into the cage, bellowing, "This way! Now do you understand how it was?"

"I think I am beginning to understand," said the jackal. "But why did you not let yourself out?"

"Because the gate was closed!" moaned the tiger.

"This gate?" said the jackal.

"Yes!" roared the tiger.

Then the jackal pushed on the gate a little and it swung closed with a loud click.

"And that clicking sound?" said the jackal. "What does that mean?"

"That means the cage is locked," said the Brahman.

"Does it?" said the jackal. "Does it, really? Well, in that case, Brother Brahman, I would advise you to leave it locked. And as for you, my friend," he said to the tiger, "I suspect it will be a good long time before you can find anyone to let you out again."

Then the jackal made a little bow to the Brahman and went on his way.

How Wendy Met Peter Pan

PARENTS: The Peter Pan stories were written by James M. Barrie in the early 1900s. Some children today may know the story of the boy who refuses to grow up from the Disney animated movie or the Broadway musical. Here we retell the opening episodes, in which we meet the Darling family children and Peter Pan. We encourage you to check your library for more adventures of Peter Pan to share with your children.

Once upon a time there were three children, named Wendy, John, and Michael Darling, who lived in a lovely house with lots of toys and picture books. They had a most unusual nurse to look after them, called Nana, and she was really a large dog. She bathed and dressed the children, and saw that they got up and went to bed at the proper time.

One night, when the children had been bathed and put to bed, the bedroom window flew open and a boy dropped in. He was dressed in a ragged shirt of leafy green and brown, and he had wild, uncombed hair. When Nana saw him, she growled and jumped at him. She did not catch him, for he leaped back out the window. But she did catch his shadow. When Mrs. Darling found it on the floor the next morning, she rolled it up carefully and put it away in a drawer.

Nothing more happened until about a week later. Mr. and Mrs. Darling were dressing to go to a party, and Nana was busy getting the children ready for bed. Now, the only person at number 14 (which was the Darlings' house) who did not much care for Nana was Mr. Darling. And on this night, when Nana happened to rub up by accident against Mr. Darling and a lot of her long hairs came off on his nice new pants, Mr. Darling shouted, "I won't have a dog in the house! I shall tie her up in the backyard!" And he did.

Poor Nana whined, for it was starting to snow. Then she barked, for she could smell danger in the air.

It was all dark and quiet in the room where Wendy, Michael, and John lay sleeping. But it was only dark for a moment. For as soon as Mr. and Mrs. Darling had left for the party, a bright light flew in at the window and darted to and fro around the room. It was Tinker Bell, a lovely little-girl fairy, come to search for the shadow that belonged to Peter Pan.

In a moment, through the window came Peter Pan himself. "Oh, Tink," he called softly, "have you found my shadow?"

She answered in a voice like a tiny bell with a silvery tinkle, which is the fairy language.

She said that his shadow was in the big box—she meant the chest of drawers—but it was too big for her to open. Peter had his shadow out in a second, and he was so excited at getting it back that he did not notice he closed Tinker Bell in the drawer!

"Bother!" said Peter, because his shadow wouldn't join to him again. He tried to stick it back on with some soap, but that didn't work. He was so disappointed that he sat on the floor and cried.

His sobs woke Wendy, and she sat up in bed. She had seen Peter before in dreams, so she was not surprised to see him now. She asked politely, "Boy, why are you crying?"

Peter got up, and they bowed to each other. "What's your name?" he asked.

"Wendy Moira Angela Darling," she replied. "What is your name?"

"Peter Pan."

"And where do you live?" asked Wendy.

Peter answered, "Second to the right, and then straight on till morning."

"Does your mother know you are here?" asked Wendy.

"Don't have a mother," said Peter.

"Oh!" exclaimed Wendy. "No wonder you were crying."

"I wasn't crying about mothers," Peter snapped. "I was crying because I can't get my shadow to stick on. Besides, I wasn't crying."

Wendy fetched her needle and thread, and she sewed the shadow onto Peter's foot. Peter danced about and crowed with joy. And instead of saying, "Thank you, Wendy, how kind you are," he crowed, "Oh, how clever I am!" For, to tell the truth, Peter was very conceited.

"Peter," said Wendy, "how old are you?"

"Don't know," said Peter.

"If you did have a mother," said Wendy, "she could tell you how old you are."

"Oh, she *might*," said Peter, "but I ran away the day I was born! It was because I heard my father and mother talking about what I would be as a grown-up man. And I don't ever want to grow up! I want to stay a little boy and have fun for ever and ever and ever! That's why I ran away to live with the fairies."

"Fairies!" exclaimed Wendy. "Really and truly? Oh, Peter, where do they come from?"

"Well," said Peter, "when the first baby that ever was laughed for the first time that ever was—"

"What was the baby's name?" asked Wendy.

"Don't interrupt," said Peter. "Anyhow, its laugh broke up into a thousand little tiny pieces, and they all went skipping about and turned into fairies. But there are only a few fairies now, because children don't believe in them. They can't live unless they're believed in. And every time a child says, 'I don't believe

in fairies,' then another fairy falls down dead." Then Peter got a surprised look on his face. "Oh!" he said. "I wonder where—Tink! Tink! Where are you? Listen, Wendy. Do you hear anything?"

"I hear a sound like tiny bells," said Wendy. "It seems to be coming from the chest of drawers."

"That's Tink!" said Peter. He opened a drawer and Tinker Bell flew out. And she was in a rage!

"Tink," said Peter, "watch your language! You shouldn't say such things. Yes, of course I'm sorry, but how could I know you were in the drawer?" Tink settled for a moment on top of a clock. She glared at Wendy and made a sharp jangling sound.

"What did she say?" asked Wendy.

"She says you are a big ugly girl," said Peter. "But you mustn't mind her."

Wendy did not like this, so she decided to talk about something else. "Tell me about where you live, Peter," she said.

"Mostly I live in the Never-Land with the Lost Boys," he said.

"Are they fairies?" said Wendy.

"No," said Peter. "They are the children who fall out of their carriages when their nurses aren't watching them. Then the fairies pick them up, and if nobody comes for them in seven days, they are brought to the Never-Land. And I am their captain."

"But why are they all boys?" asked Wendy.

"Because girls are too clever to fall out of their carriages," said Peter.

Then he asked, "Wendy, do you know any stories? I don't know any," he said, "so I come here to hear them. But sometimes I have to leave before I hear the end. Oh, Wendy, your mother was telling such a lovely story the last time I came, all about a prince who couldn't find the lady who wore a glass slipper."

"That was the story of Cinderella!" exclaimed Wendy. "And the prince *did* find her in the end, and they lived happily ever after. Oh, Peter, I could tell you so many wonderful stories!"

Peter got a greedy look in his eyes. "Wendy," he said, "come back with me and tell us stories. You could be a mother for us."

"Oh, but I can't," said Wendy. "What would my mother say? And besides, I can't fly."

"I'll teach you," said Peter. "We just jump on the back of the wind, and away we go. And when we get to the Never-Land, there are mermaids, and fairies, and Indians, and—"

Peter was going to say "pirates," but he thought it better not to mention them.

"Oooh, it would be splendid!" cried Wendy. "But would you teach Michael and John to fly, so that they could come too?"

"If you like," said Peter. So Wendy shook her brothers and woke them up. "Peter Pan is here," she cried, "and he's going to teach us to fly!"

Peter blew some fairy dust on each of them and said, "All you have to do is think lovely, wonderful thoughts, and wriggle your shoulders, and let go."

In half a minute the three little Darlings were flying around the room, their heads bumping against the ceiling. "Come on!" cried Peter. And out the window they flew.

This is just the beginning of the story. To read about the children's adventures in the Never-Land, check your library for a book about Peter Pan.

American Tall Tales

Pecos Bill

The greatest cowboy that ever lived was the one they called Pecos Bill.

Bill was born in East Texas and might have lived there forever, but one day his pa came running out of the house shouting to his ma, "Pack up everything we got, Ma! There's neighbors moved in near about sixty miles away, and it's gettin' too crowded around here."

So Bill's folks loaded a covered wagon with everything they owned and headed west. It was a long, hard journey. The children were packed into the back of the wagon, all eighteen of them. They fussed and hollered and fought as the wagon bounced along. The children were so loud that Bill's ma said you couldn't hear the thunder over the noise of the children.

One day the wagon hit a rock and little Bill fell right out. With all the fussing and fighting, nobody noticed. The wagon just kept on going. So little Bill found himself sitting in the dirt along the banks of the Pecos River, and that's how he came to be named Pecos Bill. But that was later.

Little Bill was not your average baby. He didn't cry. He just crawled along on the dusty plain, keeping his eyes peeled for whatever came along. And the first thing that came along was a coyote.

When the coyote saw this dirty, naked little creature crawling around on all fours, she thought he was a cute little animal, even if his ears were mighty small. Little Bill reached up and patted the coyote's head and said, "Nice doggie!"

The doggie—I mean the coyote—liked Little Bill. She took him home and raised him with her pups. The coyotes taught Bill to roam the prairies and howl at the moon. They taught him the secrets of hunting. They taught him how to leap like an antelope and run like the wind. They taught him how to chase lizards and lie so still that he was almost invisible.

The years went by—seventeen of them, to be exact—and Bill grew up strong and healthy. One day he was out hunting along the Pecos River when he saw a most unusual sight. It seemed to be a big animal with four legs. Or was it six legs? And why did it have one head in front and another up on top?

Well, it turned out to be a horse with a man riding it, something Bill had never seen before. Bill scurried around the horse a few times. Then he slowly crept forward and took a sniff of one of the man's boots.

"Boy," said the man, "what are you doin' scampering around down there in your birthday suit?"

"Sniffin'," said Bill. "I'm a coyote!"

"No, you ain't," said the man. "You're a man, like me."

"Nooo!" howled Bill. "Coyoteeeee!"

"What makes you think you are a coyote?" said the man.

"I have fleas!" said Bill.

"So what?" said the man. "Lots of men here in Texas have fleas."

But Bill was not persuaded. He was sure he was a coyote.

"Here's the thing," said the man. "Coyotes have big pointy ears and big bushy tails. And you don't."

"Yes, I do!" cried Bill. He felt sure he had a tail, just like all the other coyotes. He looked over his shoulder but couldn't see one. He reached back to grab his tail but he could not feel one. He backed up to the river and looked for his tail in the reflection, but it was not there.

Bill was surprised. He thought for a few moments. Then he decided the man must be right. If he didn't have a tail, he couldn't be a coyote. If he wasn't a coyote, he must be a man.

Bill decided he'd have to say farewell to his four-legged friends and try living as a man. He went to stay with the man, who happened to be a cowboy.

The man gave Bill some clothes to wear and a horse to ride. He also gave him a nickname: Pecos Bill. At first Bill had trouble living like a man. He couldn't stand the way his clothes scratched and pulled at his skin, or the way his boots came between his bare feet and the good old dirt. And he couldn't see the need for a knife or fork when it was so much easier to pick up your meat with your fingers and tear it with your teeth.

Bill learned to act like a man, but he still had a spark of wildness in him, and it would flash out from time to time. One day he was out riding on his horse when he was surprised by a mountain lion. The mountain lion scared Bill's horse away and charged right at Bill. But Pecos Bill was too quick for that cat. He dodged him once or twice; then he hopped right onto his back.

The mountain lion was not happy, no sir. He bucked. He snarled. He tried to twist around and bite Bill. Bill held on to the lion's neck with one hand. With his other hand, he waved his cowboy hat in the air and shouted, "Yahoo!"

The mountain lion did everything he could to shake Bill off, but it was no use. Finally he gave in and let Bill ride him. Then Bill put a saddle on the lion and rode him like a horse. Bill had tamed the mountain lion.

Another day, Pecos Bill was attacked by a giant rattlesnake. This particular rattlesnake was a mean old fellow who thought he was the king of the desert. He struck at Bill's heel, but Pecos Bill was too quick for that rattler.

Pecos Bill grabbed the rattlesnake by the neck and squeezed him hard. The snake wriggled and writhed in Bill's grip.

"Say 'uncle' if you've had enough!" said Bill.

"G-g-g-uncle!" said the snake, gurgling out the sounds as best as he could.

Bill relaxed his grip a bit and asked the rattler, "Who's the boss around here?"

"I was," said the snake. "But now you are."

"Well then," said Pecos Bill, "how'd you like to work for me?"

"Sure thing!" said the rattler.

From then on, the rattler was a different kind of critter altogether. He gazed at Pecos Bill with admiration and purred like a kitten. Pecos Bill had squeezed all the meanness right out of that snake!

Pecos Bill rolled the rattler up into a coil and rode away on his mountain lion.

On the way back to camp, he spotted a runaway cow. He grabbed the rattler and tied a loop at one end of him to make a lasso. Then he rode after the cow, swinging his lasso above his head. When he was close enough, he tossed the looped end of the snake over the cow. Pecos Bill jumped off the mountain lion and pulled the lasso tight, stopping the runaway cow right in his tracks.

Pecos Bill brought the cow back to his friend the cowboy. After that he taught all the cowboys at the ranch how to use a lasso to catch a runaway cow. He taught them other things, too. He taught them how to tame wild horses by riding them, just as he had done with the mountain lion. He even taught them how to sing cowboy songs around the campfire at night, in a voice that sounded a lot like a lonesome coyote howling at the moon.

Pecos Bill was famous for his riding skills. He once rode a wild mustang called the Backbreaker that no one else could ride. But that story pales in comparison to the time he rode something that no other man had before, and I reckon no man ever will again—a cyclone!

That's right. Pecos Bill lassoed a cyclone with his rattlesnake lasso and jumped on its rip-roaring back. The cyclone spun furiously, trying to throw Bill off. It went spinning this way and that way across the deserts of Arizona, trying to knock Bill off by rising up into the air and digging down into the ground. But Pecos Bill didn't let go. He held on tight until the cyclone spun itself out of energy, and by that time the two of them had carved out a deep canyon. If you ever go to Arizona, you can still see that canyon today. It's called the Grand Canyon.

John Henry

In the 1860s, the United States was growing quickly. Immigrants were pouring in, and railroad companies were laying train tracks that would carry settlers west.

The engineers who built the railroads had to overcome many challenges. They had to build bridges over rivers, and they had to dig tunnels through mountains.

Sometimes, when the mountains were more like hills, the workers were able to lay tracks over the top of them. Other times they were able to lay track that zigzagged around the mountains, like a snake. But some mountains were too tall to go over and too big to go around.

In those cases, the only solution was to dig a tunnel right through the mountain. Digging tunnels was dangerous work. The tunnels were dark and poorly ventilated. That means that there was barely enough fresh air inside the tunnels for the workers to breathe. Many workers were killed when the tunnels caved in.

To dig the tunnels as fast as they could, railroad workers worked in teams of two. One man would crouch down and hold a steel spike. Then the other man would hit the spike with a hammer. The first man would twist the spike as much as he could. Then his partner would hit the spike with the hammer again. The two men would work together, banging and twisting, banging and twisting, until they had driven the spike deep into the rock. Then they would pull out the spike, move to another spot, and start digging a new hole. After a while, the side of the mountain would be full of holes, like a piece of Swiss cheese.

Next, the dynamite men would take over. They would pack dynamite into the holes and blow up the explosives—*kaboom!* The explosions would break up the solid rock into rubble. The workers would haul away the rubble. Then they would start digging again.

To make the days go by faster, the railroad workers used to have contests. They would pick two teams and see which team could drive its spike farther into the mountain in a set amount of time. The winners of these contests became heroes. People would tell stories about these "steel-driving" men and their amazing feats. Another thing the railway workers did to pass the time while they worked was sing songs. Sometimes they would even sing songs about other steel-driving men.

One of these steel-driving men was named John Henry. No one knew for certain where John Henry was from. Some said he was from Georgia. Some said he was from Tennessee. Others said he was a Virginia man. It seems likely that he was a former slave who started working on the railroads sometime after the end of the Civil War.

One thing we are sure of is that John Henry was a legend among railway workers. They sang a song that tells the story about how he was born with a hammer in his hand. John Henry became known as the most courageous man who ever worked on the railroad. Even as a young boy he could do the work of a man. They said he had never been defeated in a steel-driving competition. They said he hit the spike so hard that sparks flew through the air. They said John Henry could swing a ten-pound hammer from sunup to sundown and not even get tired.

At first, almost all of the work on the tunnels was done by hand by workers like John Henry. Eventually, however, this began to change.

People invented machines that could do some of the work. One of the machines they invented was a steam drill. This was a drill that was powered by a steam engine. The first steam drills were pretty good, but they were not great. The steam drills could drive a spike into the mountain for sure, but not as well as two strong, experienced railway workers like John Henry and his partner. Over time the machines got better and better, and they eventually began to replace the men who worked on the railroad tunnels.

One day, the captain of John Henry's work team brought a steam drill to the worksite. He bet that the steam drill could drive steel better than John Henry could. John Henry agreed to compete against the steam drill, and he swore he would do his best to beat it. John Henry said to the captain:

"Well, a man ain't nothin' but a man.
But before I let a steam drill beat me down,
I'll die with a hammer in my hand.
Oh, oh! I'll die with a hammer in my hand."

One of the bosses blew a whistle. John Henry went to work driving steel the old-fashioned way, with a hammer and a spike. The captain started up the steam drill. It rattled away beside John Henry, belching steam and banging away at the mountain. The man and the machine worked side by side for several hours. Then the boss blew his whistle again. The bosses took measurements, and then they announced the results. John Henry had driven his spike a total of fifteen feet into the mountain. And the steam drill? It had only drilled nine feet. John Henry had won! He had beaten the steam drill!

Now the man that invented the steam drill,
He thought he was mighty fine.
But John Henry drove his fifteen feet
And the steam drill only made nine.
Oh, oh! The steam drill only made nine!

The other railway workers roared. They were excited that John Henry had won. He had shown that a hard worker was better than a machine! But John Henry himself was in no condition to celebrate. He had worked so hard that he had suffered a heart attack.

John Henry hammered in the mountains,
And his hammer was strikin' fire.
Well, he hammered so hard that it broke his poor heart,
And he laid down his hammer and he died.
Oh, oh! He laid down his hammer and he died.

The railway men carried John Henry out of the tunnel. They laid him to rest with other workers who had died. But the legend of John Henry lived on.

They took John Henry down the tunnel,
And they buried him in the sand.
And every locomotive comes a-roarin' by
Says, "Yonder lies a steel-drivin' man!
Oh, oh, yonder lies a steel-drivin' man."

Paul Bunyan

Even as a baby, Paul Bunyan was mighty big. How big? Well, he was so big that his parents had to use a covered wagon for his cradle.

As you might imagine, young Paul had a big appetite. He gobbled up six barrels of porridge a day, and his parents had to milk three dozen cows every morning and every evening just to keep his baby bottle filled.

Paul was so big it caused some problems in the little town in Maine where he grew up. When he sneezed, he blew the birds from Maine to California. When he snored, the neighbors ran out of their houses hollering, "Earthquake! Earthquake!"

After a while, Paul's father decided that it might be safer for the townsfolk if Paul didn't sleep in town. He built a large raft for Paul and floated it off the coast. Paul slept on the raft for a few nights, but things didn't work out. When Paul turned over in his sleep, he created gigantic waves that knocked down houses along the coast.

Eventually, Paul's father decided that the East Coast was just too small for Paul Bunyan. The only sensible thing to do was to move out west. So the Bunyan family moved to Minnesota.

In those days Minnesota was full of logging camps, sawmills, and lumberjacks. Americans were moving west and "building the country." They had to cut down a lot of trees to make their homes, not to mention their schools, churches, boats, and furniture.

When he grew up, Paul Bunyan went to work as a lumberjack, and what a lumberjack he proved to be! He made himself a giant ax, with a handle carved out of a full-grown hickory tree. He could bring down the tallest tree with a single swing of his ax. As the tree tipped over, he would yell, "Timber!" so the other lumberjacks had time to get out of the way.

Everyone looked up to Paul Bunyan—way up! The other lumberjacks admired him. The bosses were grateful for the amazing amount of work he could do in a day. Paul had a big heart, too, but one thing he always wished for was a true friend. There simply wasn't anybody else his size who could be his friend.

That all changed during the winter of the Big Blue Snow. It was called the winter of the Big Blue Snow because it was so cold that everyone shivered and turned blue. Even the snow shivered and turned blue. One day, as Paul made his way through the snowdrifts, he heard a muffled whimper. He followed the noise until he saw two big blue furry things sticking up out of the snow. He reached down and gave a pull.

It turned out that the two big blue furry things were two big blue ears. And connected to the big blue ears was a giant blue baby ox!

"The poor little fellow!" Paul exclaimed. "He's half frozen." He carried the blue ox home, wrapped him in blankets, and fed him.

The baby ox was so content that he took a long nap in Paul's big, strong arms. When he woke up, he looked up at Paul, and do you know what he said? "Mama! Mama!" Then he gave Paul a big, slobbery lick on the face. Paul laughed and said, "Babe, we're gonna be great friends!"

And they were. In fact, Paul Bunyan and Babe the Blue Ox were soon inseparable. Everywhere Paul went, Babe went, too. The two of them worked together in the lumber camps. Paul chopped down the trees. Then Babe hauled them to the river and dropped them in so they could float downstream to a sawmill. Between the two of them, Paul and Babe did the work of a hundred men.

The lumber company didn't want to lose Paul, and they figured the best way to keep him happy was to keep him well fed. So they hired a special cook to feed Paul and Babe. The cook's name was Sourdough Sam. Sourdough Sam was known for the giant flapjacks he cooked in the world's biggest frying pan. The colossal pan sat on an enormous cast-iron frame. Every morning Sourdough Sam would build a raging forest fire underneath the pan. Then he would call for his two Swedish helpers, Lars Larson and Pete Peterson. Lars and Pete would grease up the pan by tying slabs of bacon to their feet and skating back and forth across the sizzling pan. Then Sourdough Sam would make a giant stack of pancakes for Paul and an even larger stack for Babe.

Thanks to Sourdough Sam and his gigantic flapjacks, Babe eventually grew to be even bigger than Paul. He was so big that if you were standing at his front legs, you had to use a telescope to see all the way to his back legs. In fact, he was so heavy that his footprints filled up with water and turned into lakes. There are more than ten thousand lakes in Minnesota today, and most of them were created by Babe the Blue Ox back in the frontier days.

Babe and Paul helped the lumberjacks solve all sorts of problems. Once there was a river that was full of twists and turns. Sometimes the trees would get stuck in the turns and never make it downstream to the sawmill. But Paul Bunyan thought of a way to fix that! He went to one end of the river and sent Babe to the other end. Paul grabbed the river and pulled in one direction. Babe bit down on the other end and pulled in the opposite direction. Then—*snap!* Just like that, all of the kinks were pulled out, and the river was as straight as an ax handle.

Of course, this tightening operation left the river a good deal longer than it had been before, and there was a lot of extra water lying around. Paul and Babe worked together to dig five big holes to hold all the extra water. Nowadays these are called the Great Lakes.

One day, the logging bosses got to talking. One of them said that the United States was a fine country, to be sure, but it could still stand a little improvement. For one thing, it could use a few more rivers. And what it really needed was a big river running right down the middle of the country, all the way from Minnesota down to the Gulf of Mexico. "If we had a river like that," the man said, "we could ship timber down to New Orleans and all around the world!"

Paul Bunyan happened to overhear this conversation. He told the bosses he would see what he could do. He hitched up Babe and they started plowing south. As they plowed, they threw a great mound of dirt and rocks to the right and a smaller mound to the left. On the right side they made the Rocky Mountains, and on the left side they made the Appalachian Mountains. Paul Bunyan and Babe didn't stop until they had plowed a channel all the way south to the Gulf of Mexico. And the river that flows in that channel nowadays, that's what we call the Mississippi River.

From that day on, Paul and Babe went around the country, using their size and strength to help anyone who needed it. A few years later, they dug the Grand Canyon out west. And when the wind blows just right from the west, you can still smell those famous colossal pancakes cooking on the frontier.

Myths from Ancient Greece

Heroes and Monsters, Gods and Goddesses

Here are some stories that have been around for two thousand years or more. These stories come to us from ancient Greece. (In the World History and Geography section of this book, you can read about the great civilization in ancient Greece.) We call these stories "myths." Many myths tell about brave heroes, great battles, terrible monsters, or gods and goddesses. Some myths explain why we have seasons, or why there are volcanoes, or how constellations got in the sky. Of course today we know the real reasons that all these things happen. But long, long ago, many people believed the myths were true. Even though we no longer believe in the old myths, we like to tell them because they're such wonderful stories.

Like the people in the other ancient civilizations you've learned about, the ancient Greeks believed in many gods and goddesses. The Greeks built beautiful temples, like the Parthenon, to honor their gods. In the Greek myths, the gods and goddesses sometimes act like normal people—like you and me. They need to eat, drink, and sleep. They can be happy one moment and angry the next. They fall in love and get married. They play tricks on each other. They argue and fight with each other.

Unlike people, however, the Greek gods had magical powers. Some gods could change into an animal or hurl lightning bolts from the sky! Also, the Greeks believed the gods were immortal, which means that they never died but lived forever.

The ancient Greeks believed the gods and goddesses lived on a mountain that rose high above the clouds, called Mount Olympus. From there, they looked down on the earth, and they used their powers to help the people they liked or hurt the people they didn't like.

Let's meet some of the main Greek gods and goddesses.

Zeus [ZOOCE], the king of the gods, controlled the heavens and decided arguments among the gods. He could change his shape in an instant. If he wanted, he could come to earth as a swan or as a fierce bull. When he was angry, he had the power to throw lightning bolts down from the heavens!

Poseidon [poe-SIDE-un], the god of the sea, was an especially important god to the Greeks. Can you think of why? (Look at a map and see what's around Greece.) Poseidon could make the oceans as calm as a sleeping baby, or he could stir up high waves to crush a ship to pieces. In pictures, Poseidon often has a long beard and holds a trident, a kind of long pitchfork with three prongs.

Hera [HAIR-uh], the wife of Zeus, was queen of the gods and the goddess of marriage. She could be a very jealous person. But her husband, Zeus, had a habit of falling in love with many other goddesses and women, so Hera usually had a good reason to be jealous.

Apollo [uh-PAUL-oh], a son of Zeus, was the god of light. He is sometimes called Phoebus [FEE-bus] Apollo. "Phoebus" means "brilliant" or "shining." He was also the god of poetry and music. No one could sing so beautifully or play so sweetly on the lyre (an instrument like a small harp). He was also the god of healing, as well as the god of archery.

Artemis [AR-tuh-miss], the twin sister of Apollo, was the goddess of the moon and the goddess of hunting. She loved the woods and the wild creatures that lived there. She loved to be free and on her own. So she asked her father, Zeus, to promise that he would never make her get married, which is a promise Zeus kept.

Ares [AIR-eez] was the cruel and merciless god of war. Wherever he went, death and destruction followed. No one liked him, not even his parents, Zeus and Hera!

Aphrodite [af-roe-DIE-tee] was the goddess of love and beauty. When she was born, she rose out of the sea from the gentle waves on a cushion of soft foam. She had a son called **Eros** [AIR-oss], though you may know him by a more familiar name, Cupid. Maybe you've seen a picture of him on Valentine's Day cards. The Greeks said that when Aphrodite wanted someone to fall in love, she ordered Eros to shoot that person with one of his magic arrows. If he hit you with an arrow, then you would fall in love with the first person you saw! No one could resist the power of his magic arrows, not even Zeus.

Athena [uh-THEE-nah; "TH" as in "thin"] was the goddess of wisdom. For the people of the Greek city called Athens, she was a special goddess, for they believed she protected their city. She had a most unusual birth. One day Zeus had a terrible headache. He complained to Hephaestus, who took his hammer and struck Zeus on the head! Out of Zeus's head jumped Athena, already grown-up and fully dressed in a suit of armor.

Hermes [HER-meez], the messenger god, carried commands from the gods to humans on earth. In pictures, he often has wings on his hat or sandals to show how fast he traveled.

New Word

Does your child know what "lame" means? Lame means unable to walk because of an injury or illness.

Hephaestus [hih-FES-tus] was the god of fire and the forge. He could cause volcanoes, making the earth spit up hot flames and lava. (The word "volcano" comes from the Roman name for this god, Vulcan.) But most of all he used fire to make things. He used it to heat metal and make armor, swords, and spears, or beautiful cups and shining jewelry. Hephaestus was lame, and spent his time working at his fiery forge.

Hades [HAY-deez] was the grim god of the underworld, the dark and shadowy underground place that the Greeks believed people went to when they died. The Greeks often called this place Hades, the same name as the god who ruled there over the dead.

Same Gods, Different Names

The gods and goddesses of the ancient Greeks were later worshipped by the people of ancient Rome. (You'll learn more about the Romans in the third-grade book in this series.) If you look in your library for books of myths, you may find that some books use the Greek names for the gods, while others use the Roman names. Here's a chart to help you keep track of who's who. Are you familiar with some of the Roman names?

Greek Name	Roman Name
Zeus	Jupiter (or Jove)
Hera	Juno
Poseidon	Neptune
Apollo	Apollo
Artemis	Diana
Aphrodite	Venus
Ares	Mars
Hermes	Mercury
Hephaestus	Vulcan
Athena	Minerva
Hades	Pluto
Dionysus	Bacchus
Demeter	Ceres

Gods of Nature and Mythical Creatures

The Greeks believed in other gods and goddesses connected to the earth and nature.

Dionysus [die-un-NIE-sus] was the god of wine. Everywhere he went he taught people how to grow grapes and make wine. But sometimes Dionysus and his helpers made people act wild or do crazy things.

Demeter [dih-MEE-ter] was the goddess of grain and the harvest. The Greeks believed that because of her, corn and other grains grew in the fields, trees grew tall, and flowers bloomed. By the way, the Roman name for Demeter was Ceres [SEER-eez]. From that name we get our word for a food that you might often eat for breakfast—cereal!

In Greek myths you might meet some curious creatures. Some are beautiful, like the winged horse called **Pegasus.**

Some are scary, like **Cerberus** [SIR-bur-us], a dog that belonged to Hades, the god of the underworld.

This dog was not man's best friend! He had three snarling heads. He guarded the gate to the underworld. He let in the spirits of the dead and then made sure they didn't get out.

Some mythical creatures are part human and part animal. The **Centaur** [SEN-tar] was part human and part horse.

An odd-looking fellow named **Pan** had goat horns on his head, and his feet were goat hooves. He was a wild and frisky creature who loved to dance through the forests and mountains. He played lively music on a set of pipes that we now call "panpipes," or a "pan flute."

Prometheus Brings Fire, Pandora Brings Woe

Here is a myth about how a good thing happened, followed by a very bad thing.

Once, only the gods on Mount Olympus had fire. On earth, the people had nothing to give them light in the darkness, or warm them on a cold night, or cook their food.

A brave and powerful giant named Prometheus [pruh-MEE-thee-us] felt sorry for mankind. He stole fire from the gods and took it to the people on earth.

When Zeus, king of the gods, found out what Prometheus had done, he was furious. To punish him, he had Prometheus tied to a rock with unbreakable chains. Day after day, a fierce eagle flew down and ripped and clawed at the body of poor Prometheus. (Much later, Prometheus was finally set free by a hero named Hercules—but that's another story.)

Then Zeus looked down on the earth and said, "Let the people keep their fire. I will make them a hundred times more miserable than they were before

they had it." And so he told Hephaestus to use his skills to make a woman at his forge. Zeus called this woman Pandora, and when he breathed life into her, she was as sweet and lovely as the flowers in the spring. He sent Pandora to earth, and he gave her a closed box and told her never to open it.

But Pandora was very, very curious. Every time she looked at the box she wanted to know what was in it. She knew very well that Zeus had told her not to open it. But, she said to herself, what harm could it do to take one little peek inside? And so she lifted the lid. Out from the box flew all the bad things in the world—pain, disease, disaster, sorrow, jealousy, and hatred.

But some people say there was one more thing in Pandora's box—hope. Hope is what keeps people going despite all the bad things in the world.

Oedipus and the Sphinx

Long ago, near the Greek city of Thebes, there lived a terrible creature called the Sphinx. She had the face of a woman but the body of a lion with wings. When travelers came to the city, she would swoop down upon them. Then she would ask them a riddle. If they could answer the riddle, she would let them go. But if they couldn't, she would eat them! So far, no one had been able to answer the riddle. Everyone in Thebes lived in fear of the monster.

Then one day a very smart and brave young man named Oedipus was on his way to Thebes. When the Sphinx saw him, she smiled, for she thought she would soon have a tasty lunch.

"Answer this riddle," she said to Oedipus, "or meet your doom. What creature goes on four feet in the morning, on two feet at noon, and on three feet in the evening?"

Oedipus looked up at the Sphinx and said, "Man. In childhood he crawls on his hands and knees, which is like four feet. In the middle of his life, when he is grown up, he walks on two feet. And in the evening of his life, when he is old, he uses a cane, which is like walking on three feet."

Oedipus had solved the riddle! The Sphinx was so angry that she threw herself into the ocean and drowned. And the people of Thebes were so grateful to Oedipus that they made him their new king.

Theseus and the Minotaur

Once upon a time, not far from Greece on the island of Crete, there lived a king named Minos [MY-noce]. King Minos led a war against the Greek city of Athens. He burned the ships of the Athenians, and destroyed their fields and gardens. Then he sent a cruel message to the ruler of Athens, King Aegeus [uh-JEE-us]. "Every nine years," said King Minos, "when the springtime comes, you shall choose seven of your youths and seven of your maidens and send them to me in a ship. If you fail to do this, my soldiers will burn your city to the ground."

"But," the Athenians asked, "what shall happen to the youths and maidens?"

"In Crete," said King Minos, "there is a giant maze, called the Labyrinth, designed by the master inventor Daedalus [DED-ah-lus]. Whoever goes in the Labyrinth can never find his way out. Deep inside there lives a monster, half man and half bull, called the Minotaur [MIN-oh-tar]. I will put your youths and maidens into the Labyrinth, and there they will be eaten by the Minotaur."

And so, when nine years had passed and the flowers began to bloom in the spring, there was no joy in Athens, but only tears and sadness. Seven youths and maidens were put on board a black-sailed ship and sent to their terrible fate in the Labyrinth.

Now, another nine years had almost passed when a young man arrived in Athens. His name was Theseus [THEE-see-us; "TH" as in "thin"], and he was a prince. In fact, he was the son of King Aegeus. He had been raised by his mother in a faraway town. Now that he was grown he had come to Athens to meet his father, the king. King Aegeus embraced his son with great happiness.

Theseus arrived in Athens just a few days before seven youths and seven maidens were to be sent to the Minotaur. When Theseus learned of this, he said, "I will take the place of one of the youths. I will kill the Minotaur and all of us shall return safely." King Aegeus begged his son not to go. But Theseus promised his father, "When I return, I will change the sail of the ship from black to white, so you will know that I have succeeded."

The ship sailed to the island of Crete. When they arrived, the young victims were marched through the streets on the way to the Labyrinth. And that is when

Ariadne [ar-ee-ADD-nee], the lovely daughter of King Minos, saw Theseus. She could not bear the thought of sending this young, handsome prince to his death. And so she went to Daedalus, the inventor of the Labyrinth. She asked him how anyone who entered the great maze could get out again. Daedalus gave her a clever idea, and she rushed to the prison where Theseus was locked up.

Ariadne whispered, "Listen, Theseus. If you will promise to marry me and take me with you to Athens, I will help you." Theseus gladly agreed. Then Ariadne gave him a ball of string and told him to tie one end to the gate of the Labyrinth and unwind the ball as he went along. That way, he could follow the string to find his way back out.

Theseus soon found himself deep in the dark, winding halls of the Labyrinth. He heard a rumbling, growling sound. It was the Minotaur, snoring in his sleep. Theseus leaped on the beast. He had never wrestled so strong or savage an opponent. With fierce roars, the Minotaur fought back. But Theseus had taken the beast by surprise, and in the end the Minotaur lay dead.

Theseus followed the string back out of the Labyrinth. With Ariadne's help, he freed the other Greek youths and maidens. Then they all boarded the ship and set sail for Athens.

But oh, what a sad mistake followed! In his rush, Theseus forgot to replace the ship's black sail with a white one. His father, who had been sitting for days on a cliff looking out over the sea, awaited the return of his son. Now, when King Aegeus saw the black-sailed ship, he fainted and fell forward into the sea. And ever since then the sea where he drowned has been called the Aegean Sea.

Daedalus and Icarus

As you know, the master inventor Daedalus designed the Labyrinth for King Minos. Daedalus also showed Ariadne how Theseus could escape from the Labyrinth. When King Minos found this out, he was so angry that he threw Daedalus in the Labyrinth, along with his young son, Icarus [IK-er-us].

Not even the man who invented the Labyrinth could find his way out of it. Would the father and son die there? No—for when Daedalus saw the seagulls flying overhead, he got an idea.

Little by little, he gathered many feathers. He fastened them together with wax, and so made two pairs of wings like those of a bird. He put one pair on himself and the other pair on Icarus. He showed his son how to move his arms and catch the wind with his wings.

"Now, son," he said, "let us fly away from here. But listen carefully. Do not fly too high, or you will get too close to the sun, and the wax on your wings will melt."

Daedalus and Icarus flew up out of the Labyrinth, over the sea, away from the island of Crete. "Oh," cried Icarus, "it's wonderful to be free and flying through the air!"

"Yes," said Daedalus, "but do not fly too close to the sun."

A puff of wind lifted Icarus up. He was so excited that he forgot what his father told him. Higher and higher he flew, toward the highest heavens.

The warm sun began to melt the wax, and one by one the feathers fell from his wings. Then down, down, down fell Icarus into the sea. Daedalus cried out in grief because he saw the waters close over his son far below.

Arachne the Weaver

In all of Athens, no one could spin such fine thread or weave such wonderful cloth as the young woman named Arachne [uh-RAK-nee]. People from miles around came to admire her cloth. Arachne grew so proud of her weaving that she began to boast, "I am the most wonderful weaver in the world!"

"Yes, of course," said her friends, "next to the great goddess Athena."

"Athena? Ha!" said Arachne. "Can she spin thread so fine, or weave it into cloth as beautiful as mine? Why, I could teach her a thing or two!"

An old woman in a dark cloak spoke to Arachne. "Be careful, my dear," she said. "You must show respect for the gods. Your boasting may anger Athena."

"I'm not afraid of Athena," snapped Arachne. "Let her come here and we'll see who is the better weaver."

Then the old woman threw back her cloak. There was a flash of light, and before Ariadne stood the gray-eyed goddess, Athena. "I am ready," said Athena quietly. "Take me to a loom, and let us begin. When we are finished, if your work is best, then I will weave no more. But if my work is best, then you will never weave again. Do you agree?"

"I agree," said Arachne. "Let us begin." She went to one loom and Athena to another. The people looked on in wonder as the goddess and the young woman wove brilliant designs into their cloth.

With threads of many colors, Arachne wove cloth as fine and light as a silken web. "How beautiful!" said the people. "It almost seems as if she could weave sunlight and rainbows into her cloth."

Arachne stepped back from her loom and turned to look at Athena's work. Into her cloth the goddess had woven flowers that seemed to bloom, and a stream that seemed to ripple by, and clouds that seemed to float peacefully in a blue sky, and above them the dazzling figures of the immortal gods themselves. When the people looked at it, they were so filled with wonder that they gasped. Arachne herself had to admit that Athena's work was more beautiful than her own. She hid her face in her hands and wept. "Oh, how can I live if I must never spin or weave again?" she cried.

When Athena saw that Arachne would never have any joy unless she could

spin and weave, she said, "I cannot break the agreement we had, but I will change you so that you spin and weave forever." And with a touch, she turned Arachne into a spider, which ran to a corner and quickly began to spin and weave a beautiful, shining web.

And that is why some people say that all spiders in the world are the children of Arachne.

Make a Connection
Today, scientists use a special name for the class of animals that spiders belong to. Spiders are not insects but *arachnids*. Learn why spiders aren't insects on page 440.

Swift-Footed Atalanta

Atalanta [at-uh-LAN-tuh] was a beautiful Greek maiden who could run faster than the winds. She loved nothing better than to run freely across the fields, through the woods, and up and down the hills.

Atalanta's father thought that she should get married and settle down. But she cared nothing for the many young men who came daily to ask to marry her. So many men came, in fact, that one day she announced, "If you wish to marry me, then hear this. I will marry the man who can beat me in a race."

"Fine!" the men cried. "Let's start now."

"But there is one more thing," said Atalanta. "Whoever runs this race and loses to me shall also lose his life."

"That should scare them away," thought Atalanta, "for they know that I can outrun the wind."

And indeed, many of the men began to cough and feel a cold coming on, or suddenly remembered that they had forgotten some important business that they simply *had* to attend to at once.

But a few men stayed. Yes, they had heard about Atalanta's swiftness, but after all, could they be beaten by a *girl*? Nonsense!

And so these men raced Atalanta. She even gave them a head start of a hundred paces. But for each, it was a race to his doom.

Then one day there arrived a young man named Hippomenes [hip-POM-eh-neez]. Atalanta liked his fair features, his gentle eyes, and his brave spirit, and she felt pity for him. "Do not run against me," she said, "for I shall surely beat you, and that will be your end."

"Let me try anyway," said Hippomenes. Of course he knew that he did not have a chance at outrunning her. But he had prayed to Aphrodite, the goddess of love, and asked for her help to win Atalanta as his wife. And Aphrodite had answered his prayers by giving him three golden apples and telling him what to do with them.

The race began. Even though Atalanta started a hundred paces behind Hippomenes, she quickly

caught up to him. When he heard her breath close behind him, he took one of the golden apples and threw it over his shoulder.

When Atalanta saw the glittering apple, she left the path to pick it up. Hippomenes pulled ahead a little. But Atalanta easily caught up with him again. As she did, he threw the second golden apple even farther from the path. Again Atalanta left the path to get the apple, for she knew that she could still win. Again she caught up with Hippomenes, who was puffing and gasping. He took the third apple and threw it as far as he could. With an invisible nudge from Aphrodite, the apple rolled down a hill.

Atalanta could see that if she chased this apple, she might fall too far behind to win. But she dashed aside and grabbed the apple. Then she strained every muscle to catch up with Hippomenes. They were coming closer and closer to the finish line. She could see his face and hear his hard breathing. With one last burst of speed, she could pass him.

Suddenly, however, Atalanta felt something for Hippomenes that was not pity, but something warmer and more generous. And so she did not speed up, and the young man crossed the finish line first. With a laugh, Atalanta took his hand and led him to her father's house, where they were married that very day. And from above, Aphrodite looked down and smiled on the happy couple.

Demeter and Persephone

Demeter [dih-MEE-ter] was the goddess of all that grows from the ground. She made the corn and grain ripen, the orchards bear fruit, and the flowers bloom.

More than anything else, Demeter loved her daughter, Persephone [per-SEF-un-nee]. Once, when Demeter was away looking after the crops in the fields, Persephone was playing in a field of flowers. As she stopped to pick a flower, she happened to pull the plant by its roots, leaving a little hole in the ground. Then suddenly the hole grew wider and deeper, and Persephone heard a rumbling like thunder below her.

From the dark hole, four coal-black horses burst forth, pulling a golden chariot with a tall, sad-eyed driver wearing a golden crown. "I am Hades, king of the underworld," he said. "Come with me and be my queen." Then he snatched Persephone into his arms and carried her to his kingdom below.

When Demeter returned home, she could not find her daughter. She asked everyone, but no one had seen her. Then she asked the Sun, who sees all. And he told her that he had seen Hades take Persephone to the underworld to be his queen.

When Demeter heard this, she wept. She was so sad that the golden corn and waving wheat died, the trees dropped their leaves, and the grass turned brown. All the earth was cold and bare. And Demeter cried out, "Nothing shall grow upon the earth until my daughter is returned to me."

Then Zeus, king of the gods, saw that the people and animals were hungry, for they had no grain or fruit to eat. And so he sent Hermes, the messenger god, to tell Hades to let Persephone go back to her mother. "You know the law, Hermes," said Zeus. "As long as the girl has not eaten any food of the underworld, she may leave. But anyone who eats down there must stay there forever."

Hermes flew from the heights of Olympus to the depths of the underworld. "King of this dark place," said Hermes to Hades, "even you must obey the will of mighty Zeus. Bid farewell to your queen."

Then Hermes turned to Persephone. "Take my hand, and let us go," he said. "But first, tell me, have you eaten anything while you were down here?"

"No," said the girl, "nothing but a few seeds from that bright red fruit, the pomegranate, which I plucked from a tree."

Hades smiled. "Then you must stay with me," he said.

But Zeus gave a command. He said that for each seed Persephone had eaten, she must spend one month of every year in the underworld with Hades. But she would be allowed to spend the other months with her mother.

And that is why every year, when Persephone must leave her mother and return to Hades, we have winter on earth. But while Demeter has Persephone with her, then she is happy, and brings forth the flowers and trees and crops from the warm earth.

The Labors of Hercules

Most people know the Greek hero Heracles by the familiar Roman name Hercules, which we use here.

Hercules was the strongest man on earth. But he did not always use his strength wisely. Once, in a fit of anger, he struck and killed someone, though he did not mean to. He went to the temple of Apollo to ask what he could do to make up for his terrible mistake. He was told to go to the home of his cousin, a king named Eurystheus [yur-ISS-thee-us], and do whatever the king asked him to do.

King Eurystheus was a weak, mean man, and he was jealous of his big, strong cousin. So when Hercules came to serve him, he tried to think of the most difficult and dangerous tasks he could.

"Hercules," said the king, "for your first labor, go to the land of Nemea [neh-ME-ah]. A terrible lion has been killing both cattle and people there. He is so strong that he can kill a man with one blow of his huge paw. His hide is so tough that no sword, spear, or arrow can pierce it. You are to kill the Nemean lion and bring its skin back to me."

"Well," thought the king to himself, "that should be the end of Hercules."

But he did not know his cousin's strength. When Hercules found the lion, he jumped on the beast and grabbed him. Then he squeezed with all his might until at last the lion was dead. But how could he take off the lion's skin? When he tried to use his knife, the blade broke into pieces. Then Hercules got an idea: he used one of the lion's own sharp claws, and sure enough, it cut the skin. After he had cleaned the skin, he wrapped it around him like a coat, with the head as a hood.

When Hercules returned, looking like a lion walking on two legs, the king was frightened. "Stay outside the palace," he said, "and I will call out my orders to you."

The king ordered Hercules to kill a fire-breathing, nine-headed monster called the Hydra. Hercules used his huge club to knock off one of the monster's heads, but then two heads grew back in its place! So he grabbed a large stick and set one end on fire. Then, as he swung his club to knock off each head, he held the fire to the neck to keep any other heads from growing back.

When King Eurystheus heard that Hercules had killed the Hydra, he thought, "He kills beasts and monsters so easily that I must think of another kind of labor. Ah, I know! I will send him across the mountains to clean the stables of King Augeas [aw-GEE-us]. They are the biggest and dirtiest stables in the world, filled with the waste of thousands of oxen and cattle."

When Hercules reached the Augean stables, he saw that it would take many years for a single man to clean them, even a man as strong as himself. But as he looked around he saw a river that ran nearby. "Why not use that?" he thought. So he asked King Augeas to have all the animals taken out of the stable for a day. Then he dug a ditch from the river to the stable, and let the water run through the building. The water washed away all the filth in no time. Hercules filled the ditch and set the river back on its normal course.

"Very clever, Hercules," said King Eurystheus. "But now it's time for a real challenge. For your next labor, I order you to bring me the golden apples guarded by those three magical maidens, the Hesperides" [heh-SPARE-ih-deez]. The king chuckled because he knew that these apples belonged to Hera, queen of the gods, and were kept in a secret garden that no one had ever found.

Hercules knew that he could not find the Hesperides. But he could find their father, Atlas, the great giant who carried the heavens and earth upon his shoulders.

"Mighty Atlas," said Hercules, "will you tell me where to find the golden apples of the Hesperides?"

"I cannot tell you such a secret," said Atlas. "But I could get the apples for you myself, if only I did not have to hold the heavens and the earth on my shoulders."

"Go and get the apples," said Hercules, "and I will hold the heavens and earth for you."

"I would be glad to have someone else carry this load for a while," said Atlas. So Hercules took the heavens and earth upon his own shoulders. His knees shook and he gasped, "Hurry, Atlas, for I do not know how long I can hold this."

In a short while Atlas came back with the golden apples, but he did not hand them over. "Hercules," he said, "I will take these apples to King Eurystheus myself."

Hercules could see that Atlas did not plan to come back. So he said, "Thank you, Atlas, that is kind of you. But before you go, would you please hold the heavens and earth for just a moment? I'm not as strong as you, so I need to put a pad on my shoulders to ease the pain."

"All right," said Atlas. He put down the apples and took the load from Hercules's shoulders.

"Thanks for the apples," said Hercules, and he hurried off.

After Hercules completed these and other labors, the gods allowed him to leave King Eurystheus. He traveled all over Greece, doing many great deeds wherever he went.

> **Make a Connection**
>
> In your school classroom or library you may have a book full of maps called an atlas. The word "atlas" comes from the name of the mythical character who held the heavens and earth on his shoulders.

Learning About Language

Grammar

PARENTS: Written language has special characteristics that children need to learn in order to be able to talk about language and make progress in their writing. The section that follows introduces a number of terms and rules of written language, but children will need to practice in school for these terms and conventions to sink in. In this book we introduce some terms and concepts that will be built on in later books. For example, in this book we introduce some parts of speech, and later books will introduce other parts of speech, as well as explain more about the parts introduced here.

Sentences

PARENTS: Point to these sentences as you read them to your child:

When I read this, I am reading a sentence. Now I am reading another sentence. What is a sentence? It's a group of words that expresses a complete thought.

Here are three groups of words. Are they all sentences?

(1) Tasha has lots of colored pencils.
(2) She likes to draw.
(3) Pictures of her dog.

Both (1) and (2) are sentences, but not (3)—it does not express a complete thought. It leaves you wondering, "Who made the pictures? Why?" But let's change (3) "Pictures of her dog" by adding some words.

Tasha likes drawing pictures of her dog.

Now, is that a complete sentence? Yes, it is. It expresses a complete thought. Every sentence has a *subject and a predicate*. Here are some examples.

subject

Tasha

She

Jennifer and her dog

predicate

has lots of colored pencils.

likes to draw.

likes drawing pictures of her dog.

Can you tell me which words make up the subject and which words make up the predicate in these sentences?

Our teacher baked cupcakes for a class party.
The alien spaceship landed in our yard.
Peter Piper picked a peck of pickled peppers.

Two Rules for Writing Sentences

First, every sentence must begin with a capital letter. Look at the sentences on this page. Notice that every sentence begins with a capital letter.

Second, you must end a sentence with a punctuation mark. You use a different mark for different kinds of sentences.

Most often you use the little dot called a period. You use a period to end sentences that tell something. The sentences you are reading here end with a period.

Some sentences ask a question. If you write a sentence that asks a question, you end it with a question mark. *Is it raining today?*

To show excitement, you use an exclamation point. *We won! What an amazing shot!*

Nouns Name a Person, Place, or Thing

Look around you. What do you see? A book? A chair? A window? A yard or a street?

"Book," "chair," "window," "yard," "street"—all those words are *nouns*.

A noun names a person, place, or thing. In the sentences below, the nouns are printed in blue:

The new boy from Texas brought his rabbit in a cage to school.
The rabbit got out. It ran to the cafeteria and ate a big salad.

Can you pick out the nouns in these sentences?

My sister likes slimy frogs.
The basketball swished through the net.
We saw amazing paintings and statues in the museum.

All these are nouns, too:

Elm Street
Fido
Johnson Elementary School
George Washington

Did you notice that all those nouns just named begin with a *capital letter*? That's because they don't name just any person, place, or thing, like "school," but a certain place, like Johnson Elementary School, or a certain person, like George Washington.

We call nouns that name a certain person, place, or thing *proper nouns*. You begin a proper noun with a capital letter. Your own name is a proper noun, too, so you begin each word in it with a capital letter.

Singular and Plural Nouns

A noun can name one thing, or it can name more than one. Another name for just one of something is *singular*. All of these are singular nouns:

car
pencil
pig

Another name for more than just one is *plural*. All of these are plural nouns:

cars
pencils
pigs

You can see that to change most singular nouns to plural, all you have to do is add the letter *s*. But for nouns that end in *s*, *ss*, *ch*, *sh*, or *x*, you need to add *es* to show more than one, like this:

singular	**plural**
bus	bus**es**
dress	dress**es**
lunch	lunch**es**
wish	wish**es**
fox	fox**es**

For some plural nouns, you don't use *s* or *es*, but instead you spell the word in a new way, like this:

singular	plural
foot	feet
tooth	teeth
child	children
woman	women
man	men

Verbs: Action Words

sing dance **eat** laugh **jump**
shout imagine **throw**

All of those words are *verbs*. Verbs usually show actions.

Jake **eats** a pizza.   Hannah **opens** a present.

Can you tell me which word is the verb in each of these sentences?

Lisa eats a banana.
The monkey slips on a banana peel.
The monkey chases Lisa.

Verbs: Past and Present

Verbs can tell about actions that happen now, or actions that happened before. We say that an action that happens now is in the *present*. We say that an action that happened before is in the *past*.

These verbs are in the present. (Notice how some end in *s* and some don't.)

Today I **dance**.
Sherry **dances** with me.
Ben **dances** with Alice.
We all **dance** together.

These verbs are in the past:

Yesterday I **danced**.
Sherry **danced** with me.
Ben **danced** with Alice.
We all **danced** together.

You can change many verbs from present to past by adding *ed*, like this:

present	past
Today I laugh.	Yesterday I laugh*ed*.
Juanita walks to town.	Last week she walk*ed* to school.
Today we watch a movie.	Yesterday we watch*ed* a movie.

But some verbs are different. Here are some verbs to watch out for. Try making up some sentences using these verbs in the past and in the present.

verb in the present	verb in the past
I see, you see	I saw, you saw
he sees	he saw
I do, they do	I did, they did
she does	she did
I come, you come	I came, you came
he comes	he came
I run, we run	I ran, we ran
she runs	she ran

verb in the present	verb in the past
he runs	he ran
I go, you go	I went, you went
she goes	she went

verb in the present	verb in the past
we give, you give	we gave, you gave
he gives	he gave
you sing, they sing	you sang, they sang
she sings	she sang

You need to pay special attention to make sure you use two verbs correctly. These verbs are **be** and **have**.

be		have	
present	**past**	**present**	**past**
I am	I was	I have	I had
he, she, it is	he, she, it was	he, she, it has	he, she, it had
we are	we were	we have	we had
you are	you were	you have	you had
they are	they were	they have	they had

Adjectives Describe Things

You know two kinds of words, nouns and verbs. Now let's find out about another kind, *adjectives*. Adjectives are the words we use to *describe* nouns (people, places, or things). Adjectives can tell how something looks or tastes or feels or sounds.

a **cute** puppy with **black** and **white** fur

a **slippery** fish   a **loud** noise

Can you pick out the adjectives in these sentences?

Sara loves her old, soft, fuzzy blanket.
The brown cow ate a large pizza.
Let's tell scary stories.

Sometimes adjectives tell how many. The words in blue in these sentences are adjectives that tell how many:

I have **many** pets.
I have **two** cats, **one** hamster, and **some** goldfish.
I take good care of **every** pet.

You can use adjectives to compare. Often all you have to do is add *er* or *est*, like this:

My cat is small.   Jane's cat is smaller.   Allie's cat is
                                                                             the smallest.

More About Words: Antonyms and Synonyms

Let's play a word game. I'm going to tell you a word, then you tell me an *antonym*. Antonyms are words that mean the opposite of each other. What is the opposite of cold? Hot. So "cold" and "hot" are antonyms. "Tall" and "short" are antonyms. Now, can you tell me an antonym for each of these words?

happy   fast   small   win

Okay, let's change the game a little. This time I'm going to tell you a word, and I want you to tell me a *synonym*. Synonyms are words that mean the same or almost the same thing. "Pretty" and "beautiful" are synonyms. "Big" and "large" are synonyms. Can you tell me a synonym for each of these words?

fast   angry   powerful   leap

Now, look at these pairs of words. Are they synonyms or antonyms?

love   hate
thin   skinny
begin   start
shout   whisper
loud   quiet
shiny   dull
calm   peaceful
wild   tame

loud   quiet

Contractions

When you write, sometimes you combine two words into one short word called a *contraction*. To show that letters have been left out in a contraction, you use the punctuation mark called an *apostrophe*, like this:

I am = I'm
you are = you're
do not = don't
is not = isn't
cannot = can't
are not = aren't

Abbreviations

Have you ever looked at the address on a letter? You might see something like this.

Mr. Reginald Doodleplum
14 Castaway St., Apt.3
Topeka, KS 66614

The address uses many *abbreviations*. Abbreviations save time by making words shorter. Here are the words that go with the abbreviations in that address:

Mr.	Mister
St.	Street
Apt.	Apartment
KS	Kansas

In addresses you may see other common abbreviations, such as Rd. (Road), Ave. (Avenue), or Ct. (Court). Every state, including your own, has a two-letter abbreviation, which is written in addresses before the zip code as two capital letters without a period. What is the postal abbreviation for your state?

Many abbreviations begin with a capital letter and end with a period. When you write to someone and you want to be polite, you might use an abbreviation like this:

Dear Mrs. Grundy,
Dear Ms. Greet,
Dear Mr. Chips,
Dear Dr. Frankenstein, ("Dr." stands for "Doctor")

The word "Miss" is not an abbreviation and does not end with a period.

Using Capital Letters

You already know that you always use a capital letter when you start a sentence. When else do you use a capital letter? You use a capital when you write names of particular people, places, or things, such as:

Cindy **G. S**mith
Lassie
Alberto's **R**estaurant

When you use an initial in a name, you write it as a capital letter followed by a period. For example, in Cindy G. Smith, the *G* stands for "Gail." How do you write your middle initial? Here are some other rules for using capital letters when you write.

- When you refer to yourself, use a capital *I*.
- Capitalize the months of the year and the days of the week.

> **J**anuary
> **F**ebruary
> **M**onday
> **T**uesday

- Capitalize the names of holidays.

> **T**hanksgiving
> **I**ndependence **D**ay
> **M**other's **D**ay

- Capitalize the names of countries, cities, states, and landmarks.

> **C**anada
> **L**os **A**ngeles, **C**alifornia
> **S**tatue of **L**iberty

- Capitalize the name of a sports team.

> **C**hicago **B**ulls
> **G**reen **B**ay **P**ackers
> **M**iddletown **P**atriots

Notice that when you write the name of a city and the state together, you put a comma between them, like this:

Orlando, Florida
Denver, Colorado
Seattle, Washington

Also, when you write a date, you put a comma between the day and the year, like this:

May 31, 1998
July 4, 1776

Try writing today's date.

Capitalize all the important words when you write the title of a book. You don't capitalize little words like *a, an, the, in,* or *of,* unless it's the first word of the title, because you always capitalize the first word. Also, when you write the title of a book, underline it, like this:

<u>Little House in the Big Woods</u>

Familiar Phrases

Back to the drawing board.

People use this saying when something they're doing doesn't work out, and they feel as though they need to start over from the beginning.

"Ahmad, what are you doing?" asked his mother.

"I'm trying to write a poem for Kim's birthday. But it doesn't sound right. I think I need to go back to the drawing board."

Better late than never.

People use this saying to mean that it's better that something happens late than not at all.

"Mario, I'm sorry I'm so late getting to your birthday party. I had a flat tire!"

"That's okay, Dad. Better late than never!" said Mario.

Cold feet.

People say that someone gets "cold feet" when that person decides not to do something because he or she is afraid.

"I want to jump off the diving board, but every time I try I get cold feet."

Don't cry over spilled milk.

People use this saying to mean that once something is done or something is lost, you shouldn't keep feeling sorry or worrying about it.

"Hey, Greg, why so sad? You aren't still disappointed about losing the spelling bee, are you? Come on, don't cry over spilled milk."

Don't (or you can't) judge a book by its cover.

People use this saying to mean that the way something looks may not tell you much about what it's really like. They also use it to mean that the way a person looks may not tell you much about what that person is really like.

"Bill, pick Margaret for our baseball team," said Johnny.

"Margaret? Are you kidding?" said Bill. "She's so quiet and shy. What does she know about baseball?"

"Bill, you can't judge a book by its cover," said Johnny. "She may be quiet and shy, but I've seen her play. She can really hit!"

Easier said than done.

People use this saying to mean that sometimes it's easy to say what should be done but harder to do it.

Rachel and Tom found an old, bent bicycle frame in a trash pile. "Let's take it home and fix it," said Rachel.

"Easier said than done," said Tom. "Where are we going to get two wheels and a chain to fit this bike? And how are we going to straighten the frame?"

Eaten out of house and home.

People use this phrase, often humorously, to mean that a huge amount of food gets eaten—so much, in fact, that someone may have to sell a home to pay for all the food!

"Are you excited that your sister is getting married?" Marie asked Mary Jo.

"I am. My grandpa and grandma are coming to the wedding, and my aunts and uncles and cousins, too. But my dad seems a little worried. He says all Mom's relatives are going to eat us out of house and home."

Get a taste of your own medicine.

People use this expression to mean that someone who has been bothering or mistreating others gets treated in the same way.

"So, did Sakir play any tricks on you guys at school today, Rosa?" asked her sister.

"Nope," replied Rosa. "And I don't think he will for a while. He finally got a taste of his own medicine. During the school assembly we presented him with a medal for playing mean tricks. And he was *really* embarrassed."

Two heads are better than one.

People use this saying to mean that when one person is having trouble with a task or problem, a second person can often help out.

Pete was playing a geography game on the computer. "Rosie," he asked his friend, "what goes next to California?"

"Well," said Rosie, "Nevada and Utah? Or maybe Arizona?"

"Nevada and Arizona both fit. Hey, thanks."

"Anytime," Rosie replied. "After all, two heads are better than one."

In hot water.

People use this phrase to mean in bad trouble.

"What was your favorite part of the movie?" Ryan asked Rita.

"I liked the part when they fell into the snake pit and the snakes were slithering all over them, and then the bad guys found them and sealed the pit," Rita said.

"Yeah," Ryan agreed, "they were really in hot water."

Keep your fingers crossed.

People use this expression in several ways. They say it to keep off danger. And they say it to try to help make a wish come true.

"What are you nervous about, Carmen?" asked José.

"Well, I studied so hard for the chemistry test last week. We get our grades back today, and I'm really keeping my fingers crossed that I did well."

Practice what you preach.

People use this saying to mean that you should act the way you tell others to act.

"Mom. Mom! *Help!* Ben took my train. He shouldn't grab my toys," Chris wailed. Then Chris yanked the train out of his little brother's hands.

"That's enough, boys," said their mother. "Ben, you shouldn't take the toy Chris is playing with. And, Chris, if you grab things back from him, he will think it's okay to grab things from you. Please try to practice what you preach."

Get up on the wrong side of the bed.

People use this phrase to mean someone is in a bad mood.

"Boy, was my mom a grouch this morning. I think she got up on the wrong side of the bed."

Turn over a new leaf.

To turn over a new leaf is to make a big change in the way you act.

"I've been late to school nine times already this year. But starting today, I'm going to turn over a new leaf. No matter what happens, I'm going to be on time."

Where there's a will, there's a way.

This saying means if you're determined to do something, you'll find a way to do it.

"I can't believe our Girl Scout troop needs to sell six hundred boxes of cookies to top last year's record," said Hilary. "That's impossible."

"Oh, no, it's not," said Tina. "Where there's a will, there's a way!"

You can't teach an old dog new tricks.

People use this saying to mean that as you get older you get more set in your ways. Once you get used to doing something in a certain way, it becomes very hard to learn a different way to do it.

"Grandfather, why are you going this way to the market? Why don't you take the new road?" asked Mei Jing.

"Oh," laughed her grandfather, "I always forget that new road because I've gone this way all my life. I guess you can't teach an old dog new tricks."

II
History and Geography

Introduction

For many years American elementary schools (especially in kindergarten through third grade) have taught "social studies" rather than history. Social studies have typically been made up of lessons about the family, neighborhood, and community. This focus on the personal and the local can be of value, but it is only a beginning.

As anyone knows who has witnessed children's fascination with dinosaurs, knights in armor, or pioneers on the prairie, young children are interested not just in themselves and their immediate surroundings but also in other people, places, and times. An early introduction to history and geography can foster an understanding of that broad world beyond the child's locality and make him or her aware of varied people and ways of life. Such historical study can also begin to develop our children's sense of our nation's past and its significance.

Parents and schools following the *Core Knowledge Sequence* can also build on the knowledge children have gained in kindergarten and first grade—knowledge about the world and how it is represented on maps and globes, knowledge of ancient Egypt, the American Revolution, and much more. (See *What Your Kindergartner Needs to Know* and *What Your First Grader Needs to Know.*)

In the following pages, we *introduce* a variety of people and events, most of which will be treated more fully in later grades. The idea in second grade is to plant seeds of knowledge that can grow later. The purpose is not for the child to achieve deep historical knowledge but rather to become familiar with people, terms, and ideas in such a way that, in later years, when the child hears them mentioned or reads about them, she enjoys the satisfying sense that "I know something about that!"

Learning history is not simply a matter of being able to recall names and dates, though the value of getting a firm mental grip on a few names and dates, such as 1492 and 1776, should not be discounted. While second graders have not developed a sophisticated sense of chronology, the development of a chronological sense is aided by having at least a few dates fixed in mind and associated with specific events, so that later, as children grow, they can begin to place these dates and events into a more fully developed sense of what happened when.

While it's good to help children grasp a few important facts, for young children the best history teaching emphasizes the "story" in history. In some cases, it is hard to separate history from legend, such as, for example, the story of how a young Alexander the Great tamed the wild horse Bucephalus. While we have made every effort to respect historical accuracy, we have also tried to put the facts, when possible, into the form of a good story. We encourage parents and teachers to go beyond these pages to help children learn about history through art projects, drama, music, and discussions.

In the World History and Geography section, we introduce children not only to ancient civilizations but also to topics in the history of world religions. Religion is a shaping force in the history of civilization, and thus it should be part of what our children know about. The pages on religion have benefited from critiques by religious scholars and representatives of various faiths. In introducing children to the history of world religions, we focus on symbols, figures, and stories. Our goal is to be descriptive, not prescriptive, and to maintain a sense of respect and balance.

We encourage teachers and parents to place special emphasis on the geographical topics in the following pages. The elementary years are the best years to gain a lasting familiarity with the main features of world geography, such as the continents, the larger countries, the major rivers and mountains, and the major cities of the world. These spatial forms and relationships, when connected with interesting stories, are not likely to be forgotten. Such knowledge may be reinforced by regular work with maps, which should include a lot of active drawing, coloring, and identification of place names. Drawing maps is a fun way to help students begin to develop the geographical knowledge they will need to understand the modern world.

World History and Geography

Geography: A Quick Review

Can you name the seven continents? Trace the map below. Then locate each continent and write its name on the map.

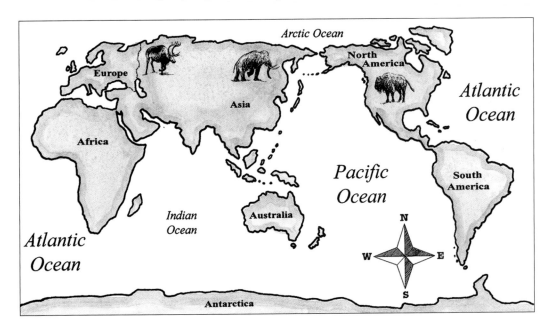

There are seven continents. They are, from biggest to smallest, Asia, Africa, North America, South America, Antarctica, Europe, and Australia. See if you can locate each of these continents on a map or globe.

Take a Look

Get a globe or world map and ask your child to locate the following:

- the seven continents.
- the Atlantic, Pacific, Indian, and Arctic Oceans.
- the North Pole and the South Pole.
- the continent where Christopher Columbus grew up.
- the continent Columbus was trying to reach, and the two continents that blocked his path.
- the continents where the Egyptian and Mesopotamian civilizations developed.

What about the major oceans of the world? Can you find the Atlantic, Pacific, Indian, and Arctic Oceans? Which ocean would you have to sail across to go from North America to Asia? Which ocean would you have to sail across to get from Europe to North and South America? Can you remember any historical figures who made that trip?

Of course, you remember that the earth is shaped like a ball. If you went north until you could not go north any farther, you would be at the place called the North Pole. If you turned around and went south until you could not go south any farther, you would be at another pole, the South Pole.

Halfway between these two poles there is an imaginary line that divides the earth into two hemispheres. This line is called the equator. The half of the earth north of the equator is called the Northern Hemisphere. The half south of the equator is called the Southern Hemisphere. Which hemisphere do you live in?

You can tell a lot about a place just by where it is located on the earth. For example, if a place is located near the equator, it will probably have warm or hot weather much of the year. On the other hand, if a place is close to one of the poles, it will probably experience long, cold winters.

Settle Down!

Let's think back to some history you may have learned in first grade. Do you remember learning that long, long ago, before there were any towns or cities, people lived by moving from place to place to find food? They looked for plants they could eat, and they followed herds of animals they could hunt.

But then a big change happened: people learned to grow large amounts of food. And when they could grow enough food to eat, they didn't have to

keep moving around. So the people settled down. As more and more people settled in one place, cities began.

The first cities were built along the banks of some famous flooding rivers. Do
you remember the important river in Africa that's the world's longest river? (It's
the Nile River.) And do you remember the two big rivers in the part of Asia that
mark the boundaries of Mesopotamia? (They are the Tigris and Euphrates Rivers.) The water and rich soil left behind by these rivers when they flooded helped
people grow large amounts of food, so they could stay in one place and build the
first cities.

The first cities were the beginning of civilization. What does "civilization"
mean? To answer that, let's look at what happened in the first cities. When people began to settle down and raise crops, they found that planting crops could
be a very efficient way of raising food. That means it was a good way to raise a
lot of food. In some places, ten people working on a farm could raise enough
food to feed twenty or thirty people. This meant that the other people were freed
up to do something else. For example, some of them might learn how to build
houses.

Here is part of an ancient city. What different sorts of work are the people doing?

Now, you might think the house builders would have a problem, because they were not growing any food of their own. But if a house builder agreed to build a house for a farmer, the farmer could pay him by giving him some of the food she had grown on the farm. And it would be the same with other kinds of workers. A person who made jugs out of clay could trade his jugs for food or a house. A person who made bowls out of metal could trade his bowls for other things he needed.

In cities, different people do different jobs. This man is using a stone to pound a metal bowl into shape.

So, one of the first things that happened in cities was that people started to do many different kinds of jobs besides the old work of getting food, taking care of children, and fighting in wars. Some built houses. Some made clothes, cooked, or cleaned. Some made things out of clay or metal. Some sold things, such as cloth, tools, or jewelry. Others became artists, musicians, teachers, or scholars.

Making Laws

When large numbers of people live together, they need rules to get along. They need laws. Long ago, who made the laws? Usually the laws were made by a powerful ruler, like a pharaoh or a king. Sometimes these rulers made fair laws. But sometimes they made unfair laws that took away the people's freedom and made their lives very hard. Do you remember the strong ruler named Hammurabi? In a great city called Babylon, Hammurabi made many laws.

One reason we know about the laws of Hammurabi is that they were written down; in fact, they were carved in stone. Writing is one of the most important developments in human history. Writing allows us to save and pass on knowledge. Do you remember what we call the writing of the ancient Egyptians? (It

This writing from ancient Mesopotamia is called cuneiform, which means "wedge-shaped."

was called *hieroglyphics*.) Do you remember what the writing used in ancient Mesopotamia was called? (It was called *cuneiform*.)

So civilization means many things, including:

- learning how to farm
- living in one place
- building cities
- different people doing different jobs
- making laws
- in some places, learning to write

Early Asian Civilizations

The Indus Valley

In the first-grade book in this series, you learned about King Tut and the civilization of ancient Egypt. Thousands of years ago, while the pharaohs in Egypt built pyramids along the banks of the Nile, another civilization was growing in another part of the world. Let's go there now.

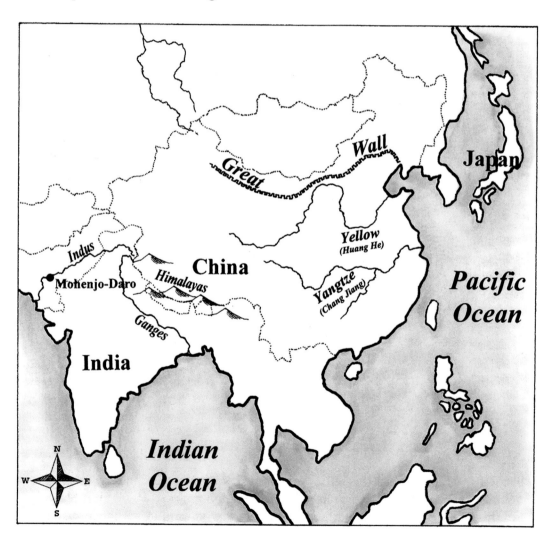

Look at the map on page 138 and find India. Can you find the Indus River? The Indus River, like the Nile in Africa, overflowed its banks every year. These yearly floods made the land around the river very fertile ("fertile" land is land that's good for growing many big, healthy plants). So, like the people in ancient Egypt and Mesopotamia, the people in the Indus Valley could grow lots of food because of the flooding river, fertile soil, and warm weather.

The people who lived alongside the Indus River built canals to control the river. They planted seeds using a plow drawn by oxen.

After they learned how to farm, what do you think the people in the Indus Valley did next? If you said "Settle down and build cities," you're right. The people of the Indus Valley built a whole string of cities along the Indus River. One of the most successful of these cities was Mohenjo-Daro [moe-HEN-joe DAH-roe].

Mohenjo-Daro was built on a hill not far from the Indus River. The highest part of the city was called the citadel. In the lower city, below the citadel, the streets were set out in a rectangular, gridlike pattern. The houses in Mohenjo-Daro were built of brownish bricks. These bricks were made by scooping mud from the Indus River and then baking it until it was hard.

In the ancient city of Mohenjo-Daro, the citadel looked down on the lower city.

Everyone in Mohenjo-Daro had a job to do. Some farmed the land outside the city walls. Some made bricks. Some used those bricks to build walls and houses. Some worked with clay or metal. In the center of the city was a large marketplace where merchants could sell the things they made.

Civilization Along the Ganges

Historians, the people who study history, know that long, long ago, the people of ancient India began to leave their cities along the Indus River. But why did they leave? Was there some great disaster, such as a terrible flood or earthquakes? That is something we just don't know.

The city of Mohenjo-Daro was lost for thousands of years. Then, about a hundred years ago, it was rediscovered by archaeologists. Do you remember what archaeologists do? They look for and study the ruins of ancient cities.

But we do know that after the people left the cities along the Indus River, a new civilization developed in another part of India. This civilization grew along the banks of yet another flooding river, called the Ganges [GAN-jeez]. Can you find the Ganges River on the map on page 138?

The Ganges is the longest river in India. In ancient India, many people made their home near the Ganges. But then new people came to this region, and they did not come as friends. These new people, who came from the northwest, were called Aryans (AIR-ee-uns). The Aryans had large and powerful armies. They conquered and ruled over the Indian people living along the Ganges. They changed the way the Indian people lived. Let's look at some of the biggest changes, starting with their religion.

Hinduism

The Aryans changed the religion of the Indian people. Over many years, the gods of the Aryans combined with the gods worshipped by the Indian people. This was the beginning of Hinduism.

Hinduism is the oldest religion still practiced in the world today. Before we learn more about Hinduism, think back to the religions you've already learned about (in the first-grade book in this series). Do you remember learning that the ancient Egyptians believed in many gods, while the followers of Judaism, Christianity, and Islam all believed that there is only one God?

Well, Hinduism is different, and may seem a little confusing at first. That's because most Hindus believe in one God *and* in many gods. For Hindus, the one God is called Brahman. Hindus believe Brahman is a spirit in everything in the universe—in people, animals, trees, water, the ground, the stars, everything.

So Brahman is the one God of Hinduism. But in Hinduism there are also thousands and thousands of different gods. For Hindus, these thousands of gods are like different faces or names of Brahman.

Among the many thousands of gods in Hinduism, there are three main gods. Most Hindus believe that these three main gods are in charge of all the others. They are called Brahma [BRAH-mah] (not to be confused with Brahman), Vishnu [VISH-noo], and Shiva [SHEE-vah].

Brahma

Vishnu

Shiva

Hindus believe Brahma is the creator of the world and all creatures—the god who made everything. He is often shown with four heads and four arms, as in the statue shown on page 142. Today in Hinduism, Brahma is not worshipped as much as Vishnu or Shiva.

Vishnu is the god who preserves and defends life. Vishnu is often associated with light and the sun.

Shiva's role is to destroy the universe in order to re-create it. Shiva is sometimes shown dancing in a ring of fire. Why fire? Fire can destroy, but it can also help make new things.

Besides having many gods, Hinduism is different from Judaism, Christianity, and Islam in other ways. Hinduism has no single leader or teacher. You may remember that believers in Christianity follow the teachings of Jesus. And Muslims follow the teachings of Muhammad. But Hinduism has no one leader or teacher that every Hindu is expected to follow.

For Hindus, the Ganges is a sacred river. Believers come from miles away to bathe in the river, say prayers, and wash away their sins.

Hindus along the Ganges River

For Hindus, some animals are sacred, and none is more sacred than the cow. Hindus are strictly forbidden to kill a cow or eat its meat. Many Hindus are vegetarians, which means they do not eat any meat.

The Holy Books of Hinduism

You've learned that many religions have a book of sacred writings. For Jews, the holy book is the Hebrew Bible, the first part of which is called the Torah. For Christians, the holy book is the Bible. And, for Muslims, the holy book is the Qu'ran. Hinduism does not have one holy book; instead, it has several sacred books.

One of the oldest sacred books of Hinduism is the Rig Veda [RIG VAY-da]. It is filled with beautiful poems, and it tells Hindus how to celebrate weddings, funerals, and holy days. If you lived in India today, you could still hear many people saying hymns from the Rig Veda at important times in their lives.

Another important holy book for Hindus is the Ramayana [RAHM-ah-YAHN-ah]. It is full of stories of great deeds and adventures. Many stories in the Ramayana tell about the hero, Prince Rama [RAHM-ah].

The Tale of Rama and Sita

One of the stories about Prince Rama in the Ramayana shows the importance of being courageous, and reminds people that evil can be hard to defeat, but good can win in the end.

According to the story, Prince Rama was born to the king of the holy city of Ayodhya [a-YOD-ya]. He was intelligent and kind, as well as an excellent archer and noble warrior. One day Ravana, the king of the demons, disguised himself as a wise old man, allowing him to trick people and capture Rama's wife, Sita.

Ravana carried off Sita in a chariot to his home, which was far away on an island in the middle of the sea. Rama soon realizes what Ravana has done, and so he begins a journey to find his wife. He is helped on this journey by an army of monkeys. On their journey, Rama and his army find their way toward the island where Sita is being held. They use trees and rocks and anything they

Ravana, the king of the demons, had ten heads and twenty arms, but he appeared to Sita disguised as a wise old man.

can find. When the bridge is finished, Rama leads his army across, and a great battle is fought. During the battle, Rama kills the evil Ravana with a magic arrow. Rama and Sita are reunited at last, and the whole world celebrates the triumph of good over evil.

Diwali: The Festival of Lights

When Rama and Sita returned to their home in Ayodhya, the people of the city lit small, oil-burning lamps called diyas [DEE-yahs]. They placed the diyas in their windows, by their doors, and in the rivers and streams. The light from the candles symbolized good, replacing darkness and evil.

> **New Word**
>
> What is a "custom"? A custom is anything that people do or the way they act that is common among a certain group or in a certain place.

Now every year, many Hindus repeat the **custom** of lighting lamps, to honor Rama and to celebrate goodness and light. This is part of a festival in late fall in India called Diwali [dih-WAH-lee]. Sometimes people will also put on plays telling the story of Rama and Sita during this festival.

The purpose of the festival of Diwali is not just for Indians to celebrate Rama, but to celebrate goodness in one another. For four or five days, the lamps and candles illuminating windows and doorways, and the tiny lights adorning walls and gateposts throughout the cities and countryside, stand for the good inside each person who lit it.

Lakshmi (LUHKSH-mee), the Hindu goddess of wealth and prosperity, is also welcomed into the homes of the Hindu people during Diwali. In the weeks before the festival begins, families clean their homes in anticipation of pleasing Lakshmi's spirit when she visits. Flowers adorn homes and businesses and even cars, in hopes that Lakshmi will bless their owners with prosperity. Diwali is a time of new beginnings, much like New Year's celebrations around the world.

Make a Connection
You can read about how people in China celebrate their New Year later in this chapter.

Buddha: The Enlightened One

Make a Connection
To see the Great Stupa, a Buddhist temple, look at page 285 in the Visual Arts section of this book.

You've just learned about one great religion that began in India—Hinduism. Now let's learn about another, called Buddhism [BOO-diz-um].

Today Buddhism is the religion of millions of people, but most of them do not live in India. Today many of these people live in Southeast Asia, China, and Japan. But Buddhism began in India, and it grew out of Hinduism. It began a long time ago, with a young prince named Siddhartha Gautama [sih-DART-tah GOW-tah-mah].

Siddhartha was born the son of a very rich king and queen. His father ruled a kingdom in the foothills of the high Himalayan Mountains. Siddhartha wore soft, beautiful clothes made of the finest silk. Servants stood by him, playing soft music and fanning him. When he walked, they held umbrellas over him to keep off the sun or rain. When he was sixteen years old, he married a beautiful princess.

What a life—all pleasure and no pain! Siddhartha's father, the king, tried to make sure that his son was always happy. He even ordered that no one who was sick, old, or poor should ever come near the prince. That way, thought the king, the prince would live in a world without suffering, a world filled with beautiful things and happy people.

Make a Connection

You can learn more about Indian culture by reading "The Tiger, the Brahman, and the Jackal" and "The Blind Men and the Elephant" in the Language Arts section of this book.

But one day, when Siddhartha was riding in his chariot outside the palace walls, he saw an old, gray-haired man, bent over and wrinkled, leaning on a stick. Soon after, he saw two women weeping for a man who had died. During another chariot ride, he saw a sick man begging for food by the side of the road. And later, for the first time in his life, he saw a dead person. Finally, he saw a holy man with a shaved head and a peaceful expression on his face.

Now Siddhartha knew what his father had tried so hard to hide from him. He saw that there is pain in the world, and that people grow old and die. He was troubled by what he had seen, and he thought for a long time. Was it right that just because he was born rich, he should be comfortable and happy while other people were unhappy and miserable?

Then he made a hard decision. He made up his mind to leave his family, his home, and his easy, comfortable life. He set off to try to understand why there was suffering and what to do about it. He cut off his long hair. He gave his soft silk gowns to a poor man and put on the poor man's old, ragged clothes. He wandered for years and years, looking for answers to his questions.

Then one night he sat down under a tree to be quiet and think. He sat and thought for a long time, and in the morning when the sun rose, he felt that now he understood. He had become *enlightened*, which means wise and aware. And so he was called Buddha, which means "the enlightened one, the one who knows."

What did Buddha know? He said that he now understood that suffering and death are part of life. He said that life is like a great wheel in which birth, suffer-

The Buddha is often shown meditating (deep in thought), with his legs crossed, as in this sculpture.

ing, and death come round and round again. And he said that the most important thing is to live a life of goodness. Buddha taught people how to be good, and many people, including his wife and his father, began to follow his teachings. He said, for example, that people should harm no living thing. He told his followers to be kind and merciful to humans and animals alike.

King Asoka: From War to Peace

About two hundred years after Buddha died, a king helped spread Buddha's teachings. King Asoka [uh-SHOW-kah] didn't believe in Buddha's teachings at first. You remember that Buddha said people should harm no living thing. But King Asoka was a warrior. He led his soldiers in fierce battles, in which many men were hurt or killed. Through these wars he brought the northern and southern parts of India together under his rule.

But after one fierce and bloody battle, King Asoka looked around and saw the death and hardship caused by war. He remembered that Buddha had said,

"Harm no living thing," and he felt ashamed. He decided to stop making war and instead to devote himself to spreading Buddha's teachings throughout his kingdom. All over India he built hospitals for both people and animals. He told his workers to plant trees and dig wells for freshwater. He even set up houses along the road for travelers who were tired from walking great distances.

King Asoka wanted the people of India to learn more about Buddha's teachings, so he had Buddha's words carved on tall pillars and put them in places where many people would see them. Even though Asoka strongly believed in Buddha's teachings, he also believed that kings should let their people worship as they wanted to. So many Indian people felt they could worship their different gods and also listen to Buddha's words.

This is one of the pillars King Asoka put up to spread the teachings of the Buddha.

King Asoka sent Buddhist priests across Asia to tell people in other lands about Buddha's teachings. Buddha's ideas spread all over Asia, and Buddhism remains one of the largest religions in the world today.

China

Look at the map on page 138. You know where India is. Now look north and east of India and find the big country called China. You can see that China is separated from India by the high Himalaya Mountains.

Where do you suppose civilizations sprang up in China? If you said "along the banks of the rivers," you got it right. In China, as in ancient India, Egypt, and

Mesopotamia, the first cities were built near rivers that regularly flooded and left rich soil, good for growing crops.

In China, two rivers were especially important—the Yellow River and the Yangtse River [yang-see]. In China, the Yellow River is known as the Huang He and the Yangtse is known as the Chang Jiang. On the map on page 138, trace each of these rivers from its source near the Himalaya Mountains to where it pours into the Pacific Ocean.

As the Yellow River makes its way to the sea, it collects a lot of silt, a fine mixture of soil, sand, and clay, and this silt gives the river a yellowish color.

The Yangtse River is located farther south, where the weather is warmer. The people who settled along the Yangtse found that it was a very good place to grow rice. Rice has been very important to the Chinese people ever since. Even today, much of the world's rice is grown along the banks of the Yangtse, in flooded fields called rice paddies.

Farmers living along the banks of the Yangtse River cleared trees to make rice paddies.

Confucius

Long, long ago, about the same time that Buddha lived in India, another wise man was teaching in China. His name was Confucius. Confucius was a very peaceful man. But during his life, China was not a peaceful country. Instead, many groups were fighting one another. They rode around the countryside and robbed and hurt the people in the villages.

Confucius, who was wise, gentle, and thoughtful, grew tired of all this fighting. He said that the fighting should stop and that all the people should come together under a single wise ruler. The people, he said, should obey a good ruler, while a good ruler should take care of the people. He said to the rulers, "You are there to rule, not to kill. If you desire what is good, the people will be good."

Confucius said many other things about how people should live and treat each other. For example, he said that you should respect your parents and teachers, and honor your ancestors.

You know the Golden Rule, don't you? It says, "Do unto others as you would have them do unto you." Confucius was the first person we know of to teach the Golden Rule, although he put it this way: "What you do not wish for yourself, do not do to others."

Many people in China began to pay attention to the teachings of Confucius and speak of "Confucianism." Confucianism is not a religion, like Islam or Christianity, because Confucius did not have anything to say about God or the gods. Confucianism is a way of thinking about how to live a good life and how to treat others.

Observing the Master

"Would you like to hear Confucius speaking with his students? You would? Very well. If you will agree to listen quietly and be respectful, this man will lead you out on the porch, where you can observe the master teaching his students."

A man in a robe leads you out onto a porch. You see Confucius standing in front of a half dozen students. The students are wearing robes and kneeling at small desks. Some of them are asking Confucius questions, and some of them are

Chinese is written using characters. Each character stands for a single syllable, and sometimes for a whole word. The characters shown here record some of the teachings of Confucius.

writing down the answers the master gives them. You kneel down in the back row and listen.

"Master," says one of the students, "what is the key to success in life?"

"The greatest glory," Confucius says, "is not in never falling, but in getting up every time you do."

"Master," says another one of the students, "how can a man learn to be wise?"

Confucius replies: "There are three ways to attain wisdom—by thinking, which is the noblest way; by imitation, which is the easiest way; and by experience, which is the bitterest way."

"Master," says a third student, "what accounts for the differences among men? Why can some men paint well while others are not as good? Is it because some are born with a special ability to paint?"

Confucius replies: "By nature, men are nearly alike; by practice, they get to be wide apart."

After a few moments of silence, another student speaks up. "My mother says that I ask too many questions. She says that a man who asks questions all the time is telling the world that he is a fool who knows nothing."

Confucius replies: "The man who asks a question is a fool for a minute; the man who does not ask is a fool for life."

"Master," says an older man, "I am trying to teach my son the skills I have learned. I have told him fifty times what he must do, but still he does everything the wrong way. How can I make him understand what he must do?"

Confucius replies: "I hear and I forget. I see and I remember. I do and I understand."

The Great Wall of China

The people of ancient China built great cities. Some of them built large houses, created art, made fine clothes, and sent their children to schools. But many people remained poor, and the rulers kept fighting one another to try to become the one all-powerful ruler.

Finally, one strong and very strict ruler brought China together under his leadership. He was China's first emperor, and he was called Qin Shihuangdi [CHIN shih-hwahng-DEE]. The name China comes from his family name, Qin.

Qin stopped the rulers from fighting among themselves. But he still had to worry about outsiders who were attacking China from the north. These people were ferocious warriors called Mongols.

Qin decided that one way he could protect the Chinese people would be to build a wall big enough and strong enough to keep out the Mongols. There were already some

The emperor Qin Shihuangdi brought people from all parts of China together under his leadership.

big walls made of packed dirt, and Qin ordered many people to do the hard work of connecting these walls, as well as building new walls. The work was very hard, since the emperor wanted a wall that went on for more than a thousand miles, up mountains, down valleys, and along the curving paths of rivers.

But this was too big a job to finish in one lifetime. The work that Qin had begun was carried forward by other emperors who came after him. They ordered workmen to make the wall longer and stronger. The workmen also built towers so that guards could look out for invaders from the north. The wall they built is known as the Great Wall of China. Much of this wall is still standing today. It is so long that if you stretched it out across the United States, it would reach from Maine to Florida!

The Great Wall of China

An Army for the Afterlife

Not long ago, archaeologists discovered the tomb of Qin Shihuangdi, the first emperor of China. Here you can see some of the thousands of life-sized terra-cotta (clay) soldiers they found in the tomb.

An Important Invention

Long ago, the Chinese came up with some important inventions. You can see a Chinese invention right in front of you. The Chinese invented paper! They made paper from a plant called hemp. Chinese travelers showed people in other countries how to make paper. As the years went on, more and more people, in Asia and even in faraway Europe, learned how to make paper. Think about this: why was paper such an important invention?

These tools are used to smash plant fibers into a pulp that is used to make paper.

Smooth as Silk

Here is an old legend from China.

Once upon a time, an empress was having tea in her garden under the shade of some mulberry trees when *plunk*—something splashed into her teacup. She looked in and saw a small white fuzzy thing. It was a cocoon! It had fallen from the mulberry trees above, where little worms lived and ate the leaves.

Now, you might expect the empress to say "Yuck!" and throw out her tea, but she was a calm and curious person. She noticed something coming off the cocoon. When she looked closer, she saw it was a thread. When she touched the thread, it felt smooth and strong. And she thought, "If we had a lot of this thread, and if we could weave it, we could make a very special cloth."

Soon the empress and her servants were feeding all the worms in the mulberry trees and gathering many cocoons. And from the thread they wove a new kind of cloth. It was like no cloth that anyone had ever felt before. It was smooth, soft, and shiny, and it felt cool against the skin. The empress, the emperor, and all the noble people began wearing

Make a Connection

In the Language and Literature section of this book, you can read a folktale from China called "The Magic Paintbrush." In the Visual Arts section, you can see a sculpture known as *Flying Horse*.

In this photograph you can see silkworms, the mulberry leaves they eat, and the pinkish cocoons they weave. The strands from cocoons like this one can be untangled and woven to make silk.

clothes made of this new cloth, called silk. Visitors from other countries saw these fine silk clothes and said, "We want silk, too."

That's the legend, and parts of it are really true. Silkworms do eat mulberry leaves. When the worms make their cocoons, they do produce a thread that can be made into silk cloth. And many people did want silk from China.

The Chinese people made a lot of silk and traded it with people from other countries. Merchants from as far away as Europe and Arabia traveled to China to buy silk and then took it back home to sell.

Talk and Think
Explain that silk feels so fine and smooth that even today, if things are going very well, people say that everything is "smooth as silk." Ask your child to name other things that are smooth.

Chinese New Year

From as long ago as the time of Confucius up to the present day, the Chinese people have enjoyed celebrating the New Year Festival. On New Year's Day, Chinese families gather together—grandparents, parents, and children. They decorate their homes and shops with bright colors, especially red, and often wear

These dancers have dressed up as dragons to celebrate the Chinese New Year.

The Chinese Lunar Calendar

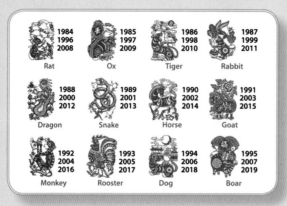

1984 1996 2008 Rat	1985 1997 2009 Ox	1986 1998 2010 Tiger	1987 1999 2011 Rabbit
1988 2000 2012 Dragon	1989 2001 2013 Snake	1990 2002 2014 Horse	1991 2003 2015 Goat
1992 2004 2016 Monkey	1993 2005 2017 Rooster	1994 2006 2018 Dog	1995 2007 2019 Boar

In the Chinese lunar calendar ("lunar" means "of the moon"), each year is said to be under the protection of one of twelve different animals. The picture to the left shows the twelve animals and lists some birth years for each animal. Can you figure out which animal goes with the year you were born? Were you born in the year of the dog? Or maybe the year of the boar?

Do It Yourself

Do you have a Chinese restaurant near your home? An easy way to learn a little more about Chinese culture is to visit a Chinese restaurant.

red outfits, because in China red is the color of good luck and happiness. The New Year Festival can go on for many days. There are fireworks and parades. People dress up in dragon costumes and dance in the streets.

The Chinese New Year does not happen on the first day of January, because the Chinese New Year is based on a special calendar that follows the cycles of the moon. Usually the Chinese New Year happens on a day somewhere between the middle of January and the middle of February.

Modern Japan

Let's Visit Japan

You've been learning about the long-ago times in India and China. Now let's jump ahead in time and look at life as it is today in an important Asian country, Japan.

Japan is a country far to the east in Asia. Since the sun rises in the east, Japan has long been called "the land of the rising sun." A rising sun is pictured on the flag of Japan, which has a red circle on a white background.

Compared with China, Japan is a very small country. Japan is made up of many islands. The four main islands are really the tops of a great mountain range. There are many volcanoes in Japan, and there are many earthquakes.

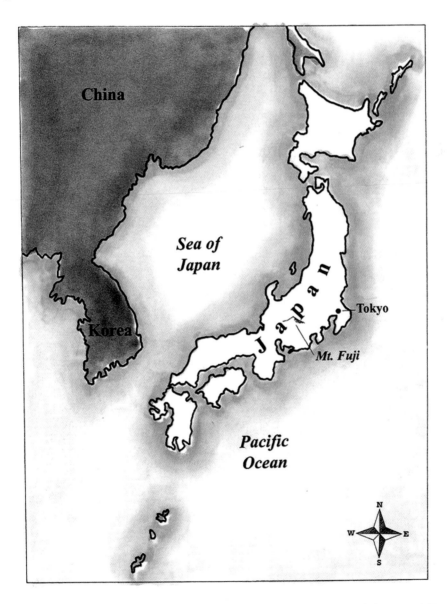

Tokyo is a busy city.

In Japan you'll find one of the largest cities in the world, called Tokyo. Tokyo is a busy, crowded, modern city, with many banks, stores, restaurants, museums, colleges, and apartment buildings.

If you were to visit a Japanese family living in an apartment in Tokyo, the first thing you would do when you entered their home would be to take off your shoes. You would wear socks or special slippers, but you would never wear your outside shoes indoors!

If your Japanese friends invited you to stay for dinner, you might not sit in a chair but instead kneel on a cushion around a low table. To pick up your food, you would not use a fork, and no,

Make a Connection

In the Language and Literature section of this book, you can read a folktale from Japan, called "The Tongue-Cut Sparrow." See also Hokusai's *The Great Wave* (page 269) and Himeji Castle (page 286) in the Visual Arts section.

When entering a Japanese home, you take off your shoes.

you wouldn't use your fingers; you'd use two slender pieces of wood about the size of pencils, called chopsticks.

In many ways, Japan is a very modern country. It has busy factories that make cars, televisions, radios, cameras, and other products that are bought by people around the world.

But there is more to Japan than a lot of modern business and industry. In Japan the people also care about their old ways and customs. For example, children in Japan learn a very old art form called origami. To do origami, you fold paper in special ways, without cutting or pasting it, to make lovely figures such as a swan.

This woman is wearing a kimono.

On special holidays, many Japanese people, both men and women, wear a kimono, a beautiful robe that is tied at the waist.

In Japan, Shogatsu, New Year's Day, is a special holiday. The Japanese also celebrate two holidays that we don't have in America: one is called Girls' Day (in March), and the other is Boys' Day (in May). On these days the children dress in bright costumes, play games, and often receive presents.

Do It Yourself
Instructions and patterns for simple origami projects can be found online.

These origami elephants were made by folding paper.

Ancient Greek Civilization

· ·

Birthplace of the Olympics

Have you ever watched the Olympics on television? If you have, then you know how exciting it can be to see some of the best athletes from all around the world come together to compete in many sports, such as running and swimming in the Summer Olympics, or skiing and bobsledding in the Winter Olympics.

These men are competing in the 100-meter dash, one of the most popular events in the modern Olympics.

Do you know where the Olympics got started? In a land that is now the country called Greece. Did you know that the first Olympics were held in Greece more than 2,500 years ago?

The ancient Greeks loved athletics. Every four years, they would hold a week of games at a place called Olympia. The best athletes would gather to run, jump, wrestle, throw weapons, and race chariots and horses.

The Olympics of the ancient Greeks were in some ways different from our Olympics today. The ancient Greeks held contests in music and poetry, which are not part of our modern games. In ancient Greece, only men were allowed to compete, and they did not wear uniforms; in fact, they didn't wear anything! Today, the winners get medals, but in ancient Greece winners were crowned with a wreath made of wild olive leaves.

Athletes who won at the ancient Olympics were crowned with a wreath of olive leaves.

The ancient Greeks gave us the Olympics, but they also gave us much more. Ancient Greece is the birthplace of many ideas and beliefs that are still important to us today. Let's find out more about the civilization of the ancient Greeks.

A Civilization of City-States

In ancient Greece, did civilization begin by a big river? No! Greece is different. Greece has no flooding river like the Nile in Egypt. Greece is mostly a rocky, dry land, broken by many hills and mountains. The hills and mountains kept groups of people apart. The people in one valley might not have much to do with the people in the next valley. Some of these groups of people grew into large communities, which were called city-states. Look at the map on page 166 to find some of the most important city-states: Athens, Sparta, and Thebes.

Greece is a rocky country where only some plants will grow.

The people in these separate city-states all spoke the Greek language. They told many of the same stories and worshipped many of the same gods. (Like people in other ancient civilizations you've learned about, the Greeks believed in many gods, whom you can read about in this book, starting on page 84.) But the Greeks did not have a single ruler. In fact, the city-states often argued and sometimes fought against each other.

Most people in ancient Greece lived near the sea. Look at the map below and find the Mediterranean Sea and the Aegean [uh-JEE-un] Sea. Can you also find the island in the Mediterranean called Crete [rhymes with "street"]?

Take a Look

When you look at Greece on the map, you will see that it is a peninsula. A peninsula is a large piece of land that sticks out into the water and is almost surrounded by water. Look at a map of the United States and you will see that Florida is also a peninsula.

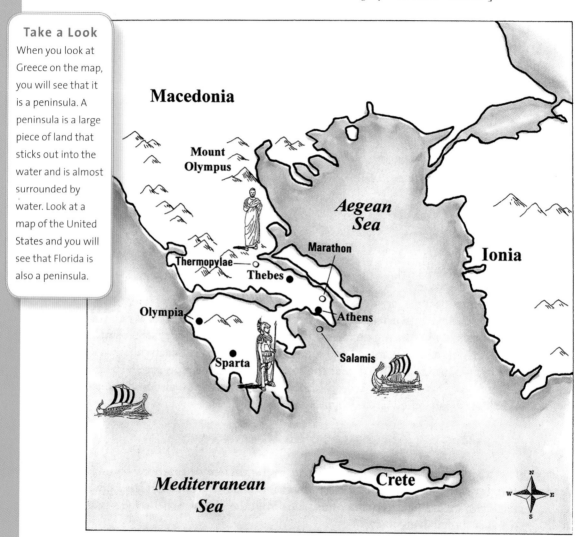

Ancient Greece and nearby regions

Athens: Birthplace of Democracy

Many things important to us today got their start in the ancient civilizations—things like agriculture (growing food crops), cities, and writing. From the ancient

Greeks, we got many new ideas, including a very important idea from the city of Athens. Let's find out about this idea called *democracy*.

For hundreds of years, the Athenians had tried different ways of governing their city. They argued a lot about the best way. Some Athenians got tired of being ruled by a small group of powerful and strict leaders. They spoke up and said, "Why should just a few people make laws for everyone else, especially when they make bad laws?"

The people of Athens elected their leaders, including Pericles, shown here.

Leaders who make bad laws and are cruel to the people are called "tyrants." Many Athenians got tired of being ruled by a few tyrants. "Let's get rid of the tyrants and rule ourselves!" they said. And that is what the Athenians did. They invented a new kind of government, in which the people chose their leaders. And if those leaders began to act like tyrants, then the people had the power to choose new leaders. This new kind of government, born in Athens and still with us today, is called democracy. It means "rule by the people."

In Athens, democracy was not perfect. Not all the people had power. Not all the people were allowed to take part in the government. Only citizens were allowed to vote, and not every adult was a citizen. Women and slaves were not citizens, so they could not vote. It would take many more years for human beings to come to believe that all people—not just men who own property—are created equal and should have equal rights.

Still, even though democracy in Athens left out women and slaves, it was the beginning of an idea that is very important today in our own country—the idea that ordinary people can and should help to make the laws and choose their own leaders. This idea of democracy made ancient Athens different from most other places on earth at that time, where the laws were made by a king, an emperor, or a small group of warriors or priests. Where would you rather live? In a place where you help make the laws and pick the leaders, or in a place where you never have any say?

Rough, Tough Sparta

Not far from Athens there was another Greek city-state called Sparta. The Spartans were tough. They were great warriors. When Spartan boys were only seven years old, they were taken from their families and trained to be soldiers. Their heads were shaved and they were given only rough clothing, no shoes, and very little food to eat. They slept on hard beds with no covers. Why? It made them tough and ready for war.

Even the Spartan girls were trained to compete in sporting events. To the people of Athens, this was shocking. The Athenians believed that young girls should learn to take care of the home and children and should grow up to be quiet and gentle, but not the Spartans. They wanted the girls to grow up to be strong and tough. Still, like the Athenians, the Spartans did not let women vote or take part in the government of the city-state.

Today, people use the word "Spartan" to describe something that is very plain and basic, with nothing fancy or frilly about it. To live a Spartan life means to live a life with very few comforts. For example, if you lived a Spartan life, you might get up very early, take only a cold shower, wear plain clothes, and never eat any sweet snacks.

The Spartans were trained to be brave warriors.

The Persian Wars

While the city-states of ancient Greece, such as Athens and Sparta, were growing bigger and stronger, another civilization was growing to the east. These people were the Persians. The Persians had conquered the people of Babylon and Egypt.

When a country conquers and takes charge of other lands, it makes those lands part of its empire. About 2,500 years ago, the Persian Empire was the mightiest empire in the world. The Persians ruled over most of the lands between the Indus River and the Mediterranean Sea. Wherever the Persians went, they spread their civilization. They gave the different peoples they conquered one government, one kind of money to use, and even a postal system.

As the Persians pushed farther west, their empire came closer and closer to Greece. The Persians came first to some Greek cities in the area called Ionia [eye-OH-nee-uh]. Look at the map on page 166 and you'll see that Ionia was not far to the east of Athens and Sparta. The Persian armies conquered Ionia. But then the Ionian people surprised the Persians: they didn't just act sad and defeated. The Ionians wanted to be free, so they fought back. The Ionians asked Athens for help, and the Athenians sent ships and soldiers. The Persian king, named Darius [duh-RYE-us], was furious: "Who do these Greeks think they are?" he roared. "Nobody

Darius, king of Persia, led a huge army against the Greeks.

stands against Darius, the king of Persia, and lives to tell the tale! I will teach these Greeks a lesson they will not soon forget!"

Darius gave orders for many soldiers and a large fleet of ships to attack the mainland of Greece. He believed that he would easily defeat the Greeks because, after all, the Greek city-states were always fighting each other. But, as you will see, Darius was wrong.

Marathon

Darius sent six hundred ships with thousands of soldiers to conquer Athens. The Athenians knew they needed help. So they turned to a city-state that was known for its brave fighters but had sometimes been an enemy of Athens—Sparta.

Back then, there were no telephones, computers, or other ways of quickly getting a message to someone far away. The fastest way to get a message to Sparta was to send a runner. The Athenians chose a runner named Pheidippides [fie-DIH-pih-deez]. For two days and nights, he ran, swam, climbed, and ran some more until he reached Sparta.

When Pheidippides asked the Spartans for help, they said, "We will send two thousand men to help you, but we cannot send them until the next full moon, when they are finished with our religious festival." Pheidippides ran back to Athens with the news. The Athenians said, "We cannot wait. The Persians are close by. Get ready for battle."

Meanwhile, the Persians had sailed their ships to a place on the Greek coast called Marathon. From there they planned to march to the city of Athens. (Find Marathon and Athens on the map on page 166.)

The Greek general knew that the Persians had many more soldiers, so he came up with a daring plan. He ordered the Greek soldiers to attack the Persians! The Greeks ran furiously right into the Persian lines. The Persians were surprised, and many of them ran back to their ships. By the end of the Battle of Marathon, many Persians lay dead.

The Greek general then turned to Pheidippides, who was already weary from the battle, and said, "Run to Athens with the news of our victory." Pheidippides ran and ran, as fast as he could. He ran about twenty-six miles before he reached

Pheidippides ran twenty-six miles to Athens to tell the people of Athens about the victory over the Persians at the Battle of Marathon.

the city and managed to gasp out the good news: "We are victorious!" Then the poor man dropped dead.

Today, people still run in long-distance races called marathons. A marathon is a little more than twenty-six miles, about the distance from Marathon to Athens.

Thermopylae

Defeated at the Battle of Marathon, the Persian army had to retreat to Persia.

"The Greeks have won for now," said King Darius, "but I promise, I will crush them!"

Before he could keep his promise, however, Darius died. His son, named Xerxes [ZURK-seez], became king. Xerxes swore that he would keep the promise his father had made, and he prepared an even larger army to attack the Greeks.

Xerxes marched his troops to the narrow body of water called the Helles-pont, which separates Asia and Europe. In order to get the soldiers across to the European side, he arranged dozens of ships side by side, like beads on a necklace, so they made a kind of floating bridge.

While the soldiers were crossing this bridge of boats, a storm blew in and broke up the boats. Xerxes was furious. He was so angry that he ordered his men to whip the water for disobeying him! Then he rebuilt his bridge of boats and marched the rest of his army across.

Xerxes marched his army around the Aegean Sea. Then he turned south to attack Athens and the other city-states of Greece. For a while, it did not seem like the Greeks could do anything to stop the Persian army. But there were some "pinch points" along the way to Athens—some places where the vast Persian army would have to squeeze through a narrow pass. One of these was a place called Thermopylae [ther-MOP-ih-lee]. There the Persians would have to march along a narrow strip of land with mountains on one side and the sea on the other. At this place, a group of about three hundred Spartan soldiers, with some other Greeks to help them, decided to wait for the Persians. There was no chance that three hundred Spartans could defeat the vast Persian army, but in the narrow pass at Thermopylae they could at least slow them down.

The Spartans faced their foes bravely. Wave after wave of Persians came forward, only to meet death at the points of the Spartan spears. But there were so many more Persians than Spartans that, one by one, the Spartans fell. At last their spears were broken. Yet still they stood side by side, fighting to the last. Some fought with swords, some with daggers, and some with only their fists. All day long they fought and held back the Persians. But when the sun went down, not one Spartan was left alive. Each and every one had died fighting to protect Greece from the Persians.

The bravery of the Spartans gave the Greeks a little more time to get ready. The Persians were able to capture Athens, but the Greeks attacked the Persian navy at a place called Salamis. The Greek ships rammed the Persian ships and sank them. A little later the Greek army defeated the Persian army in a land

At the Battle of Salamis, the Greeks smashed into the Persian ships and sank many of them.

battle. That was the end of Xerxes's invasion of Greece. The Persians had been defeated a second time, and they never came back.

Great Thinkers in Athens

After the Persian wars the people of Athens enjoyed some years of peace, and they worked hard to rebuild their city. Under the leadership of a wise man named Pericles [PER-ih-cleez], they built a big new temple and dedicated it to Athena, the goddess they believed watched over their city. They built this temple out of marble and filled it with beautiful statues. It was called the Parthenon.

Make a Connection
You can learn more about the Parthenon in the Visual Arts section of this book (page 278).

Many great thinkers lived in Athens during these years. These thinkers were called philosophers, which means "lovers of wisdom." The philosophers asked big questions, such as, *How should we live? What are our duties? What is the best form of government?*

Let's meet three of the most important Greek philosophers: Socrates [SOCK-ruh-teez], Plato [PLAY-toe], and Aristotle [AIR-iss-tot-ull].

Socrates

Young men from all over Greece came to Athens to learn from Socrates. Socrates once said, "There is only one good, knowledge, and one evil, ignorance." He loved to ask questions. He made his students think by asking lots of questions and then questioning their answers. Some people felt that Socrates asked too many questions, and they got angry at him and threatened him. But Socrates did not stop asking questions. He wanted to know the truth.

Plato was a student of Socrates, and he

wrote down much of what he learned from his wise teacher. Plato believed in the importance of education. Near Athens, he started a school called the Academy. Plato said, "The direction in which education starts a man will determine his future life."

Plato's best student was Aristotle. Aristotle was interested in everything around him. He loved to look closely at plants and animals, and to think about how things work. He thought a lot about people as well and asked: What makes a person a good ruler? What are the best ways for people to live so that they get along with each other? Aristotle gave lectures on many subjects, and his students wrote down some of the things he said.

Plato

Aristotle

The ancient Greeks wrote a lot about philosophy and history. They also wrote many poems and plays. The ancient Greeks used an alphabet that is still used in Greece today. Here are its first four letters.

A B Λ Δ
alpha beta gamma delta

The first two letters are called alpha and beta. Do you see where our word "alphabet" comes from?

Alexander the Great

Aristotle had a student named Alexander. When he grew up, Alexander became so powerful and famous that he was called Alexander the Great.

From the time that he was very young, Alexander's mother told him that he would do wonderful things. From his teacher, Aristotle, Alexander learned much about the world, about people, and about how a good king should rule. From others, Alexander learned how to fight well.

Alexander was the son of King Philip, the ruler of Macedonia [mass-ih-DOE-nee-uh], in the northern part of Greece (see the map on page 166). By the time Alexander was a young man, his father had already led his armies to the south and conquered many Greek city-states, including Athens.

There is a story that one day King Philip took the twelve-year-old Alexander to a place where horses were bought and sold. One of the horses kept snorting and bucking furiously. "No one can ride so wild and savage a beast," the men said. King Philip ordered the servants to take the horse away, but Alexander spoke up. "Those men do not know how to treat him," he said.

"Perhaps you can do better?" said his father doubtfully.

"Yes," said Alexander confidently. He ran to the horse and quickly turned the animal's head toward the sun, because he had noticed that the horse was afraid of his own shadow. He then spoke gently to the horse and patted him with

Alexander the Great tamed Bucephalus, a wild horse nobody else could ride.

his hand. When he had quieted him a little, he quickly leaped onto the horse's back.

Everybody expected to see the boy tossed to his death. But Alexander held on tight and let the horse run as fast as he could. By and by, the horse became tired, and Alexander rode him back to where his father was standing.

"My son," said King Philip, "Macedonia is too small a place for you. You must seek a larger kingdom that will be worthy of you."

A few years later, after his father died, that is just what Alexander did. When he was only twenty-two years old, he set off on his horse, which he named Bucephalus [byoo-SEF-ah-lus], to conquer the world.

Alexander was a strong, intelligent ruler, but he could also be hot-tempered and cruel. Not long after he became king, the Greek city-state of Thebes decided that it no longer wanted to be ruled by Alexander. The young king moved quickly to show his strength: he burned the city to the ground and ordered that the citizens be sold as slaves.

Alexander and his army could not be stopped. With Greece under his control, he marched eastward.

The Gordian Knot

There is a famous legend about Alexander the Great. The legend says that hundreds of years before Alexander, a king named Gordius made a knot with so many twists and turns that nobody could untie it—a knot a hundred times more tangled than the worst knot you've ever gotten in your shoelaces. This famous knot was called the Gordian knot. People said that anyone who could undo the knot would have the world for his kingdom.

Alexander the Great cutting the Gordian knot

When Alexander heard about the Gordian knot, he said, "Take me to it." The people took him to a little temple and showed him the famous knot.

"Tell me again," said Alexander, "what you believe about this knot."

"It is said," one man replied, "that the man who can undo it shall have the world for his kingdom."

Alexander looked carefully at the knot. He could not find the ends of the rope, but what did that matter? He raised his sharp sword and, with one stroke, sliced through the knot. The rope fell to the ground, and the people cheered.

"The world is my kingdom," said Alexander.

What Lies Beyond?

Over the next few years, Alexander conquered a huge empire. He led his armies into Egypt. There, near the Nile River, he built a splendid new city, which he named Alexandria after himself. He then attacked the heart of the once mighty Persian Empire, near the Tigris River. After many battles, the people of Persia ac-

Alexander the Great on his horse Bucephalus

cepted Alexander as their king. Alexander the Great even conquered part of India, despite the fact that the Indians rode into battle on armored attack elephants.

Eventually Alexander conquered most of the ancient world. (See the map below.) But that was not enough for him. As soon as he had conquered one land, he would ask, "What lies beyond?" He pushed his army forward into battle after battle. But, after years of fighting, the soldiers were tired. They grumbled and argued and often drank too much wine. Finally, they refused to go any farther. Alexander was furious, but many of his men had been marching and fighting for eight years, and they had had enough. And so Alexander gave the order to return home.

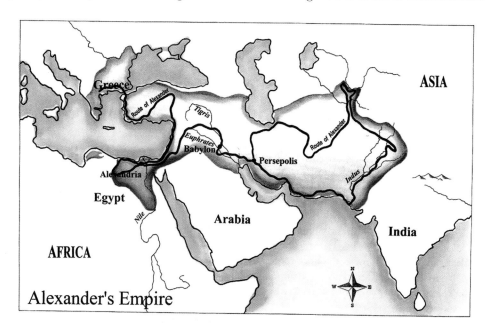

Alexander's Empire

We will never know whether Alexander would have been a good ruler of his empire because he soon fell ill and died. He was only thirty-three years old.

In just ten years, Alexander had conquered the largest empire the world had ever known. But soon after his death, his empire fell apart. Other leaders got into fights about who should rule, and none of these leaders was as strong as Alexander. Still, even though his empire did not last, Alexander had a lasting effect on the world because everywhere he went, he spread Greek ideas and learning that are still important today.

American History and Geography

A Quick Look Back

If you've read the first-grade book in this series, then put on your thinking cap, and let's see what you remember.

Let's take a quick look back to long, long, long ago, all the way back to prehistoric times. Way back then, wandering groups of people followed the animals they were hunting. The wandering hunters who lived on the continent of Asia followed the animals across what was, back then, a land bridge. Where did this land bridge lead them? It led them to another continent—our continent, North America.

Over many years, these people kept moving south. After a long time, they settled down and started civilizations. Can you tell me something about some of the earliest American civilizations, like the Aztec, or the Maya, or the Inca?

Now, think about some of the first explorers who came from Europe to North and South America. (Find these continents on a world map or globe.) In 1492, who "sailed the ocean blue"?

After Columbus, people from England crossed the Atlantic and settled in Virginia. In 1607 they arrived at a place they called Jamestown. They soon met the Powhatan Indians. Do you remember the brave young woman named Pocahontas?

More people came here from England. The Pilgrims and the Puritans settled in the Massachusetts Bay colony. Over the next hundred years, thirteen English colonies grew in America. Can you name some of these colonies? (If you don't

A Pilgrim family aboard the *Mayflower*

remember their names, look ahead to the map on the right.)

As the American colonies grew, they decided that they no longer wanted to be ruled by England and King George III. They wanted to be their own country and rule themselves. And so, one day in the year 1776, representatives of the thirteen colonies signed the Declaration of Independence, which said that from now on, the thirteen colonies would be their own country. Now Americans celebrate that day as Independence Day, the birthday of the nation. Do you remember the exact date? (It was July 4, 1776.)

After the Americans declared their independence from England, they had to fight for it. Many lives were lost in the American Revolution. But in the end a new country was born: the United States of America.

You've learned a lot about American history. Now it's time to find out more. We're going to begin by going back to the years just before George Washington became our first president. Let's start with what happened to our country just after the American Revolution.

After the Revolutionary War, the thirteen colonies became the first thirteen states of the new United States of America. The dotted lines show the state boundaries as they exist today.

The Constitution

Democracy: A Big Challenge

You might think that after our country gained its freedom from England, everything was just fine. After all, we won the Revolutionary War. We were no longer ruled by a faraway king. We were no longer thirteen colonies of England. We were our own country. We could choose our own leaders. So democracy was safe and sound in our new country, right?

Well, not quite. Democracy doesn't just happen. Do you remember what the word "democracy" means? It means "rule by the people." But the people don't always agree. Just think about your own family, or your classroom. Do you always agree?

Back in the 1780s, Americans did not always agree. They had fought hard to become the United States of America, but they did not act very united. "United" means "joined together, working together." But each of the first thirteen states wanted to be in charge of itself. None of the new states wanted a strong central government telling them what to do. Each state wanted to make its own laws and have its own rulers. Pennsylvanians wanted to make their own laws for Pennsylvania, but Virginians wanted to pass laws for Virginia, and Georgians would take care of themselves, too, thank you. Rhode Island disagreed so much with its neighbors that once the little state almost got into a fight with Massachusetts and Connecticut!

So the new states couldn't agree on much. They couldn't even agree to use the same kind of money.

During the colonial period, and even after the colonies gained independence, each colony, or state, issued its own money.

With each state looking out for itself, how could the United States be united? After all, sometimes the states would have to join together. What if England or another country attacked the United States? Then who would organize an American army? Who would pay the soldiers? Who would be in charge? Who would watch out for the whole country, not just each state on its own, but all together, united?

Many of the leaders knew they had to figure out some way for the states to work together. Fortunately, we had some very smart leaders. And one of the smartest was James Madison.

James Madison: Father of the Constitution

James Madison was the oldest of the twelve children in the Madison family. His father called him Jemmy. As a boy, he was often sick, but that didn't stop him from reading. On the big plantation in Virginia where he grew up, his father had a room with eighty-five books—not children's books but big books about science and history. James started reading them when he was nine. By the time he was eleven, he had read every one!

Madison's father sent him to a school to learn more. There young Jemmy learned math and science. He learned to read in other languages, including French, Latin, and Greek. Later, James Madison went to college in New Jersey. Most students took four years to finish their college studies, but James finished in only two.

All this reading and studying came in handy after the Revolutionary War. James Madison knew that if the United States was to be strong, the states had to learn to work together, but how? He started thinking, and, of course, he read some more. He asked his good friend Thomas Jefferson to send him books about history and government. Jefferson sent the books—hundreds of them! James Madison read them. He thought very hard, and he came up with a plan.

His plan was shared at a meeting in the city of Philadelphia. There, about fifty men from twelve of the thirteen states met in a building now called Independence Hall. (No one came from Rhode Island; they still disagreed with almost everyone else!) Along with James Madison, George Washington was at this meeting. So was Benjamin Franklin. Even though it was a terribly hot summer, they kept the windows closed because they didn't want people outside to hear what they were arguing about.

Leaders from the states met at the Constitutional Convention in 1787. Do you recognize the tall man standing on the platform at the right? (He would soon become our first president.)

And oh, how they argued! Although James Madison was usually a quiet person, even a little shy, he spoke up often at this meeting. Many men disagreed with him. But finally, after months of arguing in the hot, sticky building, the men accepted many of Madison's ideas.

They wrote down those ideas, and when they were finished, they had produced the Constitution of the United States. In the Constitution, they said how they wanted to set up the government of the new nation. They said:

The United States Constitution states the basic rules, the most important laws, of our country. Even today, the Constitution is the highest law in our land. This means that others cannot pass laws that go against the rules in the Constitution.

When the men in Philadelphia finished writing the Constitution, they sent copies to all the states. The American people read it. Many people liked it. Just as many people argued loudly against it. But after all the arguing was over, the representatives from each state voted to accept the Constitution. Because James

James Madison

Madison worked so hard to get the Constitution written, and because so many of his good ideas are in it, he is remembered as "the father of the Constitution."

Look closely at the picture of the Constitution below. Can you see what the biggest words are? They are the first three words:

We the People

Why are they so important? Because they say that we Americans ourselves chose this new kind of government. They say that the Constitution is not a law laid down by a mighty king. It's not what some all-powerful pharaoh or emperor says that everyone must do. Instead, the United States Constitution is the law We the People have created.

The opening words of the U.S. Constitution

The War of 1812

. . . .

Trouble on the High Seas

Not long after the Revolution, our young country faced another war. A war against whom? Oh, no, not again! Yes, Great Britain!

It happened like this. In the year 1812, our president was "the father of the Constitution," James Madison. At this time, Great Britain and France were at war, again. (These two countries had a long habit of fighting each other.) But Great Britain and France are across the Atlantic Ocean in Europe. How did America get drawn into a faraway war?

It happened partly out on the rolling waves of the Atlantic Ocean. There, American ships were stopped by both French and British ships. You see, the British didn't want Americans selling supplies to the French, and the French didn't want Americans selling supplies to the British. So they both stopped American ships, sometimes shot cannonballs at the American ships, and sometimes even captured American ships and sailors.

In 1811, France let go all the American ships she had captured, but Great Britain did not. The British navy kept on stopping American ships and sometimes "impressing" American sailors. That doesn't mean they did something to impress or amaze them! This kind of impressment means that the British captured some of our sailors and forced them to serve in the British navy.

Many Americans were angry at the British for impressing our sailors. They cried, "Let's fight the British!" But President Madison knew that the American navy was still young and not very strong, while the British had the most powerful navy in the world. So at first he did not want America to get into any fights with Great Britain.

But other people were saying, "We should fight the British anyway, for another reason." These people, who were called the "War Hawks," had their eyes on the land to the north of the United States. They had their eyes on Canada.

Back then, Canada was still a British colony, just as the United States had been a British colony before we won our independence in the Revolutionary War.

The War Hawks said, "Look, the British are busy fighting against France, so they won't be able to defend Canada. This is our big chance. Let's declare war on the British. Then our American soldiers can march north and take over Canada. That will teach the British a lesson!"

The War Begins

Eventually President Madison came to agree with the War Hawks. With the battle cry of "On to Canada!" the United States declared war on Great Britain. The War of 1812 had begun.

At first, things did not go well for the Americans. The attack on Canada fizzled. The British sent many soldiers across the Atlantic and fought hard to protect their northern territory. They beat back the American soldiers.

American soldiers during the War of 1812

Even though the British were beating the Americans badly, the Americans did win some important battles at sea. That was a big surprise because the British had the most powerful navy in the world, but the Americans had some very good ships and commanders, too. The ship called USS *Constitution* won several naval battles. The sailors liked to say that British cannonballs bounced off her sides as if she were made of iron. So they nicknamed her "Old Ironsides." Old Ironsides is docked in Boston Harbor for tourists to see. She is the oldest warship afloat in any of the world's navies.

Old Ironsides is still sailing today!

Dolley Madison

The Americans won some battles at sea, but things were not going well for the Americans elsewhere. British ships sailed into Chesapeake Bay, bringing more soldiers. The soldiers were headed to our nation's capital, Washington, D.C.! What if they were to capture President Madison? What a disaster that would be!

Fortunately, James Madison was not in Washington at the time. But his wife, Dolley Madison, was there. From the president's house, she could hear gunfire as the British soldiers approached. The British had already burned the Capitol, the building where Congress met. Now they were heading toward the president's

Dolley Madison

house. Dolley Madison acted quickly. A servant and a slave removed a famous painting of George Washington while she grabbed silverware and hurried off to a horse-drawn carriage. Then she disguised herself as a farmer's wife and rode quickly out of town.

Just in time! The British arrived soon after she left. They ate the dinner that Dolley had left on the table. Then they burned the president's house, as well as many other buildings in Washington. On the other side of the Potomac River, Dolley Madison met her husband. Because of her bravery and quick thinking, part of America's past had been saved.

Oh, Say, Can You See . . .

For three days, fires blazed in Washington. Then the British troops sailed north to Baltimore. Baltimore was a very important city for the Americans because many American ships sailed out of Baltimore Harbor. The British wanted to stop those ships. They wanted to smash Baltimore to the ground.

But this time it was the British who were surprised, because the Americans were ready. As the British ships sailed into Baltimore Harbor, they approached Fort McHenry, which guarded the harbor. There they saw an American flag flying, and what a flag! It was huge! It measured forty-two feet by thirty feet.

The British ships were met by an American ship. But this ship did not come to fight. It came in peace. On it was an American lawyer named Francis Scott Key. He was sent to ask the British to release an American doctor they were holding as a prisoner. The British released the doctor, but they would not allow the American ship to go back to Baltimore, at least not until after the battle.

Imagine that you're with Francis Scott Key on that ship. The battle begins. Cannons boom like thunder. Through the night the British ships keep bombing

The White House

This picture shows what the president's house looked like after it was burned during the War of 1812. Can you see the dark spots where the walls were burned? The house was not repaired until several years after the war ended. Even then, the workmen could not remove the burn marks the fire had made on the outside walls. So they covered the marks by painting the walls white. Pretty soon people started calling the president's house by the name we still use today—the White House.

Fort McHenry. You wonder, "What is happening to the Americans?" Through the darkness, the smoke, and the noise, you can't tell. As the bombs keep bursting in the air, you fear the worst. Maybe Fort McHenry has fallen to the British.

Finally, the morning comes. By the dawn's early light, you look through the misty air. You strain your eyes to see Fort McHenry. What's that you see? Yes, our flag is still there! When you see that big American flag, with its broad stripes

When Francis Scott Key saw the American flag still waving over Fort McHenry after a night of bombardment, he sat down and wrote a poem. That poem was later set to music and became the national anthem.

and bright stars, still flying, you want to shout, "Hooray!" And you know that Baltimore is safe—the British have not won.

Francis Scott Key must have seen something like that. He wrote a poem about what he saw. People liked the poem and began to sing its words to a familiar tune. And in time that poem became the song that is our national anthem, "The Star-Spangled Banner." It has four parts; you may know the first part well:

> Oh, say, can you see by the dawn's early light,
> What so proudly we hailed at the twilight's last gleaming?
> Whose broad stripes and bright stars, through the perilous fight,
> O'er the ramparts we watched were so gallantly streaming?
> And the rockets' red glare, the bombs bursting in air,
> Gave proof through the night that our flag was still there.
> Oh, say, does that star-spangled banner yet wave
> O'er the land of the free and the home of the brave?

The Battle After the War

The War of 1812 dragged on. In fact, it was now late in 1814, and both sides were tired of fighting. In Europe, British and American leaders were talking and trying to find a way to end the war. They finally signed a peace treaty on December 24, 1814.

Now, if America were in a war today, and the war ended, you would know the news right away. That's because we have satellites, televisions, telephones, computers, and other ways to send news around the world in the blink of an eye. But none of those things were around in 1814. So the news of the peace treaty traveled slowly from Europe across the big Atlantic Ocean to America. Before the news arrived, American and British soldiers fought another big battle.

The Battle of New Orleans happened in early January 1815, a couple of weeks after the peace treaty had been signed. General Andrew Jackson was in charge of the American troops. He and his men dug trenches around the city. They crouched down and waited.

Our Changing Flag

The flag that Francis Scott Key saw waving over Fort McHenry (pictured below) was not exactly the same as our flag today. Since Key's time, our flag has changed many times.

What are some of the differences between the flag that Key saw and our flag today? Compare the number of stripes on each flag. Our flag today has thirteen stripes. They stand for the thirteen original states of our country.

Notice the hole in the middle of the Fort McHenry flag. This flag had fifteen stars on it during the War of 1812. Over the years, the American flag got more and more stars. Our flag today has fifty stars. Do you know what they stand for? (The fifty stars stand for the fifty states now in the United States of America.)

Andrew Jackson, riding on a white horse and giving orders to American troops at the Battle of New Orleans

The British marched straight toward General Jackson and his soldiers. And almost as fast as they marched, they were shot down. The battle was a big victory for the United States. It made Andrew Jackson a popular hero. He became so popular that, years later, he was elected our seventh president.

After the War of 1812 ended, Great Britain and the United States would never fight each other again. Today, the two countries are good friends.

Westward Expansion

Settlers Head West

Do you remember learning about the Louisiana Purchase (in the first-grade book of this series)? It was a great bargain for the United States. France claimed a lot of land in North America but wanted to sell it. So President Thomas Jefferson bought it. And *zing*—just like that, the Louisiana Purchase doubled the size of our country! A little later, in the 1840s, the United States added even more land, including what is now Texas, California, Oregon, and Washington.

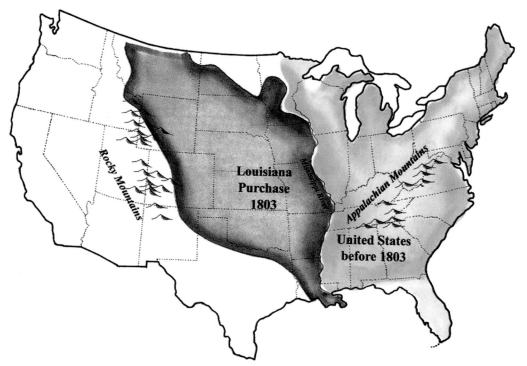

The United States at the time of the Louisiana Purchase

Many Americans wanted to go to these new lands. They wanted to farm the land and make new homes in the West. They had heard stories about how well the crops grew in the rich land west of the Appalachian Mountains and the Mississippi River. (Can you find these on the map?) Why, some people said that all you had to do was toss the seeds on the ground and jump back because big plants would start popping right out of the ground. Others said that pumpkins grown in these western lands reached the size of mighty boulders! And some said there were so many animals to hunt out west that you would trip over them when you walked!

But if you wanted to get to this land, there was something in your way—a mountain range. The Appalachian Mountains stretched from Maine to Georgia, and it was a hard, slow trip to cross the mountains on foot or in a horse-drawn wagon. If only there was some other way! Well, pretty soon there was.

To get to the West, settlers had to cross the Appalachian Mountains.

Boats and Canals

Things changed when a man named Robert Fulton developed a new kind of boat, called the steamboat. Steamboats didn't need oars or paddles or sails. You just put wood or coal into a furnace that heated water, which made steam, which ran the engine, which made the boat go! Steamboats could take settlers up and down rivers and lakes faster than people had ever gone before.

Robert Fulton's *Clermont* was the first steamboat.

But what if the rivers and lakes didn't go exactly where you wanted to go? Not even a steamboat can travel on land. For some of the settlers moving west, there was no way to go except by land. And this made their lives even harder. If they ran out of supplies like flour, or if they needed a new ax, it could take a month or more to get what they needed from the merchants back in the East.

Some people said, "It's so much faster and cheaper to move things in boats on the water. We've got lots of rivers along the East Coast and lots of lakes in the

West—really big lakes, too, like the Great Lakes. If only we could connect them together." But how?

Well, one man had an idea. The governor of New York, a man named De-Witt Clinton, wanted to build a canal—a big, man-made ditch. He wanted the canal to connect the Hudson River and Lake Erie, but such a canal would be more than three hundred miles long! It would have to be dug in hard, rocky ground, and through forests with snakes and wildcats.

At first people thought this was a bad idea. They thought Clinton was crazy, and they called his canal "Clinton's Ditch." Eventually, Clinton got people to believe that his idea would work, and they began digging the canal. Many of the workers were people who had recently come to America from Ireland. They were poor and hungry and willing to do the hard and sometimes dangerous work.

Take a Look

On this map, find the Hudson River, the Erie Canal, and the five Great Lakes. Can you see how the Erie Canal connects the Hudson River and the Great Lakes?

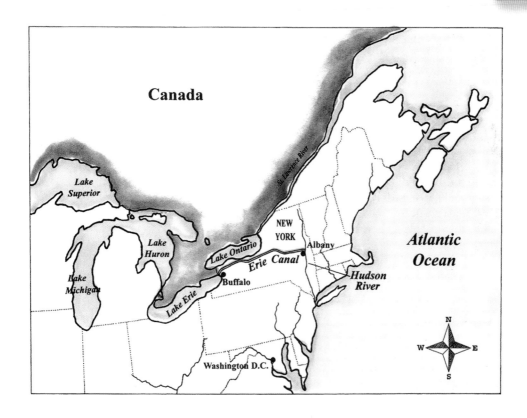

In about seven years, the work was done. The Erie Canal was finished! Look at the map on page 201 to see how the canal connects the Hudson River and Lake Erie.

The Erie Canal made traveling west a lot easier and cheaper. Things could be brought by boat from New York City up the Hudson River to Albany. Then they could be loaded onto flatboats called barges and pulled along the Erie Canal. The barges were pulled by mules or horses who walked along the banks of the canal. The barges could be dragged west, all the way to Buffalo, on the shores of Lake Erie.

A flatboat on the Erie Canal

The Erie Canal

Here's part of a well-known American folk song.

I've got a mule, her name is Sal,
Fifteen miles on the Erie Canal.
She's a good ol' worker and a good ol' pal,
Fifteen miles on the Erie Canal.

We've hauled some barges in our day,
Filled with lumber, coal, and hay,
And we know every inch of the way
From Albany to Buffalo.

Low bridge, everybody down!
Low bridge, for we're comin' to a town.
And you'll always know your neighbor,
You'll always know your pal,
If you've ever navigated on the Erie Canal.

The Iron Horse

It didn't take long for people to realize that if you could use a steam engine to power a boat, then maybe you could use it for other kinds of transportation, too. Soon steam engines were pulling trains. These early, steam-powered railroads might seem slow to us today, but back then, people were frightened to be speeding along at twenty miles per hour!

The passengers on these early trains had other reasons to be frightened, too. The engines puffed out soot that could turn your nice white shirt a dirty gray. Even worse, the engines sometimes spit out sparks. One might land on you and set your coat on fire!

When people first heard a steam-powered train puffing and snorting along, they came up with a name for it. They called it an "iron horse." When an American writer named Henry David Thoreau [thuh-ROW] heard a train go past his house in the woods, he wrote, "I hear the iron horse make the hills echo with his snort like thunder, shaking the earth with his feet, and breathing fire and smoke from his nostrils."

Hundreds and hundreds of miles of railroad tracks soon crisscrossed the eastern part of the United States. Customers could travel by train from Baltimore to Richmond or from Boston to New York. But for many years the railroad tracks did not go to the unexplored and barely explored parts of the West. If you wanted to go to those parts, you had to go by wagon train.

Wagons West

After the War of 1812, many thousands of Americans moved beyond the Appalachians. More and more people came from Europe, too. Some of these people had been poor and hungry in their old countries. In America, they hoped to find land to farm and a chance to make a better life for themselves and their children.

The people who moved west, leaving behind their old lives and heading into an unknown future, were called pioneers. The pioneers prepared the way for the millions of people who would move west in later years.

The early pioneers went west in wagon trains. A wagon train was very different from a railroad train. It was a group of covered wagons. The wagons had big wooden wheels, and they were pulled by horses, mules, or **oxen**.

Why were these wagons called covered wagons? Because they were covered by a big canvas cloth stretched over wooden hoops. Inside a covered wagon a pioneer family would pack in as much as they could. Of course there were no supermarkets out west, so they had to take a lot of food, such as flour, potatoes, beans, and dried meat. They would also take a barrel of fresh water.

What else do you think the pioneers would need to take with them? Well, they needed clothes, of course, and needles and thread to sew new clothes or fix rips in the old clothes. They needed blankets to keep them warm at night, and things to cook and eat with: pots and pans, metal plates, knives, forks, and spoons. They needed tools, like an ax to chop with, and a hammer and nails. Also, they needed some soap to wash with and some candles. A rifle was important, so that they could hunt for more food. Maybe, for the children, they would pack a favorite book or toy—no more than one or two because there just wasn't room enough in the covered wagon to hold more.

The family might also bring some animals like cows or sheep—not in the wagon, of course! The animals were tied to ropes and walked behind the wagons.

A covered wagon

Moving West

Here is a story about the journey of Molly and her family from Missouri to Oregon. Today, it would take three or four days to drive from Missouri to Oregon. It took Molly's family four months to complete the journey by wagon.

My name is Molly. In the spring of 1849, I set out for Oregon with my family. I went with my mama and papa and my two sisters. I was twelve at the time.

We started out from near Osceola, Missouri, in early May. We had one wagon for all five of us, and for all of our belongings. But we weren't alone. We traveled with several other families. Together, there were 25 wagons and 140 people in our party. About 60 of the people in our wagon train were children.

A wagon train

Our wagon was drawn by oxen. We had four teams of them. The wagon was loaded up with blankets and quilts; barrels full of flour, cornmeal, and bacon; Papa's gun and ammunition, some tin dishes and cooking pots; a few tools; and the family Bible.

There was a red bandana tied to one spoke of the wagon's rear wheel. My job was to walk beside the wagon and count how many times the bandana passed the ground. That was how we knew how many times the wheel had turned, allowing us to estimate how far we traveled. My sister Matilda's job was to take care of our two milk cows. Beatrice was too young to walk. She mostly rode in the wagon with Mama.

We traveled twelve miles the first day. Some days we covered a little more, other days a little less. At night we would draw up the wagons in a circle, to protect ourselves from Indians. We would let the cows and horses graze for a while, then bring them in and tie them up for the night.

Mama cooked dinner over the campfire. When there was firewood we used it, but sometimes there wasn't any. Sometimes we had to burn buffalo dung in place of wood. It burns better than you might think! Every family had its own campfire, and after dinner we would get together with other families to sing and dance and tell stories under the stars. Mama slept with us kids in the wagon. Papa slept in a tent. We were afraid that the Indians might attack while we were asleep, but we were fortunate and did not have much trouble from the Indians.

In the morning we would get up and have breakfast. Then we would load up the wagons and set off again.

We had only been traveling about a week when Mrs. Hawes had her baby. We stopped only for a day so she could rest. Then we started moving again.

In late May we got some bad news. Molly Pinchorn, a girl just a year older than me, died. After she died, her ma and pa decided to turn back.

We soon reached the plains. This was a lonely, deserted place, with hardly a bush for miles in any direction—nothing but tall waving grass and wind. One thing there was, though, was buffalo. There were thousands upon thousands of them on the plains, and we had fresh buffalo meat for dinner every night for a while.

In June, some terrible things happened. One of the men from our party accidentally cut himself while he was out gathering firewood. Then four women fell sick—I think Papa said it was cholera. Two died, one of them within only five hours of falling ill.

We kept going and going, day after day. The day we passed Independence Rock, some of the men went out to cut their names into the rock but got chased by a party of Sioux Indians and almost didn't make it back.

When we got to the Green River, Mama got sick, and for a few days I had to do all the cooking, wash all the clothes, and take care of my younger sisters. Papa was busy fixing up the wagons and buying supplies. By that time we were running short of food. Papa found a man who had some to sell, but he was charging such high prices, we could only afford to buy a little. We were all very hungry for a while.

We went on to Fort Hall, where we traded our wagon and our oxen for horses. We rode some of them and used the others to carry our belongings in packs. The roads in this area were not good enough for wagons.

We hired an Indian to guide us down to The Dalles, a town in Oregon, and from there we went down the Columbia River on a boat. Finally we made it to the place where we would build our new home! By the time we got there, it was late September and there was a chill in the air. It had taken us almost five months to make the journey!

Women's Work

Back in the pioneer days, many women worked hard, but they didn't leave their homes to go to work. Their work was at home, and they had their hands full.

Remember, this was before supermarkets, refrigerators, dishwashers, electric lights, and store-bought clothes. It was a big job to take care of a home and family, and the women did most of it. Women gardened and grew vegetables. They milked cows, collected eggs, and churned butter. They cooked the family meals and baked the family breads and pies. They canned fruits, made jelly, and preserved meats to last through the winter. They boiled lye to make soap and collected beeswax to make candles. They spun, knitted, and wove cloth, making blankets and much of the clothing for their families. Then, of course, the clothes got dirty, and the women washed them, too!

As if that weren't enough, pioneer women in America did one of the most important jobs done anywhere at any time—they raised the children. Their job was to teach their children how to be good people and how to be good helpers around the home and farm. Many mothers taught their children to read before they ever sent them off to school.

Pioneer women worked hard.

What About You?

Ask your child if he or she would have enjoyed living in pioneer times. Why or why not? Which parts of pioneer life would be hardest? Which would be the most enjoyable?

The Oregon Trail

Some pioneers settled on the Great Plains. Others, like Molly's family, wanted to go even farther west, all the way out to the Oregon Territory. To get there many of them followed a path called the Oregon Trail. The trail started in Missouri, then stretched west. And what a stretch! The trail went on for about two thousand miles!

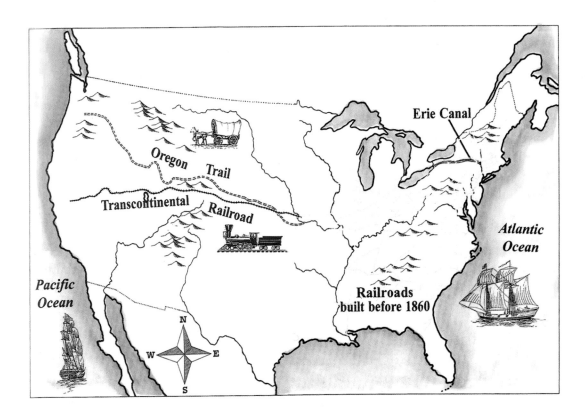

A journey on the Oregon Trail took a long time, usually five or six months. It was a hard and dangerous trip. Pioneers who traveled the Oregon Trail usually started their journey in the spring. Often they would be soaked by bitterly cold rains. Later they would have to make it through the hot, dry desert. After the desert, they came to the high, rough Rocky Mountains. It was very hard to get a covered wagon over the mountains. Sometimes a wagon would slip down a steep mountainside and a family would lose everything. Some pioneers got sick or starved and died on the way.

But many made it. With bravery, hard work, and a little luck, they pressed on until they came to the new land where they could start a new life.

West to California!

A few years after the Oregon Trail became popular, many pioneers decided to follow a different trail that led to California. Can you guess why? It wasn't the beautiful views of the Pacific Ocean that drew settlers to California; it was the prospect of getting rich. In 1848, some nuggets of gold were discovered in a stream in California. When the news was reported in the East, tens of thousands of people went west, hoping to scoop up a bunch of gold and get rich.

In the end, only a few people got rich during the California gold rush. But many of the people who went to California to find gold decided to stay. These people wanted to keep in touch with friends and relatives they had left behind, but it was no easy task to transport a letter from California to the East Coast, or from the East Coast all the way out to California. It could take a month or longer for your letter to arrive. At least, that's how long it took before the Pony Express came to the rescue.

The Pony Express

Have you ever run a relay race? That's when you run part of the race, then you tag another runner, and he or she runs to tag the next runner, and so on.

If you imagine a relay race, then you'll understand how the Pony Express worked. The Pony Express was set up to get mail to the people who were settling out west in California, and to allow those people to write back to their friends in the East. Nobody likes to wait a month to get a letter, and it seemed like a lot of people would be willing to pay a little extra to get their letters delivered more quickly. That's why two businessmen decided to set up the Pony Express, a kind of relay race on horseback from Missouri to California.

A Pony Express rider speeds past two workers raising telegraph poles. Eventually, the telegraph put the Pony Express out of business.

Here's how it worked. A young rider would grab a mailbag full of letters, jump on a horse, and ride for ten miles at top speed. Then he would jump on a fresh horse and keep going. He would change horses seven times, and then he would pass the mailbag to another rider, who would ride on seven different horses for another seventy miles until he reached the next rider.

With the Pony Express, the mail got all the way to California in only ten days! That was a big improvement. But in just a couple of years, there was no need for the Pony Express. People could use a brand-new, electric way to send messages, the telegraph. With the telegraph, you could send a message from the East Coast to California in only seconds. That was a lot quicker than the Pony Express but not nearly as exciting!

The Transcontinental Railroad

For many years, there was no way to get to California by train. Train tracks connected many cities in the East, but they did not run all the way out to California. If you wanted to send a message to California, you could use the telegraph, but if you wanted to go yourself, you had to ride in a covered wagon.

That changed when the Transcontinental Railroad was completed in 1869. Two companies worked on this railroad. One company laid tracks west from Omaha, Nebraska. The other company laid tracks east from Sacramento, California. When the two tracks were finally connected, in what is now Utah, a golden spike was driven into the ground to celebrate. Once the trains began to run on these new tracks, passengers could travel by train almost all the way from the Atlantic Ocean to the Pacific—across the whole continent. That is why the new railroad was called the Transcontinental Railroad ("trans" means "across").

The Transcontinental Railroad made it easier than ever to go west. If you lived in the East and wanted to go to California, all you had to do was buy a ticket, hop on board, and wave goodbye!

Already There: The American Indians

For countless settlers, the American West was a place where they could go to make a new start in life. They could get some land of their own, start a farm, and perhaps even become wealthy. What could be better?

For one group of people, the arrival of tens of thousands of settlers was not good news at all. For the Native Americans, it was very bad news, indeed.

Out West there were many different tribes of American Indians. Sometimes we call these people Native Americans because they were already living in America at the time Christopher Columbus and the Europeans arrived. Each tribe of Native Americans had its own way of life. For example, in the dry and hot Southwest, the Pueblo Indians were mostly farmers, and they lived in houses they made of adobe, a mixture of clay, sand, and straw. Another tribe in the Southwest, the

> **Make a Connection**
>
> Some of the songs introduced in the Music section of this book have to do with building railroads ("I've Been Working on the Railroad") or driving trains ("Casey Jones").

Make a Connection

In the Language Arts section of this book you can read stories about Iktomi, a trickster figure in the folklore of the Plains Indians.

Apache, did not settle down and farm, but instead roamed the mountains and deserts and hunted for food.

Many Native Americans lived in the big, grassy land between the Mississippi River and the Rocky Mountains, called the Great Plains. The Great Plains were home to tribes such as the Iowa, the Lakota (also called the Sioux), the Crow, the Blackfoot, and the Cheyenne.

This map shows where some Native American groups lived at the time when American settlers started moving West.

Forced from Their Lands

As the pioneers moved west, they often fought with the Native Americans. The pioneers thought of the land as their new home, and they did not want other people living on it or using it.

In some ways, the pioneers were doing what the United States government had already been doing for years, pushing Native Americans off the lands where they lived and forcing them to move far away.

One American leader who forced many Native Americans to move was President Andrew Jackson. (You may remember him as the general who led the American troops at the Battle of New Orleans.) Jackson enforced a law called the Indian Removal Act. This law said that thousands of Native Americans had to leave the lands where they had lived for generations and move many hundreds of miles away to Indian Territory, which was mostly dry, dusty land west of the Mississippi River.

In the southeastern part of our country, in what is now the state of Georgia, one tribe refused to go. The Cherokee people did not want to leave their land and their homes. But the American government

Andrew Jackson

wanted their land because there was gold on it. So American soldiers were sent in. They used rifles to threaten the Cherokee people. The soldiers forced the Cherokee people to get into railroad cars and steamboats, which took the people only part of the way to the Indian Territory.

There were still hundreds of miles to go. The Cherokee people were forced to walk the rest of the way. Many of them got very sick. Many starved. Many did not make it. Thousands of Cherokee men, women, and children died along the way. Their journey was so terrible and so sad that it is now known as the "Trail of Tears."

Sequoyah's Invention

A Cherokee man named Sequoyah did an amazing thing: he invented a writing system and taught his people to read and write. Most Native Americans did not use written language, and the Cherokee people were no exception, but Sequoyah worked for twelve years to develop a writing system for his people. He eventually

came up with a set of written symbols—one symbol for each syllable in the Cherokee language. Then he and his daughter set about teaching the Cherokee people to read and write in their own language. The system Sequoyah developed caught on and is still used today.

Indians of the Plains

Other Native Americans also suffered. As wagon trains and railroads brought more and more pioneers west of the Appalachian Mountains and then west of the Mississippi, the American government forced the Native Americans to move onto smaller pieces of land, called "reservations." Some Native Americans agreed to move to these reservations, but others resisted.

For many of the Plains Indians, the big, shaggy animal called the buffalo was very important. Thousands and thousands of buffalo roamed across the Great Plains. The Native Americans hunted the buffalo for food. They used the

Plains Indians hunting buffalo

Make a Connection

For a poem about the decline of the buffalo population, see "Buffalo Dusk" by Carl Sandburg, in the Language Arts section. Your child may be interested to know that the buffalo have made a comeback in recent years and are no longer in danger of going extinct.

buffalo's hide to make clothing. Some also used the hide to make tents called teepees.

When settlers arrived and began to hunt for buffalo, things changed. At first it was not too bad. There seemed to be enough buffalo for everyone. But as time went on the settlers killed more and more of the buffalo, and this led to more conflicts.

Only a Matter of Time

Imagine you are a Native American child who lives on the plains. What a shock it must be to see a wagon train rolling across the land, bringing people who look different, talk in strange ways, and hunt the buffalo you depend on. How alarming it must be to see a train puffing black smoke as it whizzes past, with dozens of settlers leaning out the windows, shooting buffalo.

Sometimes you feel friendly toward these strangers from the East. You trade with them, exchanging food or buffalo hides for blankets and metal fishhooks. But sometimes you do not feel friendly. You feel angry at the settlers for swarming over your native land and killing so many buffalo. Sometimes the settlers shoot buffalo for food, sometimes they shoot them for the hides, which can be sold for lots of money back East, and sometimes they shoot them just "for sport." Because they are shooting so many of them, the buffalo herds are beginning to disappear. Once there were millions of buffalo grazing on the plains. Now there are many fewer. You worry that, in time, the buffalo may disappear altogether.

These strangers come with very different ideas about the land. They say that they "claim" the land. Some say they have bought it, and so they own it. But you have lived on this land for years. You wonder: *How can anybody own the land?* You do not see the land as something that any person can keep just for himself. You have always thought of the land, and the animals and the plants on it, as a gift that should be used carefully by all.

One night, you hear the leaders of your tribe talking in serious voices around a campfire. One man sounds angry. He says that the strangers are bad. He says that they have driven away the animals your people need and that the people are going hungry. He says that you must fight the strangers and drive them away. You do not want this to happen, but something inside you knows that you cannot stop it. The fighting will come. It is only a matter of time.

The Civil War

A Nation Divided Against Itself

As you know, many years ago Americans fought the British in two wars—the Revolutionary War and the War of 1812. Now you're going to learn about another war, but this one was different. In this war, Americans fought against each other. It is called the Civil War. A civil war is a war between two parts of a single country, or two groups of people in a single country.

The U.S. Civil War was a war between the Northern states and the Southern states. Why would Americans fight against each other? There were many reasons. One big reason was that people could not agree about slavery.

Slavery in America

Slavery started early in the United States. It started when we were still a group of colonies. Not long after the English first settled in Jamestown, ships brought the first Africans to America, but these people did not come here because they

Enslaved Africans were sometimes chained at the wrists and ankles to keep them from escaping.

wanted to. They were forced to come as slaves. Many had been kidnapped, taken against their will, from their homes in Africa. Some of these enslaved people were taken to Europe, but many more were taken to North and South America. Enslaved Africans were chained to each other and crammed into ships, and many of them died on the hard voyage across the Atlantic Ocean. The Africans who survived the terrible voyage were sold into slavery.

Think about that for a minute—these were people, human beings, but they were sold, like furniture or cattle. They were mainly sold to farmers in the Southern states, like Virginia, North Carolina, South Carolina, and Georgia.

These Southern states had big farms, called plantations. On the plantations, the owners grew crops that they sold for money, such as tobacco and cotton. The farm owners wanted slaves to work on their farms. The owners were the masters, and they could do what they wanted with the enslaved Africans. Many masters forced the enslaved Africans to work hard from dawn to dark. The enslaved Africans often had very little to eat and only worn-out clothes to wear. If a master did not like the way a slave was working, he could have the slave whipped.

Spirituals

When Africans were forced to come to America as slaves, they combined their music with the music they heard in America. The songs they sang, called spirituals, often told of their hard lives and of their hopes for better times to come. Here are the words to a well-known spiritual.

Swing Low, Sweet Chariot

Swing low, sweet chariot,
Comin' for to carry me home,
Swing low, sweet chariot,
Comin' for to carry me home.

I looked over Jordan and what did I see
Comin' for to carry me home,
A band of angels comin' after me,
Comin' for to carry me home.

If you get there before I do,
Comin' for to carry me home,
Tell all my friends I'm comin' there too,
Comin' for to carry me home.

Stop Slavery or Let It Spread?

Although there were many, many enslaved Africans in America, mostly in the South, not everyone agreed that slavery was right. In fact, many people were saying that slavery was wrong and that it should be ended. They said that no one should be allowed to own people. They said the enslaved Africans should be given their freedom.

The people who wanted to end slavery lived mostly in the Northern states. But in the Southern states, where enslaved Africans worked on the big farms, most people wanted to keep slavery going. The Northerners and Southerners also disagreed about whether slavery should be allowed to spread. As more Americans moved west, some wanted to take enslaved Africans out west to work for them. They said, "We own these slaves. They are our property. You can't stop us from taking what we own." But many Northerners said, "No! Slavery should not be allowed to spread to these new lands!"

Southerners did not want to change their way of life. They said, "The United States government cannot tell us what to do. We Southern states have the right to make our own decisions."

Harriet Tubman

Another Kind of Railroad

While the North and South argued over slavery, some brave people worked to help enslaved Africans escape to freedom. One of the people who helped slaves escape had been a slave herself. Her name was Harriet Tubman.

When Harriet Tubman was a little girl, she had worked as a slave for a mistress who often beat her. Harriet wanted to run away. She dreamed of being free. As she worked in the fields, Harriet heard other enslaved Africans whispering about a railroad, but it wasn't a real railroad. It was called the Underground Railroad, and it was a way for enslaved Africans to escape to freedom. It wasn't really underground, but it was called that because it was secret. It was a secret way to go north to freedom. Along the way, many people, both white and black, took great risks by hiding and feeding enslaved Africans who had run away from their masters.

With help from people on the Underground Railroad, Harriet Tubman escaped to the North. There she was free. But she didn't just sit still and enjoy her freedom. She started to work for the Underground Railroad herself. She went back and helped her family escape, and she kept going back, over and over. It's hard to tell exactly how many people Harriet Tubman helped, but some say that she led three hundred slaves to their freedom.

Follow the Drinking Gourd

Here is part of a song that some slaves sang about the Underground Railroad and escaping to the North. The "drinking gourd" is another name for the constellation of stars known as the Big Dipper. To follow it was to go north to freedom.

When the sun comes back and the first quail calls,
Follow the drinking gourd.
For the old man is a-waiting for to carry you to freedom
If you follow the drinking gourd.

Follow the drinking gourd,
Follow the drinking gourd,
For the old man is a-waiting for to carry you to freedom
If you follow the drinking gourd.

The river ends between two hills,
Follow the drinking gourd.
Follow the drinking gourd,
There's another river on the other side,
Follow the drinking gourd.

Abraham Lincoln: A Man for the Union

In 1861, the Southern states decided that they did not want to be part of the United States anymore. They said, "We will be in charge of ourselves." They set up their own government, called the Confederate States of America, and their own army.

Many people in the North did not think the Southern states should be allowed to leave the United States. There was one man who especially wanted the United States to stay together as a union—which means to stay as one country, all united. This was President Abraham Lincoln.

If you say the Pledge of Allegiance at school in the morning, then you say the words "one nation, indivisible." If something is indivisible, it means it cannot be divided into smaller parts. That's what President Lincoln wanted for the United States: he wanted it to be a nation that could not be divided. He wanted to keep the states together in a single country.

President Lincoln said he would fight to save the Union. But he did not know how awful the fighting would be. Nobody knew. Many people thought the war would be over in a few months, but the Civil War turned out to be the largest and most deadly war Americans have ever fought! Hundreds of thousands of men and boys died—many in battle, and many more from the diseases that spread in their dirty, crowded camps.

Abraham Lincoln was president during the Civil War. He was determined to keep the states together.

Yankees Against Rebels, Grant Versus Lee

The Civil War started in 1861. It lasted until 1865. It was American against American, North against South, the United States of America against the Confederate States of America. The Southerners called Northerners "Yankees." The Northerners called Southerners "Rebels," or "Rebs" for short.

General Robert E. Lee was in charge of the Southern army. General Ulysses S. Grant was in charge of the Northern army. They were very different men. General Lee was a quiet, tall, dignified gentleman. General Grant was scruffy-looking and, to tell the truth, he drank too much. But both men were excellent military leaders.

Robert E. Lee led the Southern army.

Ulysses S. Grant led the Northern army.

Songs of the North and South

Soldiers on both sides of the war had songs they liked to sing to keep their spirits up. A popular marching song for the Northern, or Union, army was "When Johnny Comes Marching Home." The words of this song described what it would be like when the war was over and the soldiers went back to their families:

> When Johnny comes marching home again,
> Hurrah, hurrah!
> We'll give him a hearty welcome then,
> Hurrah, hurrah!
> The men will cheer and the boys will shout,
> The ladies they will all turn out,
> And we'll all feel gay when Johnny comes march-
> ing home.

A Union soldier

The most popular song in the South was actually written by a Northerner! It was called "Dixie." "Dixie" was a nickname for the South.

Confederate soldiers

> I wish I was in the land of cotton,
> Old times there are not forgotten,
> Look away! Look away! Look away!
> Dixie Land.
>
> Oh, I wish I was in Dixie,
> Hooray! Hooray!
> In Dixie Land, I'll take my stand,
> To live and die in Dixie,
> Away, away, away down south in Dixie.
> Away, away, away down south in Dixie!

Clara Barton

When the Civil War started, a brave woman named Clara Barton gathered medicine and supplies and went to nurse the wounded soldiers. Her care meant a lot to the soldiers, and she became known as the "Angel of the Battlefield." But Clara Barton's work did not end when the war was over.

After the war she formed an organization to look for missing soldiers and mark their graves. Then she began to think about people who needed help not just in wars but in natural disasters such as floods, hurricanes, or droughts. She became the founder of the American Red Cross, which provided food, clothing, and medicine whenever disaster struck. The Red Cross still does this today.

Clara Barton, the "Angel of the Battlefield"

The Emancipation Proclamation

In the middle of the Civil War, President Lincoln wrote the Emancipation Proclamation. To "emancipate" means to set someone free. To make a proclamation is to announce something. In the Emancipation Proclamation, Lincoln announced that all slaves in the Southern states were now free. The Emancipation Proclamation did not end slavery overnight, but it was a big and important step toward ending slavery.

President Lincoln wanted the country to be one nation, indivisible, with liberty and justice for all. At Gettysburg, Pennsylvania, after a terrible battle in which many soldiers died, President Lincoln made a famous speech. He said that the soldiers who died in battle died for a very important reason:

that this nation, under God, shall have a new birth of freedom—and that government of the people, by the people, for the people, shall not perish from the earth.

After Lincoln made his Emancipation Proclamation, many African Americans joined the Northern army. In this picture, you can see black soldiers fighting bravely in an attack on Fort Wagner, in South Carolina.

In the end, Lincoln and the North were victorious. Ulysses S. Grant and the army of the Northern states defeated Robert E. Lee and the army of the South. The country had made it through the worst time in its history, and the United States were united once again.

Immigration and Citizenship

A Nation of Immigrants

Let's talk about food for a minute. Do you like spaghetti or ravioli? Tacos or burritos? How about egg rolls or fried rice? Many Americans love these foods. The funny thing is that all these foods came to America from other countries. It's not just the food, it's also the people. People have come to America from all over the world.

The United States is a nation of immigrants. An immigrant is a person who leaves his or her home to settle in another country. People from countries all around the world have immigrated to America. They have chosen to come and settle here. They have come from Ireland, Italy, Poland, Cuba, Mexico, China, Vietnam, and many other countries. New immigrants are coming to America every day.

Do you know where your family originally came from? Were you born in America? What about your parents and grandparents?

Native Americans had lived in this country for many years when people from Europe began to immigrate to North America. You've learned how the English settled at Jamestown in Virginia and at Plymouth in Massachusetts. Pretty soon the English were joined by people from Holland and Scotland, who settled in New York and New Jersey. Germans began to settle in Pennsylvania. Immigrants from France made new homes in New York, New Hampshire, and Louisiana. People from Spain settled in Florida and Texas.

How could people from so many different countries settle here and live together peacefully? It wasn't always easy. People from different countries didn't always trust or like each other. Sometimes they couldn't even speak to each other, because they spoke different languages, but since the earliest days of this country, people knew that if America was going to succeed, all these different people must try to get along.

After the Revolutionary War, our country adopted a motto: *E Pluribus Unum*. Look on the back of any coin or on the back of a dollar bill and you will find the words *E Pluribus Unum*. They are in an old

An immigrant arriving in the United States

Sit down with your child and discuss your family's ethnic background. Where did your ancestors come from? Point out countries of origin on a globe or world map. Share stories and photos about your immigrant ancestors.

Talk and Think

language called Latin, and they mean "from many, one." That means Americans are determined to make one country out of people from many different countries, and we are still trying to do it today.

Why Did Immigrants Come to America?

Would you be willing to move to a faraway country and never see your home or your grandparents, aunts, uncles, cousins, and friends again?

Why would people choose to immigrate? What made them want to leave their old countries and come to the United States? For many immigrants, it was a combination of bad times at home and the hope that they could find something better in America.

Do you remember why the Pilgrims and the Puritans came to America? They wanted religious freedom. In England they were not allowed to worship in the way they believed was right. So they looked for a place where they could practice their religion and live as they wanted to. They left their homes in England and made the hard trip across the Atlantic Ocean to America.

Many immigrants have continued to come to America looking for religious

The Great Seal of the United States includes the Latin words "E Pluribus Unum," which mean "from many, one."

freedom. Quakers, Catholics, and Jews left their home countries and came to America because they wanted to be free to follow their own beliefs.

Some immigrants have come to America to get away from awful things happening in their old countries. Once in Ireland a deadly disease almost wiped out one of the most important crops, potatoes. Without potatoes, many poor families in Ireland went hungry. There was so little to eat that thousands of people were starving. Some of these Irish people decided that things were so bad, they had to leave their country, and so they came to America.

People came from other countries, too, such as Sweden and Germany and China, for the same reason—the land where they lived just wasn't producing enough food. They came to America with dreams of starting a farm, growing food, and never being hungry again.

A Land of Opportunity?

Most immigrants were sad to leave their old homes but hopeful about life in the United States. They thought America would be a land of opportunity, a place where they and their families would have a new chance for a better life. Their hopes gave them the courage they needed to make the hard trip to America.

In the 1800s, many immigrants came to America on crowded ships. For most of the passage across the ocean they were cramped in the big, dark bottom of the ship, called *steerage*. There were no separate rooms. Everybody was jammed together. There were no sinks or bathtubs. The air smelled awful. If you had hard crackers and dried cheese to eat, you were lucky. Some passengers got sick, and in the crowded spaces down in steerage, diseases spread quickly. Weaker immigrants often died of disease before they ever saw America.

When they finally came near land, the tired immigrants rushed on deck to see their new country. After 1886, immigrants who arrived in New York Harbor were greeted by a special sight: the Statue of Liberty raising her torch in welcome. But some immigrants did not feel very welcome. For example, many who arrived in New York had to stop at a big building on Ellis Island. They had to wait in long lines and go through medical examinations and answer a lot of questions. If they were sick or didn't have the proper papers, they might not be allowed to enter the

Chinese immigrants on the streets of San Francisco

country. When they were allowed to enter, their lives were still hard. Many came to America hoping to buy a little land and start a farm, but most were so poor that they had to stop and look for work in the cities where they arrived—cities such as New York, Philadelphia, Boston, and San Francisco.

Immigrants often took the low-paying jobs no one else wanted. They sold newspapers or washed clothes. They did the backbreaking work of building the canals and railroads. Many Irish immigrants worked to build the Erie Canal. Many Chinese immigrants helped build the Transcontinental Railroad. In hot factories, women and even children worked at spinning cloth or sewing clothes.

Immigrants were often treated badly. Some Americans who had been in the country for many years did not like the different languages, religions, or customs of the new immigrants. These Americans forgot that there was a time when their ancestors had been immigrants, too.

Even though many immigrants were not welcomed, they worked hard and made a better life for themselves in America. Some saved enough money to buy a little land to farm or to open their own business in the cities. They built homes. They educated their children, and they watched their sons and daughters become successful people. They became the country's teachers, professors, writers, businessmen, nurses, and doctors. They became our newest and proudest citizens.

Immigrants at Ellis Island

In New York Harbor, the Statue of Liberty welcomes newcomers to America. "Lady Liberty" was a gift from France to the United States. The statue is so large that it had to be delivered in parts.

These immigrant women are stitching clothes in a clothing factory.

An Immigrant's Story

Have you ever heard the song "White Christmas"? It begins, "I'm dreaming of a white Christmas, just like the ones I used to know." The song, along with many other popular songs, was written by an immigrant named Irving Berlin.

Irving Berlin was born in a Russian village, but his family was not Russian. They were Jews who had settled in Russia. Irving and his seven brothers and sisters lived in a tiny hut with a dirt floor. On Saturdays, Irving's father would take the children to the local synagogue, to worship and sing Jewish songs.

Then one day, a group of Russians who did not like Jewish people rode into town and burned the village to the ground. Irving's parents decided that it was not safe to remain in Russia. They traveled from village to village with only the items they could carry, and eventually they got on a boat that carried them to the United States.

After catching sight of the Statue of Liberty and passing through Ellis Island, the family settled in an immigrant neighborhood in New York City. Irving's father took a job as a butcher's assistant. When he died a few years later, the other members of the family had to get jobs to help pay the rent. Irving's mother worked as a midwife, helping women have babies. His brother worked in a sweatshop, stitching shirts. Three of his sisters rolled cigars. Irving himself worked as a paper boy, selling newspapers. When the children came home at the end of the day, they would hand the money they had made to their mother. By pulling together, they made enough to pay the rent and buy food.

Irving Berlin's family immigrated to the United States when he was just a boy. He grew up to become a famous songwriter.

A little later, Irving began to make a little extra money by singing. By the time he was eighteen, he was a singing waiter in a New York restaurant. At the end of the night, when the restaurant closed, he would stay and practice playing the piano. He wrote his first song when he was nineteen and had his first big hit when he was twenty-three. After that, there was no slowing down. He became one of the most popular songwriters in the country and made quite a lot of money.

You probably know some of the songs Irving Berlin wrote. He wrote "Puttin' on the Ritz" and "There's No Business like Show Business." He wrote "Annie Get Your Gun" and "Anything You Can Do, I Can Do Better." He also wrote "God Bless America," a song that many people think should be the national anthem. The lyrics to that song are very touching, and they are even more touching if you remember that the man who wrote them was an immigrant who came to the United States, not knowing a word of English, in the hope of finding a better life.

God bless America,
Land that I love.
Stand beside her, and guide her
Thru the night with a light from above.
From the mountains, to the prairies,
To the oceans, white with foam
God bless America,
My home sweet home.

All Together
Work with your child to memorize the words of "God Bless America."

Becoming a Citizen

What does it mean to be a citizen of a country? It means you are a legal member of a country. As a citizen of the United States, you have certain rights and responsibilities. For example, all adult American citizens have the right to vote in elections and the right to be elected to a position in the government (if enough people vote for you). All citizens have the responsibility to obey the laws and pay taxes.

How do you get to be an American citizen? If you are born in the United States, you are automatically a citizen of this country, even if your parents are not. But you don't have to be born here to be a citizen. Immigrants can become United States citizens, too, if they want to. First they have to live in the United States for at least five years. During that time, they have to obey the law and pay taxes. Then they take a test on American history and government. The test asks questions such as: *What is the basic law of our country called? Who was president during the Civil War?* (You know the answers, right?)

After passing the test, you make a pledge to be loyal to the United States, and then you are a new citizen.

Do It Yourself

Familiarize your child with democratic procedures such as campaigning and voting by having a vote on some issue relating to family life, such as what to prepare for a special meal. Allow family members to speak in support of their favorite meal; then, set up a ballot box and have them vote. Count the votes and follow the voice of the people!

These new citizens are promising to obey the laws of the United States.

Civil Rights: Fighting for a Cause

All Men Are Created Equal

You know these words from the Declaration of Independence: "We hold these truths to be self-evident, that all men are created equal."

Does that mean that all people are exactly alike? No; as you know, people differ in many ways. Instead, that part of the Declaration means that people are born with equal rights. It means that everyone should have a fair chance. It means that you should have the same freedom as everyone else to do things such as get an education, get the best job you can, and vote for the leaders you want, or even try to become a leader.

That's what it means, but that's not always the way it has worked out. The Africans who were brought here and forced to work as slaves were not given equal rights and opportunities. The Native Americans who were forced to leave their homelands were treated unfairly, too.

Our country was only just coming into existence when Thomas Jefferson wrote those words: "All men are created equal." Now, more than two hundred years later, we are still working to make this country a place where everyone has a fair chance. In our history, many brave people have worked hard to help bring equal rights to all Americans. Let's learn about some of these people who have worked for our civil rights.

Susan B. Anthony and Votes for Women

The Constitution says that "all men are created equal." Today, we understand the word "men" to include all people, but for many years, "men" meant just men, not women. For many years, women did not have the same rights as men. They were not allowed to do many kinds of jobs, and they were not allowed to vote.

Susan B. Anthony thought that was unfair. For many years after the Civil War, she made speeches and published a magazine in which she argued that women should have equal rights, including the right to vote. She asked: *Why should only men have the right to choose our leaders? Why should women be left out?*

In the year 1872, Americans were voting for a new president. Well, American men were voting. Women still weren't allowed to vote. But that didn't stop Susan B. Anthony. Bright and early, at seven o'clock in the morning, she walked to the polls (the voting place) and cast her vote for president.

Two weeks later, Anthony was arrested and charged with voting illegally. She was brought before a judge. The judge was convinced that Anthony was in the wrong. He ordered the jury to find her guilty. Then he asked Anthony if she had anything to say.

Susan B. Anthony

That was the chance Anthony had been waiting for. "I have many things to say," she announced, "for in your ordered verdict of guilty, you have trampled underfoot every vital principle of our government. My natural rights, my civil rights, my political rights, my judicial rights, are all alike ignored."

The judge tried to quiet Anthony down, but she continued to protest. Finally, the judge ordered her to pay a fine of $100.

"I shall never pay a dollar of your unjust penalty," Anthony declared. And she never did. She refused to pay the fine because she did not believe she had done anything wrong. She did not believe that it was wrong for her to vote; she believed it was wrong that her country did not allow her to vote.

Susan B. Anthony kept working for women's rights until the end of her life. Fourteen years after she died, her hard work paid off. In 1920, all American women gained the right to vote.

Eleanor Roosevelt

In the United States, the wife of the president is known as the First Lady. One of the most famous First Ladies ever was Eleanor Roosevelt, the wife of President Franklin Roosevelt (you can see his face on a dime). Eleanor Roosevelt was full of energy. She once wrote a book called *It's Up to the Women*. In it she said that women must work to make the nation better. She followed her own advice. She tried to help wherever she could.

When Franklin Roosevelt was first elected president in 1932, this country was going through a very hard time known as the Great Depression. Many people had lost their jobs and were poor and hungry. President Roosevelt started government programs to give people jobs. Eleanor Roosevelt did not stay cooped up in the White House. She volunteered to work in the soup kitchens that served meals to hungry people. She visited factories and coal mines, and she talked with the workers to see what the government might be able to do to help them.

Eleanor Roosevelt spoke out for equal rights for all Americans. In many speeches, she said that everyone in America should be given a fair chance, and she meant everyone—

Eleanor Roosevelt

women, black people, Native Americans, poor people, everyone. She said, "We are all brothers, regardless of race, creed, or color."

In 1939, Eleanor Roosevelt took a stand against discrimination. She belonged to an organization called the Daughters of the American Revolution. When the Daughters of the American Revolution refused to allow a talented African American singer named Marian Anderson to sing at a hall they owned in Washington, D.C., Eleanor Roosevelt resigned from the organization. A little later, she got permission for Marian Anderson to sing at the Lincoln Memorial in Washington, D.C. More than 75,000 people came to support Anderson and hear her wonderful voice.

Even after the death of her husband, Franklin, Eleanor Roosevelt continued

Marian Anderson singing on the steps of the Lincoln Memorial, in Washington, D.C.

to work for human rights. In 1946, President Harry Truman asked her to work at the United Nations, an organization that includes many of the countries in the world. The main goal of the United Nations, even today, is world peace, but it also works to reduce poverty and help people in need. Eleanor became the leader of the United Nations Commission on Human Rights. She helped write an important document called the Universal Declaration of Human Rights. This document states that all people should have the right to work, the right to rest, the right to an education, and the right to share in the life of their own community.

Mary McLeod Bethune

You know that enslaved Africans in the South were emancipated, or set free, during the Civil War. When the war ended, all of the enslaved Africans in the United States were set free. But life continued to be very difficult for these African Americans. Many white people did not want to give equal rights to African Americans and other people with dark skin. But there were many other people who were determined to help African Americans secure equal rights. One of those people was Mary McLeod Bethune.

Mary McLeod Bethune was an African American woman who wanted to be sure that African Americans had a chance to learn to read and get a good education. She knew how important education could be. "When I learned to read," she once remarked, "the whole world opened up for me."

In 1904 Mary McLeod Bethune opened a small school for black girls in Daytona, Florida. She didn't have much money to buy school supplies or furniture. The students used boxes for desks. And there were only five students at first.

But in the next few years, her school grew and grew. In time it became Bethune-Cookman College. Mary McLeod Bethune served as president of the college.

Later, President Franklin Roosevelt asked Mary McLeod Bethune to work for him, and when she said yes, she became the first African American woman to be in charge of a government office.

Near the end of her life, Mary McLeod Bethune wrote down what she wanted to leave behind after she was gone. In strong capital letters, she wrote, "I leave you LOVE; I leave you HOPE; I leave you a THIRST FOR EDUCATION."

Mary McLeod Bethune

Jackie Robinson

In college, Jackie Robinson was a good student, and he was an amazing athlete. He won awards in four different sports, including baseball. You would think that the major-league baseball teams would all be crying, "Play for us, Jackie." "No, play for *us*!" But that didn't happen. Back then—and this was only about seventy years ago—African Americans weren't allowed to play in the major leagues. Only white people could play in the major leagues. There was a separate league for black baseball players.

This is a little hard for kids today to believe, but there were dozens and dozens of great baseball players who couldn't play in the major leagues, simply because they were black.

But that changed in 1947, when Branch Rickey, the president of the Brooklyn Dodgers, convinced Jackie Robinson to break the color barrier. Rickey could see

Jackie Robinson

that Jackie Robinson was a great baseball player, but he wanted to make sure he was also a brave and strong person. He knew that there would be many white people who did not want Robinson to play in the major leagues. When Rickey met Robinson, he was impressed. He was confident that Robinson was tough enough to deal with criticism and abuse.

Jackie Robinson played his first game for the Brooklyn Dodgers on April 15, 1947. He became the first black baseball player to play for a major-league team.

At first Jackie Robinson had to put up with more than most people could stand. People would spit on him and call him terrible names. Pitchers would throw balls and try to hit him. It was hard, but Jackie Robinson kept his cool. He focused on the game, and he proved that he was a terrific player. During his first season in the major leagues, he got 175 hits and scored 125 runs. At the end of the year, he was named Rookie of the Year, and two years later he was named the league's Most Valuable Player.

Today African American athletes compete in many professional sports. It was Jackie Robinson who opened the way for these talented athletes.

Rosa Parks

Even after Jackie Robinson joined the major leagues, African Americans were kept out of many things. Especially in the southern states, black people were kept separate and apart from white people. In restaurants, black people were told to sit in a separate section, or they weren't allowed in at all. Black children and white children went to separate schools. There were even separate drinking fountains for white people and black people.

This separating of people just because of their skin color is called segregation.

In 1955, even the buses in southern states were segregated. If you were white, you could sit in the front. If you were black, you had to sit in the back or give up your seat to a white person if there were no empty seats left.

One day in 1955, a black woman named Rosa Parks got on a bus in Montgomery, Alabama. She had worked hard all day and she was tired. She sat down in a seat at the back of the bus, just beyond the section that was reserved for white people. Later the bus got crowded and all the seats in the white section were filled. Well, the next time the bus stopped, a few white people got on, and the bus driver told Parks and some other black people to get up and give their seats to white people.

Rosa Parks

Several of the African Americans on the bus did as they were told, but Parks did not give up her seat. She did not believe she should have to move, even if the law said she did have to. She thought it was a bad law, an unfair law.

The bus driver told Parks that if she did not stand up, he would call the police to come and arrest her. She replied quietly, "You may do that." When the driver asked her one more time to stand up, Parks responded by saying, "I don't think I should have to stand up."

And so Rosa Parks was arrested.

When people heard that Parks had been arrested, they got very angry. African Americans in the city of Montgomery decided that they would stop riding the buses. They would walk or share rides in cars, but they would not pay the bus company to ride as long as the company practiced segregation.

For a whole year, African Americans refused to ride the buses in Montgomery. This became known as the Montgomery Bus Boycott. (To boycott is to refuse to buy or use something.)

A little more than a year after Parks was arrested, the highest court in our land, the Supreme Court, said that she was right and the Alabama law was wrong. The court held that segregated seating was unconstitutional. That was an important victory for the civil rights movement, and today Rosa Parks is recognized as one of the pioneers in the struggle for civil rights.

Martin Luther King, Jr.

During the Montgomery Bus Boycott, African Americans had a strong leader. He was a young minister named Martin Luther King, Jr. King convinced the African American people of Montgomery to stand together and support the bus boycott.

When the boycott ended, King continued to work for civil rights for African Americans. He brought many people together, black and white, to help Americans understand that segregation was wrong. He said that wherever white and black people were separated by the law, it was wrong. In schools, hospitals, restaurants, or hotels, it was wrong to keep people apart just because of the color of their skin.

King believed in fighting against segregation, but he also believed in fighting peacefully. He wanted to change the bad laws, but he did not believe in using violence to change them. He told people not to use their fists, throw rocks, or shoot guns. Instead, they should join together and march peacefully. Or they could go to a restaurant for white people only and ask to be served. If the restaurant refused to serve them because they were black, they should just sit patiently.

King and other people working for civil rights began a series of sit-in protests. During a sit-in, protesters would go to a place where segregation was practiced and sit down. Black protesters would sit in areas reserved for whites, and white protesters would sit in areas designated for blacks. Usually the protesters would be asked to move, and they would refuse. Then they would be arrested, but as soon as they got out of jail, they would go to another place that practiced segregation and begin another sit-in. In some places there were so many sit-ins that the police had to spend all day arresting protesters. Newspapers and television channels began to cover these sit-ins, and soon the whole country was paying attention to segregation and the protests King and his supporters were making against it.

Martin Luther King, Jr., was arrested many times, along with other civil rights protesters. On one occasion, he was kept in a jail cell in Birmingham, Alabama. While he was there, he wrote "Letter from the Birmingham Jail." In the letter King replied to another minister who had criticized him and other civil rights activists for breaking the law and conducting sit-ins. The minister did not think it was right, or could ever be right, to break the law. In response, King argued that there are two types of laws: just and unjust: "I would be the first to advocate obeying just laws," he said. "One has not only a legal but a moral responsibility to obey just laws." But one also "has a moral responsibility to disobey unjust laws." In fact, King insisted, "an unjust law is no law at all." He continued:

In no sense do I advocate evading or defying the law. . . . That would lead to anarchy. One who breaks an unjust law must do so openly, lovingly, and with a willingness to accept the penalty. I submit that an individual who breaks a law that conscience tells him is unjust, and who willingly accepts the penalty of imprisonment in order to arouse the conscience of the community over its injustice, is in reality expressing the highest respect for law.

Martin Luther King, Jr., tried to protest peacefully. But that wasn't always easy. When he and other civil rights protesters marched peacefully or sat down in

Martin Luther King, Jr.

segregated restaurants, people who didn't want things to change shouted at them, punched them, and even tried to kill them. Once someone threw a bomb into King's home. But this didn't stop him. He kept on peacefully fighting for what he believed was right.

In August 1963, hundreds of thousands of Americans gathered in Washington, D.C., to support civil rights for African Americans. King gave a speech that is known as his "I Have a Dream" speech. Here is part of what he said:

I have a dream that one day this nation will rise up and live out the true meaning of its creed: "We hold these truths to be self-evident, that all men are created equal." I have a dream that my four little children will one day live in a nation where they will not be judged by the color of their skin but by the content of their character.

Many Americans shared King's dream of equal rights for all people. But not everyone agreed with him. Some people even hated him, because these people did not want blacks to have equal rights. And in the spring of 1968, one of these people shot and killed King.

Martin Luther King moved our country closer to its dream of equality. To honor him and his work, the United States government decided that the third Monday in January would be a holiday in memory of Martin Luther King, Jr.

Cesar Chavez

Once when he was a teenager, Cesar Chavez was arrested for refusing to leave a section of a movie theater reserved for white people only. But Cesar Chavez wasn't black. He was Mexican American.

For many years, in the southwest part of this country and in California, Mexican Americans were treated as second-class citizens, very much as black people were in the South. They had to go to separate schools and were kept out of many restaurants and hotels.

Many Mexican American people worked as migrant workers. They moved around from farm to farm, hoping to find work picking fruits and vegetables. It was very hard work. Often the migrant workers worked seven days a week, fourteen hours a day. They didn't get paid much. At night they often crowded into dirty shacks to sleep.

Cesar Chavez came from a family of migrant workers. As a boy, before he left the eighth grade, he had gone to thirty-eight different schools. When he grew up, he decided to try to make life better for migrant workers. He brought the workers together and helped them form a union that would fight for things like better pay. Like Martin Luther King, Jr., Cesar Chavez wanted to fight peacefully for equal rights. He told people not to use violence.

Have you ever walked a mile? Imagine what Cesar Chavez felt when he and many migrant workers made a march of three hundred miles across California. Chavez wanted to draw attention to the suffering of the farmworkers. He wanted more Americans to understand that the workers deserved a better life. On the television news, people across the country saw Cesar Chavez and the workers marching. Many of them decided to support Cesar Chavez and the migrant workers. They refused to buy grapes or other crops grown by farmers who were mistreating the migrant workers. (This was a kind of boycott, like the Montgomery Bus Boycott.)

In the end, the march was a success. While farmworkers were marching, they weren't harvesting. The farm owners realized that unless the workers returned, their grapes would shrivel up and die on the vines, and they would lose money. They agreed to meet with Cesar Chavez and the union to discuss higher wages and better treatment for migrant workers. Over time, the migrant workers got better pay and better living conditions, thanks largely to the dedication of Cesar Chavez.

Talk and Think

Extend this unit by talking with your child about civil rights issues in the news at the moment.

Cesar Chavez had a famous saying: *"Sí, se puede!"* or "Yes, we can!"

Geography of the Americas

The Geography of the United States Today

Here are five quick review questions. Ready? What continent is the United States on? What country is our neighbor to the north? What country is our neighbor to the south? What ocean is to the east of the United States? What ocean is to the west of the United States?

(The answers, in order, are: North America, Canada, Mexico, Atlantic, Pacific.)

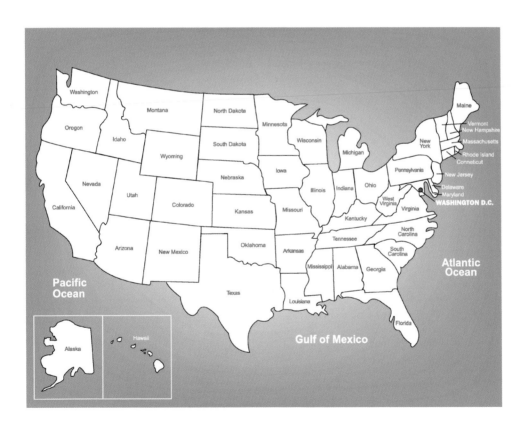

Take a look at the map on this page, which shows you the United States as it is today. Can you find the state where you live? Do you know how many states are in the United States today? There are fifty states, and that's why our country's flag has fifty stars on it.

Can you point to the original thirteen states? They are all located along the Atlantic coast, from New Hampshire down to Georgia. The thirteen stripes on our flag—seven red and six white—stand for these thirteen states.

Do you see Virginia and Kentucky? Those states and the states south of them (below them on the map) fought with the South during the Civil War. The states to the north of Virginia and Kentucky remained in the Union and fought for the North.

Can you locate Oregon and California on the West Coast? These are two states a lot of settlers went to during the period of westward expansion. If you trace a line from Illinois, in the Midwest, out to Oregon, you will see some of the states the pioneers traveled through when they made their way west on the Oregon Trail.

On the map you can see that forty-eight of the states are *contiguous,* which means "touching." But there are two states that do not touch any of the others. One of these states is Alaska, way up north. The other is Hawaii, a group of islands in the Pacific Ocean. There are little pictures of Alaska and Hawaii on the map, but to see where they really are, you will need to find them on a globe.

On the map, find the Mississippi River. (Hint: It runs right up the center of the contiguous United States and forms the border between several states.) Now find the five big lakes in the north called the Great Lakes. (To help remember their names, think of the word "HOMES," which is made up of the first letter of each lake: Huron, Ontario, Michigan, Erie, Superior.) Now look south and find the warm body of water called the Gulf of Mexico. Which states touch the Gulf of Mexico?

Take a Look
Supplement this section by sharing a map of your town or state with your child. Ask if he or she can find the place where you live. Explain the legend of the map and have your child find things identified with symbols described on the legend.

Central America and the Caribbean

On a globe or a map of the world, find the continents of North America and South America. Put your finger on Mexico; then move it down to the narrow strip of land just before South America. On a map, it looks almost like a tail hanging off the end of a kite.

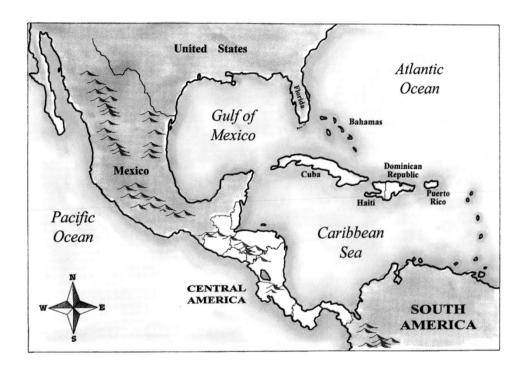

We call this narrow region Central America. Look at the map above. Central America is not a continent. In fact, it is part of North America. Central America is the name people use for the countries that are in the center, between the two big continents of North America and South America. (If you read the first-grade book in this series, you know about the ancient Maya, who lived in Central America.)

What body of water is to the west of Central America? Yes, it's the Pacific Ocean. To the east you'll find the warm, crystal-blue waters of the Caribbean Sea [CARE-uh-BEE-un or kuh-RIB-ee-un]. In the Caribbean there is a large group of islands called the West Indies. (Do you remember why Christopher Columbus called these islands the Indies?) On the map, find these big islands in the West Indies: Cuba, Puerto Rico [PWHERE-toe REE-koh], and the island with the countries of Haiti [HAY-tee] and the Dominican Republic.

Central America and the West Indies are near the equator, so what does that make you think the climate is like there? It's often very warm, except in the highlands and mountains, where it stays pretty cool. The warm, wet climate is good for growing crops such as coffee, bananas, and sugarcane. But many hurricanes also hit this region.

South America

Look at the map of South America on the right. The continent looks a bit like a triangle standing on one of its corners. It reminds some people of an ice cream cone, and two popular flavors of ice cream come from crops grown in South America: chocolate from cocoa beans and vanilla from vanilla beans!

Most people in South America today speak Spanish. That's because Spanish explorers and soldiers conquered and ruled the Native Americans living in South America. Do you remember learning about the Inca people and how they were defeated by the Spanish conquistador named Pizarro?

The Incas built their civilization high in the Andes Mountains. You can see the Andes Mountains on the map. They run along the Pacific coast of South America. Starting in the north, the Andes run through the countries of Colombia and Ecuador. They go through Peru, where the Inca Empire was located, and continue on into Bolivia, Argentina, and Chile. (Find all these countries on the map.) The Andes are the longest mountain chain in the world. They go on for more than five thousand miles!

The second-largest country in South America is called Argentina. Part of this country is a big desert, but part of Argentina is a great grassy area called the pampas. On the pampas, farmers grow crops, including wheat and cotton, and raise sheep and cattle.

The largest country in South America is Brazil. Brazil was never conquered by Spain, but it was conquered by another European country, Portugal. That's why most people in Brazil today speak the Portuguese language.

The Andes Mountains

Talk and Think

Your child may be interested to learn more about threats facing the rain forest today. These include pollution, logging, and mining.

Find Brazil on the map and run your finger along the line that shows the world's second-longest river, the Amazon. (Do you remember the longest? It's the Nile, in Africa.) The line on the map may look short, but the Amazon is almost four thousand miles long!

The Amazon River flows through the biggest rain forest in the world. In the warm, steamy rain forest, you'll find more varieties of plants, animals, and insects than you could count, even if you had years to do it.

The rain forests of the Amazon are home to many species of animals.

Suggested Resources

* *

Recommended for Reading Aloud

A Little History of the World by E. H. Gombrich (Yale University Press, 2008)

The Story of the World by Susan Wise Bauer, 4 vols. (Peace Hill Press, 2006)

India, Hinduism, and Buddhism

Anklet for a Princess: A Cinderella Tale from India by Meredith Brucker (Shens Books, 2002)

Buddha at Bedtime: Tales of Love and Wisdom for You to Read with Your Child to Enchant, Enlighten, and Inspire by Dharmachari Nagaraja (Duncan Baird, 2008)

The Cat Who Went to Heaven by Elizabeth Jane Coatsworth (Aladdin, 2008)

Diwali! by Bhakti Mathur (Anjana, 2011)

Prince Siddhartha: The Story of Buddha by Jonathan Landaw (Wisdom Publications, 2011)

China

Greetings, Asia! by April Pulley Sayre (Millbrook Press, 2003)

The Story About Ping by Marjorie Flack (Grosset and Dunlap, 2000)

Welcome to China by Caryn Jenner (DK Publishing, 2008)

The Year of the Dog by Grace Lin (Little, Brown, 2007)

Yeh-Shen: A Cinderella Story from China by Ai-Ling Louie (Puffin, 1996)

Japan

I Live in Tokyo by Mari Takabayashi (Houghton Mifflin Harcourt Books, 2004)

Suki's Kimono by Chieri Uegaki (Kids Can Press, 2005)

The Way We Do It in Japan by Geneva Cobb Iijima (Albert Whitman, 2002)

Ancient Greece

Ancient Greece (True Books: Ancient Civilizations) by Sandra Newman (Children's Press, 2010)

The First Marathon: The Legend of Pheidippides by Susan Reynolds (Albert Whitman, 2006)

Growing Up in Ancient Greece by Chris Chelepi (Troll, 1997)

Hour of the Olympics by Mary Pope Osborne (Random House, 1998)

I Wonder Why Greeks Built Temples and Other Questions About Ancient Greece by Fiona Macdonald (Kingfisher Publications, 2012)

The U.S. Constitution

A More Perfect Union: The Story of Our Constitution (and other titles) by Betsey Maestro (HarperCollins, 2008)

If You Were There When They Signed the Constitution by Elizabeth Levy (Scholastic, 1992)

Shh! We're Writing the Constitution (and other titles) by Jean Fritz (Puffin, 1997)

The War of 1812

Francis Scott Key's "Star-Spangled Banner" (Step into Reading) by Monica Kulling and illustrated by Richard Walz (Random House Books for Young Readers, 2012)

The Star-Spangled Banner by Peter Spier (Reading Rainbow, 1992)

The War of 1812 (Primary Sources of American Wars) by Georgene Poulakidas (PowerKids, 2006)

Westward Expansion

Buffalo Before Breakfast (Magic Tree House, No. 18) by Mary Pope Osborne (Random House, 1999)

Buffalo Bill and the Pony Express by Eleanor Coerr (HarperCollins, 1996)

The Erie Canal by Peter Spier (North Country Books, 2009)

Little House in the Big Woods by Laura Ingalls Wilder (HarperCollins, 2004)

Native Americans

The Girl Who Loved Wild Horses by Paul Goble (Aladdin, 1993)

Sequoyah: The Cherokee Man Who Gave His People Writing by James Rumford (Houghton Mifflin Harcourt Books, 2004)

The Civil War

Looking at Lincoln by Maira Kalman (Nancy Paulsen Books, 2012)

Show Way by Jacqueline Woodson and illustrated by Hudson Talbott (Putnam Juvenile, 2005)

Thunder at Gettysburg by Patricia Lee Gauch (Calkins Creek, 2003)

Unspoken: A Story from the Underground Railroad by Henry Cole (Scholastic, 2012)

Immigration

At Ellis Island: A History in Many Voices by Louise Peacock (Atheneum Books, 2007)

Emma's Poem: The Voice of the Statue of Liberty by Linda Glasner (Houghton Mifflin Books for Children, 2010)

My Name Is Yoon by Helen Recorvits (Farrar, Straus and Giroux, 2003)

Civil Rights

Heroes for Civil Rights by David A. Adler and illustrated by Bill Farnsworth (Holiday House, 2007)

Martin's Big Words: The Life of Dr. Martin Luther King, Jr. by Doreen Rappaport (Hyperion Books, 2007)

The Story of Ruby Bridges by Robert Coles (Scholastic, 2010)

Who Was Jackie Robinson? by Gail Herman (Grosset and Dunlap, 2010) and other titles in the series

Geography

Geography from A to Z: A Picture Glossary by Jack Knowlton and Harriet Barton (HarperCollins, 1997)

The Great Kapok Tree by Lynne Cherry (Houghton Mifflin Harcourt Books, 2000)

III
Visual Arts

Introduction

A book alone cannot adequately convey the power and excitement of visual art. While this book can provide some basic knowledge about art and introduce the language of art, it is not a replacement for looking at art, visiting museums, and creating art.

For the second grader, art should mostly take the form of doing: drawing, painting, cutting and pasting, working with clay and other materials. In the side-bars for this section, we suggest many activities your child can do, sometimes with your help. You can also find good art activities in several of the books recommended at the end of this section.

By reading this section aloud with your child and discussing the pictures, you can help him or her learn some of the ways that we talk about art. You will also introduce her to some wonderful works of art. In this way, your child will come to understand that while art involves doing, it also involves seeing and thinking. By looking closely at art and talking about it, your child will begin to develop a love of art and a habit of enjoying it in thoughtful, active ways.

Let us repeat: in addition to looking at art and talking about it, do try to provide your child with materials and opportunities to be a practicing artist!

Lines in Art

Taking a Line for a Walk

An artist named Paul Klee [pronounced "clay"] once said that drawing is taking a line for a walk. When you draw a picture, notice the different lines you use. Let's say you want to draw a tree. You might start with the trunk by drawing two straight lines. Lines that go up and down are called *vertical* lines. If you want to draw the ground under the tree, you might draw a line across the bottom of the page. Lines that run from side to side are called *horizontal* lines. You might want to draw a ladder leaning up against the tree. Lines that lean are called *diagonal* lines.

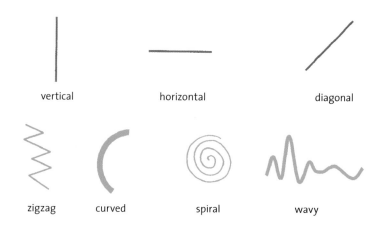

Think of where you might see these different kinds of lines. You might see vertical lines in tree trunks, telephone poles, fence posts, and skyscrapers. You might see horizontal lines on a mattress or the edge of a table, or on the horizon. You might see diagonal lines in slides, rooftops, ramps, and teeter-totters.

vertical   horizontal   diagonal

zigzag   curved   spiral   wavy

You probably know the names for other kinds of lines, too.

Lines can be thick or thin. In the picture above, which lines are thick? Which ones are thin?

Do It Yourself

Get a piece of paper and a pencil. Turn the paper so the long edge is at the top. Then fold it in half to make a dividing line down the middle. On the left side draw your favorite animal using only straight lines. They can be horizontal, vertical, or diagonal, but all the lines have to be straight. On the other side of the paper, try drawing the same animal in the same pose using only curved or wavy or zigzag lines. Now, do the same thing, but this time draw a house or building instead.

Let's look at a beautiful painting called *Mother and Child* by the Spanish artist Pablo Picasso. Take your finger and follow the lines in the picture. Do you find more straight lines or more curved lines? The many curving lines add to the gentle feel of this picture.

Sometimes an artist can *suggest* a line without actually painting one. In *Mother and Child* the tilt of the mother's head suggests a line. Look at the way the mother's head is tilted slightly to one side. If you could draw a line to follow the tilt of her head, would the line be horizontal or diagonal?

Pablo Picasso (Spanish, 1881–1973), *Mother and Child*, 1922. Oil on canvas. 39½ x 32⅟₁₆ in. (100.3 x 81.4 cm). The Baltimore Museum of Art: The Cone Collection, formed by Dr. Claribel Cone and Miss Etta Cone of Baltimore, Maryland, BMA 1950.279. Photography By: Mitro Hood

Now look at the child's body. The same diagonal line extends from the mother's head along the child's body. Picasso united mother and child with a single suggested line to show how close they feel to each other. What else in the painting shows how close they feel?

The arrangement of the figures suggests a line.
What kind of line is it?

Lines and Movement

Have you ever been swimming at the beach and been knocked down by a big wave? Well, be glad it wasn't as big as the wave in this picture by the Japanese artist Hokusai [HOE-koo-sigh]. (You can read about Japan in the World History and Geography section of this book.)

The picture on the facing page is called *The Great Wave at Kanagawa Nami-Ura*. Imagine that this picture is part of a movie. What will happen next? What is the great wave about to crash on? Can you spot the men huddled together in wooden fishing boats? What might they be thinking?

Hokusai has drawn the great wave as if it were alive, with curling fingers reaching out to grab the boats. Do you see the many curving lines in the picture? Put your finger on the top of the water on the right side of the picture. Now move your finger to the left, following the curving line up and under the big wave. Do you see how the line pushes up and around, almost as if it wants to keep on until it makes a big circle? Now put your finger on the top of the water on the left side of the page and follow the curve along the top of the great wave. This line seems to want to keep going, too. What kind of shape would it make if it did?

Ask your child if she can find a mountain in Hokusai's painting. The snowcapped mountain in the background (just to the right of the center, right where the wave seems about to crash) is Mount Fuji, the tallest mountain in Japan. How does Mount Fuji look in comparison to the wave in the foreground? Why might Hokusai have included the mountain in this picture of the watery world?

Take a Look

Have your child look at the upper left-hand corner of Hokusai's picture. The characters written there are Japanese characters. The characters in the box give the name of the work. The characters to the left of the box say, "From the brush of Hokusai." This print is actually the first in a series of prints Hokusai called *Thirty-six Views of Mount Fuji.*

The Great Wave at Kanagawa Nami-Ura, Katsushika Hokusai

The Discus Thrower

Looking at Sculptures

You can walk around a sculpture or statue. It's not flat like a picture. Sculptures can be made of stone, wood, metal, or other materials. Let's look at a stone sculpture from ancient Greece called *The Discus Thrower*. In the World History and Geography section of this book, you can read about the Olympic Games that were held in ancient Greece. One of the events in the Olympic Games was the discus throw. This statue shows a man throwing a discus. His goal is to throw the discus farther than anyone else. A discus looks like a big Frisbee, but it is much heavier than a Frisbee because it is made out of metal. Can you find the discus in this picture?

Although *The Discus Thrower* is a sculpture, not a drawing, it still has lines. To see how, put a piece of tracing paper over the picture of *The Discus Thrower* on this page. Draw a straight line from the hand holding the discus to the man's chin. Then draw another straight line from his chin to his hip. Draw a third straight line from his hip to his knee. Finally, draw a fourth straight line from his knee to the heel that sticks up in the air. Now lift the tracing paper and see what you have drawn. A zigzag line! Even though this statue does not move, the zigzag line helps show the energy of a tensed-up body about to uncoil.

Now let's look at a sculpture often called *Flying Horse*. It was found in a tomb in China and is about two thousand years old. (You can read about ancient China in the World History and Geography section of

Do It Yourself

A discus may look like a Frisbee, but it's much heavier. Throwing one takes a lot of energy. To get a sense how much, hold a big book in one hand. Then try to stand like the discus thrower. Bend your knees, move your arms to one side of your body, and look over your shoulder. Can you feel that your body would have to work hard to throw a discus?

Flying Horse

this book.) Even though the sculpture is made of a heavy metal called bronze, the horse itself seems light. Why? Look at the legs. See how thin they are? How many of the horse's legs are in the air? How many are touching the ground? Just one! This makes it look as if the horse is moving very quickly, perhaps even so quickly that it is rising above the ground!

What do you think the man is doing in this sculpture by the French artist Auguste Rodin [row-DAN]? Do you see how the man is resting his chin on his fist? Have you ever sat this way? The sculpture is called *The Thinker*. Rodin modeled this sculpture in clay first and then had it cast in bronze. Several copies have been made of it, some small and others twice as big as a real

The Thinker, Auguste Rodin

man! Look at how Rodin posed the figure. Try to sit this way with your right elbow resting on your left knee. Is this a comfortable pose? Not really. You have to strain your muscles to get into this position. The strained pose, powerful muscles, and stern expression all show that thinking can be hard work!

Looking at Landscapes

If you read the first-grade book in this series, then you learned about two kinds of painting: portrait and still life. Now let's learn about another special kind of painting called a "landscape." The most important thing in a landscape is the scenery, which includes the land, the trees, and the sky. A painter can put people in a landscape, but they are not the main focus of the painting. When you look at a landscape painting, try to notice the weather, season, location, and time of day.

The Oxbow, Thomas Cole

This painting by the American artist Thomas Cole has a very long name, but it's usually called *The Oxbow*. An oxbow is a U-shaped collar placed around the neck of an ox so that it can be hitched to a plow. Can you find something U-shaped in this scene? (Do you see the bend in the river?)

You could almost divide this painting in two parts. One part shows the landscape close up. The other shows the landscape far away. Look at the left side of the painting, which shows the close-up part of the landscape. What is the weather like here? Do you see the broken tree trunk? What do you think might have happened to this tree?

Now look at the faraway landscape on the right side of the painting. What is the weather like? This painting shows two very different views of nature. On the left, close to us, nature is dark, stormy, and wild. But on the right, nature looks bright and peaceful. Now that you've looked carefully at the weather in this painting, its real name won't surprise you: it's called *View of Mount Holyoke, Northampton, Massachusetts, After a Thunderstorm*.

Did you notice a person in this painting? The picture in this book is much smaller than the real painting, so it may be hard to find him. Look near the bottom, a little to the right of the center. Who is it? It looks like an artist in a top hat. Why, it must be Thomas Cole painting a landscape! But in this painting, it's easy to tell that the landscape is more important than the person.

Take a Look

If you can't see the painter in *The Oxbow*, you may wish to look for a larger image online. An Internet search for "Thomas Cole, Oxbow" will find several images that capture more details from the original (which is 76 inches wide and 51 inches tall).

Do It Yourself

Help your child to create his or her own landscape. First have your child decide whether it will be a real landscape or an imaginary one. Then decide what materials you will use: you could use watercolors, paint, colored pencils, or markers. Have your child think about the mood or feeling he or she wants the picture to have. Encourage your child to think about the weather, the time of day, and the light. Will it be dark and stormy? Or will it be bright and peaceful? Will it be spooky or something else? Will your child put any people or animals in this landscape?

View of Toledo, El Greco (Doménickos Theotokópoulos)

Now let's look at a landscape by an artist who called himself El Greco. El Greco means "the Greek." The artist who painted this picture was born in Greece but spent the second half of his life in Spain. This picture, *View of Toledo*, shows us the Spanish city of Toledo, where the artist lived. Can you see the town of Toledo in the background? Can you see a stone bridge arching over a river? What about a big rock in the middle of the river? What is the weather like in this landscape? What time of day do you think the artist is showing? Is it day-time with the sky darkened by a thunderstorm? Or is it nighttime with moonlight breaking through storm clouds? Either way, the sky casts a spooky light over the whole scene. What kind of mood or feeling do you have when you see this paint-ing? Is it the kind of picture you would want to use on a poster saying, "For your next vacation, visit Toledo"?

Detail from *Virgin Forest*, Henri Rousseau

Landscapes don't have to show real places. They can also show places you imagine. The French artist Henri Rousseau [on-REE roo-SO] never visited a tropical jungle, but he did many paintings like the one shown here, which is known as *Virgin Forest*. Rousseau learned about jungle plants and animals like monkeys and jaguars from encyclopedias, science books, and visits to the zoo, but he did not try to copy them in a lifelike way. Look at the plants in this picture. Rousseau painted many plants and made them very big. Does this landscape look like a place you would want to visit? Before you answer, did you notice the jaguar in the picture? It is pouncing on a man who is walking through the forest. Rousseau's colorful, dreamlike jungle is beautiful, but it is also dangerous.

Look at the painting called *The Starry Night* by the Dutch artist Vincent van Gogh [usually pronounced "van-GO" in the United States]. What do you notice first in the painting? What do you see in the bottom half of the painting? What do you see in the top half? Van Gogh's sky is full of circles. Use your finger to follow some of the curving lines that Van Gogh painted in the sky. The sky seems to be moving and swirling around, while the town below is calm and still. Van Gogh applied the paint in bold, thick strokes. Even though this is just a picture of the painting, you can almost feel its rough texture.

The Starry Night, Vincent van Gogh

Animals, Real and Imagined

Some artists want us to know exactly what an animal looks like. They are careful to include every detail and to get the colors exactly the way they are in nature.

The nineteenth-century American artist John James Audubon [AH-du-BAHN] also wanted to make very lifelike pictures of animals, especially birds. He traveled throughout North America from Florida to Canada studying and sketching birds. He became famous when his illustrations were published in a

Passenger Pigeon, John James Audubon

book called *Birds of America*. Look at Audubon's picture of two passenger pigeons. The one on the lower branch is a male and the other one is a female. Do they look alike? How do their colors differ? What do you think they are doing?

Audubon wanted his pictures of animals to look like real animals. He wanted them to look realistic. But other artists try to show us animals in a new or unusual way. Look at the painting on the next page by Paul Klee [pronounced "clay"] called *Cat and Bird*. Klee had many cats, including a tomcat named Fritzi, who inspired this painting. But does this painting show what Fritzi really looked like?

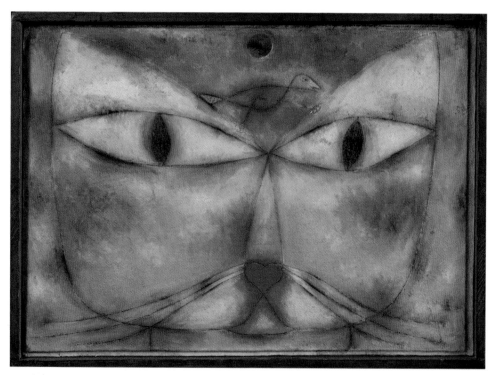

Cat and Bird, Paul Klee

Do It Yourself

Find a photograph of an animal you would like to draw. Look at it closely. Now decide if you would like to make a realistic, lifelike drawing of the animal, or just sketch its main lines and shapes and maybe add some unusual touches, the way Klee drew his cat. If you want to color your picture, then, like Audubon, you can use realistic colors; or, like Klee, you can use unusual colors, and perhaps add something that your animal is thinking about.

No! Klee painted only the cat's head, and he made it huge, with eyes that are much bigger than life, and an unusual shade of green. Klee did not try to show the cat's soft fur. Instead he used only simple lines and shapes. Also, Klee put the bird in a place it would probably not be in real life. In real life, it would not be safe for the bird to land on the cat's forehead! Why do you think Klee might have put the bird in that spot? Look for these shapes in the painting: an oval, a heart, a diamond, a triangle, and a circle.

You might have a little trouble at first seeing the animal in the picture on the facing page. It's by the French artist Henri Matisse [on-REE mah-TEECE]. Can you guess what it is?

Matisse called this picture *The Snail*. It is made from cutout pieces of colored paper stuck on a white background. At first it might look like it's just a bunch of colored shapes, but how has Matisse arranged the shapes? Put your finger on the green shape in the center, then trace a counterclockwise circle around the green shape. Continue moving your finger so that it goes to the black shape. From the black shape take your finger along the outside edges of the other shapes that curve around the central green shape. Do you see how your finger moved in a spiral path? So Matisse has arranged the shapes to suggest a spiral. His picture doesn't show you what a snail looks like in real life; instead, it shows how much the shape of a snail is made up of a spiral line.

The Snail, Henri Matisse

Do It Yourself

It's fun to use your imagination to see the basic lines and shapes in animals. You can make your own animal cutout, like Matisse. Start by tearing or cutting out various shapes from pieces of colored construction paper. Experiment with placing them in a variety of positions on a white piece of paper. If you want, arrange them in a way that reminds you of some animal's basic shape—for example, the big oval of an elephant's body. When you have made a picture you like, paste the pieces onto the paper. What title will you give your picture?

Abstract Art

We call art like Audubon's bird pictures *realistic* art, because they look very real and lifelike. There's a different name for art like Matisse's *The Snail*. We call such art *abstract* art. Abstract art doesn't look exactly like the real thing, but it may remind you of things you've seen. Or it may make you see something in a new way, not by showing you every little detail but instead by drawing your attention to basic lines and shapes.

Have you ever had a dream in which lots of crazy things happened? Some people think the next painting looks like something from a dream. Look at this abstract painting by the Russian painter Marc Chagall [sha-GALL]. What do you see? You can recognize some of the things in this painting, such as a woman milking a cow, or a man and a woman walking near a group of buildings, but how are the things in this painting arranged? Some of them are upside down and some are much bigger than others. Some, like the woman milking the cow, are in very strange places. What about the colors? What colors seem unusual to you?

Do It Yourself

Now it's your turn to make an abstract picture that shows things in a dreamlike way. What will your picture be about? It can be a place you like a lot, such as the beach, or it can be a time of year, such as autumn when the leaves fall. Think of all the things you want to include in your picture. Make some much bigger and others much smaller than they really are. What colors do you want to use? How do you want to arrange things on the page?

I and the Village, Marc Chagall

Chagall called his painting *I and the Village*. He painted it just after he left the small village in Russia where he grew up and moved far away to Paris, France. Do you think he missed home?

Sculpture can be abstract, too. Look at this sculpture by Constantin Brancusi [bran-KOO-zee], an artist from Romania. What does it look like to you? The title, *Bird in Space*, may help you see what the artist was thinking. Brancusi did many sculptures of birds. The first ones he did still looked somewhat like birds. But this one doesn't look much like a bird at all. Or does it? Have you ever watched a bird fly? Think about a bird flying, then look at this sculpture again. Brancusi made a tall, thin, pointed, gently curving shape that seems to soar. Its shiny metal surface reflects the light and seems almost weightless. So while this sculpture does not show you an image of a bird with a beak and feathers, it shows you something about a bird in flight. It gives the feeling of rising into the air in one quick swoosh!

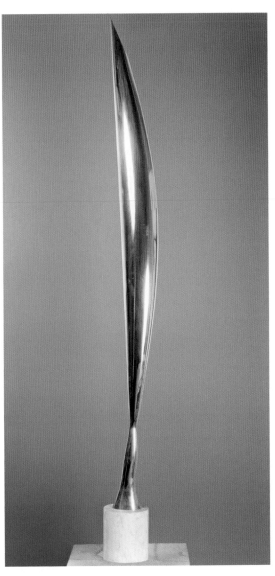

Bird in Space, Constantin Brancusi

Architecture: The Art of Designing Buildings

Architecture is the art of designing and planning buildings. A person who designs buildings is called an architect.

Here is a photograph of a very famous building in Athens, Greece, called the Parthenon [PAR-thuh-non]. More than two thousand years ago, the people of Athens built the Parthenon as a temple to honor the goddess Athena.

This is the Parthenon as it looks today.

Make a Connection

You can learn more about the ancient Greeks in the World History and Geography section of this book. And you can learn more about the gods and goddesses they worshipped—including Athena—in the Language and Literature section.

You can see that the Parthenon has been worn down through the years. At one time the Parthenon was used to store gunpowder and ammunition, and some of the gunpowder exploded, blowing the roof off the building. So the original building has seen better days. But take a look at the engraving on the next page. It shows what the building looked like when it was first built. Think about the kinds of lines you've learned about. Do you see how the roof and the steps of the Parthenon make long horizontal lines? But even more, you probably notice all the up-and-down vertical lines made by the many columns. The columns hold up the roof. They also point upward to the sky. Why does that seem right for a temple?

This engraving shows the Parthenon as it looked in ancient times.

Now look at this drawing of the front of the Parthenon. We've put a vertical dotted line right down the middle to help you see something about the way this building is designed. First, count the number of columns on the left side of the dotted line. Now count the number of columns on the right side of the dotted line. Did you get four columns on each side?

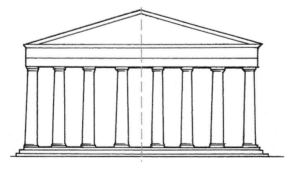

The front of the Parthenon, with a line of symmetry

Make a Connection

You can read more about symmetry in the Mathematics section of this book on page 394.

Do It Yourself

One way to learn more about symmetry is by cutting folded paper. Get a piece of blank paper and fold it in half. Then cut some triangles and other shapes into the folded side. When you unfold the paper you should see identical cutouts on either side of a line of symmetry created by the folding. To create a second line of symmetry, get a second sheet of paper, and fold it once as before; then fold it a second time in the opposite direction. Cut shapes along the sides that have at least one fold. Then unfold. You should have a page with cutout shapes arranged on either side of two lines of symmetry.

When something is the same on both sides of an imaginary line running down the middle, we say it is *symmetric* [sih-MET-rik]. We call the imaginary line running down the middle a line of symmetry [SIM-ih-tree]. The Parthenon is a symmetric building.

A Valentine heart is a symmetric figure. Where else can you see symmetry—not just in art or buildings, but in nature, too? Look at your body in a mirror. You are symmetric! Can you think of something else that's symmetric?

Learning from the Ancient Greeks

The ancient Greeks designed beautiful buildings, and many architects learned from them in later years. One person who learned a great deal from the ancient Greeks was Thomas Jefferson. You might know him as the author of the Declaration of Independence and the third president of the United States, but Jefferson was also an architect. His own

Thomas Jefferson's Monticello

house, Monticello, was based on Greek architecture. Can you see the columns in front of the house? Can you see that the house is symmetric? Try drawing an imaginary line of symmetry on the picture with your finger.

In America today you can find many buildings with columns. Are there any buildings with columns where you live?

A Building with Curves

In the World History and Geography section of this book, you can read about how Buddhism began in India. The building at the bottom of this page is a temple to the Buddha. It is called the Great Stupa, and it is in Sanchi, India.

Think of what you know about different kinds of lines. Look again at the Parthenon (on page 282), then look at the Great Stupa below. What differences do you see? The Parthenon is mostly straight lines—many vertical, some horizontal, some diagonal. But the Great Stupa has many curved lines. If you walked around it, you would walk in a circle. And if you traced your finger along the top

The Great Stupa

of the stupa, from left to right, you would be tracing a curve. In fact, you would trace half a circle.

You know what a sphere is, right? A sphere has the same shape as a ball. The Great Stupa is half a sphere. In architecture, this shape is called a *dome*. The outside of a dome may remind you of the shape of a hill. People in India say that when you walk around the Great Stupa, you are walking the Path of Life around the World Mountain.

A Beautiful Castle

You've looked at some buildings with straight lines and one with curved lines. Now let's look at Himeji [hih-MAY-jee] Castle in Japan. (You can read about Japan in the World History and Geography section of this book.) The castle is made of wood covered with white plaster. It was built more than four hundred

Himeji Castle (White Heron Castle)

years ago during a time when the Japanese were often at war. What do you think the castle's barred windows and gates were for?

Himeji Castle has many vertical and horizontal lines, but it also suggests another shape. Look at the way each story is a little smaller than the one below it. The overall shape of this building is like a pyramid, or a triangle, but with the top cut off. This shape and the curving roofs make the castle seem to point upward. Himeji Castle is also called "White Heron Castle" because it reminded people of a favorite bird, the white heron, in flight.

A Modern Museum

Have you ever been to a museum? They are wonderful places to visit. In many museums, you'll find beautiful works of art.

When Frank Lloyd Wright, an American architect, was asked to design a new museum, he decided to make the building itself a work of art!

The Guggenheim Museum

Inside the Guggenheim Museum

Do It Yourself

Did you know that many museums allow visitors to enter on certain days without paying an admission fee? In fact, some museums have free admission one day each week. Check with the museums where you live to see if they offer free admission on particular days. Also check to see if they offer children's programs.

The Guggenheim Museum is in New York City. What is unusual about it? Its shape! The outside looks like a teacup made of four circular disks. If you go inside, you're in for another surprise. A ramp spirals up to the top, leaving a tall opening in the center. To see the paintings on display, you walk along the ramp. It's like walking inside a big sculpture. Every step you take gives you a different view of the museum's inside, too.

Suggested Resources

Art Activity Books

Ed Emberly's Drawing Book of Animals (and other titles by the same author) by Ed Emberly (LB Kids, 2006)

Kids Create: Art and Craft Experiences for 3- to 9-Year-Olds by Laurie Carlson (Williamson Publishing, 1990)

Mudworks: Creative Clay, Dough, and Modeling Experiences (and other titles) by Mary-Ann F. Kohl (Bright Ring Publishing, 1989)

Reprinted Artworks for Children

Come Look with Me: Enjoying Art with Children (and other titles in the Enjoying Art with Children series) by Gladys Blizzard (Charlesbridge, 1996)

Biographies of Single Artists

Henri Matisse: Drawing with Scissors (and other titles in the Smart About Art series) by Jane O'Connor (Grosset and Dunlap, 2002)

Paul Klee (and other titles in the Getting to Know the World's Great Artists series) by Mike Venezia (Children's Press, 1991)

IV
Music

Introduction

A book alone cannot adequately convey the experience of music. While this book can hope to provide some basic knowledge about music, nothing can replace attending performances, listening to recordings, and encouraging children to sing and dance themselves.

One of the best activities, and one of the easiest, is singing with your child. We suggest some familiar children's favorites in this section. The more you sing with your child, the more you'll enjoy music together.

We also encourage you to listen to recordings with your child and attend musical performances to help build his or her love of different kinds of music. In the first-grade book in this series, we introduced jazz, classical music, and opera, as well as different kinds of dance. In this book we build on that earlier knowledge by introducing patriotic music and folk music and by extending the discussion of classical music to include more composers. We also build on the first-grade introduction to melody, harmony, and rhythm by exploring a few of the basics about how music is written down.

While some families will choose to provide lessons that will lift children to a level of musical competence beyond what we describe in the following pages, it is important for everyone to enjoy music. We hope this book will help increase that enjoyment.

In the following section we suggest a number of recordings. For more good resources, see *Books to Build On: A Grade-by-Grade Resource Guide for Parents and Teachers*, edited by John Holdren and E. D. Hirsch, Jr. (Dell, 1996).

Many Kinds of Music

People around the world love to sing and play music. Here in the United States, we have many different kinds of people, and we have many different kinds of music. If you turn on a radio, you might hear rock-and-roll, jazz, classical, soul, country, or salsa.

Let's find out more now about three kinds of music: patriotic music, folk music, and classical music. Whenever you can, sing the songs that we give the words for, and try to listen to recordings of all these kinds of music.

Patriotic Music

Have you ever been to a baseball game or a football game where, just before the game begins, everyone stands and sings "The Star-Spangled Banner"? That's our national anthem, which means our country's official song.

Songs and music that honor our country are called patriotic music. Just about every country has its own patriotic music. Patriotic music makes people feel proud of their country. Besides "The Star-Spangled Banner," do you know any

It's a tradition to sing our national anthem before the ball game begins.

other patriotic songs about America? In the first grade, did you sing "America the Beautiful"? It begins with, "O beautiful for spacious skies . . ."

Here are the words to part of a favorite patriotic song called "This Land Is Your Land," written by Woody Guthrie. What do the words say about our country?

As I was walking the ribbon of highway
I saw above me that endless skyway.
I saw below me that golden valley.
This land was made for you and me.

This land is your land, this land is my land,
From California to the New York island.
From the redwood forest to the Gulf Stream waters,
This land was made for you and me.

Woody Guthrie

Folk Music

Do you know the song called "I've Been Working on the Railroad"? Here are the words. Let's sing it.

I've been working on the railroad,
All the livelong day.
I've been working on the railroad,
Just to pass the time away.
Can't you hear the whistle blowin'?
Rise up so early in the morn,
Can't you hear the captain shoutin',
"Dinah, blow your horn!"

Dinah, won't you blow?
Dinah, won't you blow?
Dinah, won't you blow your horn?
Dinah, won't you blow?
Dinah, won't you blow?
Dinah, won't you blow your horn?

Who wrote "I've Been Working on the Railroad"? No one knows. It's a song that has been passed down from parents to children for many years. We call this kind of song a folk song. Another word for folk is "people." Folk songs have been sung and enjoyed by people for so long that most of the time we don't know who made them up. Many of the melodies of our favorite American folk songs were brought to this country by immigrants from other countries. (You can read about immigrants in the American History section of this book, beginning on page 228.)

Wherever you go in a country, people often know the same folk songs. In America, folks who have never lived near a railroad can sing "I've Been Working on the Railroad."

Just about every country has its own folk music. In France, people enjoy singing a folk song called "Frère Jacques" (Brother John). You probably know the

English words to this song: "Are you sleeping, Brother John?" You can find the lyrics in *What Your First Grader Needs to Know.*

Classical Music

Do you know who Wolfgang Amadeus Mozart [MOTES-art] is? Perhaps you've heard some of his music (and read about him in the first-grade book in this series). He was one of the greatest composers of all time. He began composing music when he was only five years old!

We call the kind of music Mozart wrote classical music. Some classical music is played by a large group, called an orchestra. An orchestra is made up of many musicians who play many different instruments—violins, clarinets, trumpet, drums, and a lot more. Do you remember what the person who leads the orchestra is called? (The conductor.) A long piece of music played by an orchestra is called a symphony. Although Mozart did not live to be very old, he wrote forty-one symphonies!

Mozart (born in Austria, 1756)

An orchestra

Meet Some Great Composers

You've met Mozart, and maybe you've heard some of his music. Now let's meet some other great composers of classical music. Try to hear their music, too.

When he was a boy growing up in Italy, Antonio Vivaldi [vih-VAHL-dee] learned to play the violin from his father. When Vivaldi grew up, he became a priest. He was nicknamed the "Red Priest" because of his curly red hair, and because he sometimes wore a bright red robe. He worked at an orphanage for girls. He taught the girls to play the violin. Many people came to the concerts given by the orchestra of orphan girls, and everyone said they played beautifully.

Vivaldi (born in Italy, 1678)

Vivaldi composed hundreds of pieces of music. One of his most famous works is called *The Four Seasons.* For each season, Vivaldi wrote a concerto [con-CHAIR-toe]. A concerto is played by an orchestra, and usually one instrument gets the most attention; the person who plays this instrument is called the soloist. In Vivaldi's *Four Seasons,* the soloist plays a violin, and he or she gets to make sounds that make you think of birds singing in the spring or lightning flashing in a summer storm.

Johann Sebastian Bach [BAHKH] came from a family filled with music. When Bach grew up, he became a great organist. He composed tons of music, including organ music, concertos, and a lot of choral music for the church. Bach had many children— twenty in all! Four of them grew up to be composers.

Bach (born in Germany, 1685)

Beethoven (born in Germany, 1770)

Ludwig van Beethoven [BAY-toe-vin] did not have a happy childhood. When he was four years old, his father started to give him piano lessons. His father made him practice for hours, sometimes late into the night. If young Ludwig made a mistake, his father would shout or hit the boy's knuckles.

You might think that Beethoven would grow up hating music. But music was his whole life. He became famous as the greatest pianist in Europe, as well as a great composer.

Beethoven wrote nine symphonies. Try to listen to his Sixth Symphony. It's also known as the Pastoral Symphony, because the music is full of peaceful feelings about Beethoven's love of nature and the countryside, but Beethoven was not a peaceful man. He was often moody and he had a fiery temper. By the time he wrote his great Ninth Symphony, a very sad thing had happened: Beethoven had become deaf. He could not hear the orchestra play his wonderful music.

Composers and Their Music

The Classical Kids series (produced by Susan Hammond) offers a fun way to get to know some composers and their music. Titles (on cassette tapes or compact discs) include *Mr. Bach Comes to Call*, *Beethoven Lives Upstairs*, *Mozart's Magic Fantasy*, and *Vivaldi's Ring of Mystery*. Each title weaves the composer's music into a lively story.

The Greatest Hits series (Sony Classics) and the Best of . . . series (Naxos) offer budget-priced compact discs with favorite works by Vivaldi, Bach, Beethoven, and more.

The classic Walt Disney animated movie *Fantasia*, available on video, features works by Bach and Beethoven, as well as other favorites.

Trumpet

Families of Instruments: A Closer Look

If you've read the first-grade book in this series, then you may remember that an orchestra is made up of different families of instruments. Can you name an instrument in the brass family? How about an instrument in the wind family? In the percussion family? In the string family?

Let's take a closer look now at the string family and the percussion family.

Clarinet

Drum

Violin and bow

The String Family

You may know two stringed instruments: the guitar and the banjo. You play them by using the fingers of one hand to press on the strings that run up the long neck of the instrument, while you use your other hand to strum or pick the strings.

The guitar and banjo are popular stringed instruments, especially for folk music, but you won't usually find them in an orchestra. The main stringed instruments in an orchestra are the violin, viola, cello, and double bass. The violin is the smallest: the others look like bigger and bigger violins.

This man is playing a banjo.

Each of these instruments has four strings. You can pluck the strings to make a sound, but most of the time you play them by sliding a bow back and forth over the strings. When you play the violin or viola, the instrument rests between your shoulder and chin. But the cello is much bigger, so you sit on a chair and hold the instrument between your legs. To play the big double bass, you either have to stand beside it or sit on a tall stool.

Of these four stringed instruments, the violin makes the highest sounds. The viola makes slightly lower sounds. The cello's sounds are even lower, while the double bass plays the lowest pitches of all the stringed instruments.

The French composer Camille Saint-Saëns [san-SAHN] wrote a work for orchestra called *The Carnival of the Animals*, in which he used the sounds of different instruments to make us think of different animals. He used a cello to make us think of a lovely swan floating gracefully on the water. And what stringed instrument do you think he used to make us think of big, heavy elephants? The double bass!

The two girls on the left are playing the violin. The girl in the middle is playing the viola. The boy on the right is playing a cello.

The Percussion Family

The instruments in the string family look similar to each other, but the instruments in the percussion family are sometimes as different as can be. The percussion family includes tiny clicking castanets, a triangle that goes *ding-a-ling-a-ling*, and a big bass drum that goes *boom-boom-boom*.

Why are all the instruments in the same family? What do they have in common?

Castanets

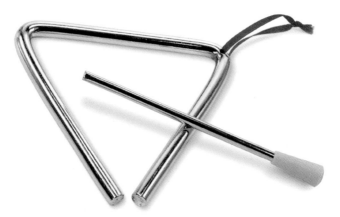

Triangle

They are all percussion instruments because you hit or shake them. You play most percussion instruments by hitting them with your hand or with a stick. You shake some instruments, like the maracas.

Maracas

Bass drum

Some percussion instruments can add excitement to music. When the French composer Georges Bizet [bee-ZAY] wrote the overture to his opera *Carmen*, he used cymbals to give a big, bright splash of sound.

Smaller percussion instruments can add a kind of decoration to music. For example, when you shake sleigh bells or hit a wooden block, you can make sounds that are just right for Christmas music, since they make you think of a horse pulling a sled down a snowy path.

The main job of percussion instruments is to beat out the rhythm. In a marching band, the big bass drum helps keep a steady beat.

Some percussion instruments can also play melodies. You can play songs on the xylophone or marimba, which have keys that you strike with mallets.

These big drums are called timpani. Sometimes they're called kettledrums because they look like big tubby kettles.

Carlos Chávez, a Mexican composer, wrote some music just for percussion instruments. His *Toccata for Percussion* is exciting to hear. (A recording is available on a compact disc on the Dorian label.)

Keyboard Instruments

Is there a piano at your school? On a piano you can play many different kinds of music: classical, jazz, or rock, as well as melodies to go along with songs you might sing at home or school.

A piano has eighty-eight keys. When you push the keys, it causes little wooden hammers covered with hard felt to strike the strings inside the piano, and that's what makes the sound. On the piano, you can push one key with a single finger, or you can play many notes at the same time.

A piano is a *keyboard instrument*. Another keyboard instrument is the organ. Some organs have two, three, or even four keyboards. That keeps the organist's hands very busy! But that's not all: really big organs have many pedals that the organist plays with his or her feet. In some churches or auditoriums, you might see a big organ called a pipe organ. When you press a key, it allows air to be sent through a pipe.

Grand piano

A big pipe organ

Bach at the Keyboard

A lot of wonderful music for the organ was composed by Johann Sebastian Bach, who was himself a great organist. Did Bach also play the piano? No, but that's because the piano had not been invented in Bach's time (about three hundred years ago). Bach played other keyboard instruments that were ancestors of the piano, such as the harpsichord. The harpsichord looks like a piano, but it makes a more plucky, jangly sound.

When Johann Sebastian Bach was only ten years old, both his parents died, so he went to live with his older brother, Johann Christoph. The whole Bach family was very musical: Johann Christoph was the church organist in the town where he lived. He gave his younger brother music lessons, but he was a very hard, strict teacher. He would not let his brother study a very valuable book of organ music that he kept locked in a bookcase, but Johann Sebastian wanted so much to learn to play the music in that book! So at night, while his brother was asleep, Johann Sebastian would creep downstairs in the dim moonlight, squeeze his hand between the bars of the bookcase door, take out the valuable book, and then copy the music, note by note! He did this every night until he had copied the whole book. But then his stern brother found the copies, and he took them away as a punishment.

Do you know what? Even without those copies, Johann Sebastian could play much of the music, because it was in his head! The music in that book was now in his memory!

Harpsichord

There is so much wonderful music written for the piano or organ that it's hard to say where to begin! For starters, try listening to these:

- Minuet in G major from J. S. Bach's *Anna Magdalena* Notebook
- Rondo "Alla turca" from Mozart's *Piano Sonata* No. 11, K. 331
- Beethoven's "Für Elise"
- "Spring Song" from Felix Mendelssohn's *Songs Without Words*
- Toccata and Fugue in D minor (for organ) by J. S. Bach

Writing Music Down

You've read about some famous composers, such as Bach and Mozart. Now, imagine that *you* are the composer. You have written a song. How can you get other people to play it as you want it to sound? Well, you could play the song for them and they could follow along. What about people far away, who can't be right there with you to hear your song? If you want them to play the song just right, then you have to write it down.

When composers write down music, they use special marks and follow rules that they all agree on. Music that is written down is like directions that tell you what to do. Here is how a part of a song you probably know looks when it's written down.

Twin-kle,   twin-kle,   lit-tle   star,   how I   won-der   what you   are.

Sing aloud the first words: "Twinkle, twinkle, little star." Now, sing it again, but clap along with the strong sounds, like this:

Twin	kle	twin	kle	lit	tle	star
clap		*clap*		*clap*		*clap*

When you clap at the strong sounds, you get the *beat*.
Now sing the words again, but this time clap on each sound, like this:

Twin	kle	twin	kle	lit	tle	star
clap	*clap*	*clap*	*clap*	*clap*	*clap*	*clap*

When you clap on each sound, you get the *rhythm*.
Now hum the tune, but don't say the words, like this:

him	hum	him	hum	him	hum	himmm

When you hum the sounds, you get the *melody*.
When you sing the song, then you get it all: the beat, the rhythm, the melody, and the words, all at once.

Follow the Notes

When composers write music down, they use special marks called notes. Here are some musical notes:

Whole note   Half note   Quarter note

The notes tell us the rhythm. They tell us how the music moves. That's because each note has a different length. Another way of saying it is that each note stands for a sound that lasts for a different amount of time. On the whole note, you count to four. On the half note, you count to two. The quarter note gets one count. (You might also hear people say that a whole note gets fours beats, a half note gets two beats, and a quarter note gets one beat.)

Try this: Find a clock with a second hand, the kind that goes *tick-tick-tick* loud enough for you to hear. Now, say one long "ahh" for four ticks. You've just made a sound that lasts as long as a whole note. (Really, in different songs, notes can last for different lengths of time, but we can use the seconds of a clock as an example of how long notes can last.) If a whole note lasts for four ticks of the clock, then how long would a half note last? Say "ahh" for two ticks—that's how long a half note lasts. Now, say "ah" four times, in time with the ticking of the clock like this: "ah—ah—ah—ah." You've just made the sound of four quarter notes.

A half note lasts twice as long as a quarter note. It takes two half notes to make up a whole note. How many quarter notes do you think it takes to make up a whole note? (Four.)

Look again at this music from "Twinkle, Twinkle Little Star." Can you put your finger on the quarter notes? On the half notes?

Twin-kle,   twin-kle,   lit-tle   star,   how I   won-der   what you   are.

Pitch: High and Low

Let's think of some high sounds and low sounds. What are some high sounds? How about a bird chirping, or the brakes on a car squeaking? Can you think of some low sounds? How about thunder rumbling, or a big dog growling?

When we talk about how high or low a sound is, we are talking about *pitch*. Pitch is how high or low the sounds are.

When you sing a song, your voice goes higher and lower. Listen to yourself as you sing just the first two words of "Twinkle, Twinkle Little Star." Do you hear how your voice goes higher on the second "twinkle"?

When composers write music, they tell us how high or low the notes should be by placing the notes in different positions on a *staff*. A staff looks like a wide ladder:

When you follow the notes as they go up and down on the staff, you get the melody. When you put notes near the top of a staff, they are high notes. The notes near the bottom of the staff are lower notes.

Often at the beginning of a staff you will see a special mark called a treble clef. When a staff has a treble clef at the beginning of it, then the lines and spaces of the staff have special names. These names tell musicians how high or low the notes are. The names for the pitches are taken from the alphabet. The music alphabet is **A B C D E F G.** Can you say the music alphabet forward and backward?

We use the music alphabet to name the lines and spaces of the staff. Count how many lines are in the staff. Now count the number of spaces between the lines. Did you count five lines and four spaces? Here are their names:

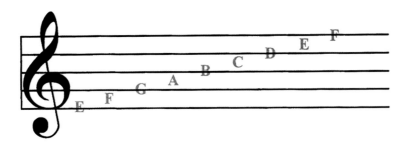

Do you see how the music alphabet is repeated? Look at the bottom line of the staff, which is an E. You go up to F, then G. What comes next? Not H. Instead, you start over again with A.

Sometimes a composer wants silence as part of the music. Then he or she writes a mark called a *rest*. A whole rest lasts as long as a whole note. It says to the musician, "Stay quiet for four counts." A half rest lasts as long as a half note. A quarter rest lasts as long as a quarter note.

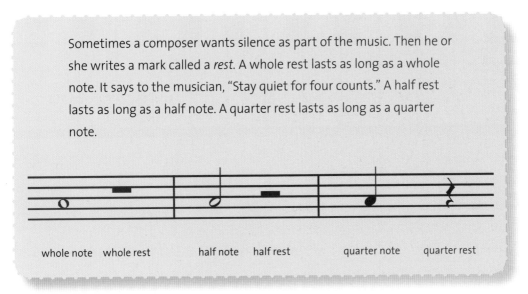

whole note   whole rest   half note   half rest   quarter note   quarter rest

A Musical Scale

You've seen that musical notes have letter names: A B C D E F G. When you sing or play these notes in a row, one after the other, you are singing or playing a musical *scale*.

On a piano or electric keyboard, you can play a scale called the C-major scale. It begins and ends with C, but the first C is a lower pitch than the last one. Begin with a white key just below two black keys, and play only the white keys. (Later books in this series will tell you what the black keys do.)

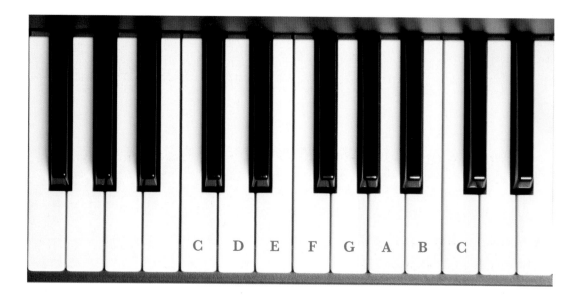

You can use letters to name the notes of the C-major scale, or you can use some special sounds. Here are the sounds that go with each letter:

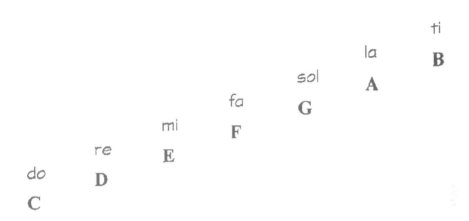

Here are the words to a song you can sing to help you learn the special names of the notes.

Do-Re-Mi

Doe—a deer, a female deer,
Ray—a drop of golden sun,
Me—a name I call myself,
Far—a long, long way to run,
Sew—a needle pulling thread,
La—a note to follow sew,
Tea—a drink with jam and bread,
That will bring us back to do!
Do-re-mi-fa-sol-la-ti-do!

Some Songs for Second Grade

PARENTS: Here we present the words to some favorite children's songs. You can find the music to these and other favorite songs in songbooks like *Gonna Sing My Head Off! American Folk Songs for Children* by Kathleen Krull (Knopf, 1992) and *American Folk Songs for Children* by Ruth Crawford Seeger (Doubleday, 1980). You might also want to play tapes or compact discs for your child to sing along with, such as:

- A Child's Celebration of Folk Music, *available on tape or compact disc from Music for Little People (800-727-2233)*
- Wee Sing America *and other recordings in the Wee Sing series by Pam Beall and Susan Nipp (Price Stern Sloan)*

You can find more songs for second graders elsewhere in this book, including:

- "John Henry," page 78
- "The Star-Spangled Banner," page 195
- "The Erie Canal," page 203
- "Swing Low, Sweet Chariot," page 221
- "Follow the Drinking Gourd," page 223
- "When Johnny Comes Marching Home," page 226
- "Dixie," page 226
- "This Land Is Your Land," page 291
- "I've Been Working on the Railroad," page 292
- "Do-Re-Mi," page 311

Clementine

In a cavern, in a canyon,
Excavating for a mine,
Dwelt a miner, forty-niner
And his daughter, Clementine.

(chorus)
Oh my darling, oh my darling,
Oh my darling Clementine,
You are lost and gone forever,
Dreadful sorry, Clementine.

Light she was and like a fairy,
And her shoes were number nine,
Herring boxes without topses,
Sandals were for Clementine.
(repeat chorus)

Drove she ducklings to the water,
Every morning just at nine,
Hit her foot against a splinter,
Fell into the foaming brine.
(repeat chorus)

Ruby lips above the water,
Blowing bubbles soft and fine,
But, alas, I was no swimmer,
So I lost my Clementine.
(repeat chorus)

Old Dan Tucker

I came to town the other night
To hear the noise and see the fight.
The watchman was a-runnin' round,
Cryin', "Old Dan Tucker's come to town."

(chorus)
So get out the way, Old Dan Tucker,
You're too late to get your supper.
Supper's over, breakfast cookin',
Old Dan Tucker standin' there a-lookin'.

Now Old Dan Tucker was a mighty man,
He washed his face in a frying pan,
Combed his hair with a wagon wheel,
And he died with a toothache in his heel.
(repeat chorus)

Home on the Range

Oh, give me a home where the buffalo roam,
Where the deer and the antelope play,
Where seldom is heard a discouraging word,
And the skies are not cloudy all day.

Home, home on the range,
Where the deer and the antelope play,
Where seldom is heard a discouraging word,
And the skies are not cloudy all day.

Goodbye, Old Paint

Goodbye, Old Paint, I'm leaving Cheyenne.

Goodbye, Old Paint, I'm leaving Cheyenne.

I'm leaving Cheyenne, I'm off for Montana,

Goodbye, Old Paint, I'm leaving Cheyenne.

Goodbye, Old Paint, I'm leaving Cheyenne.

Buffalo Gals

This American song from the 1840s is not about buffalo but about the women of Buffalo, New York—or of any other town where the boys like to dance with the girls.

As I was walking down the street,

Down the street, down the street,

A pretty gal I chanced to meet

Under the silvery moon.

Buffalo gals, won't you come out tonight,

Come out tonight, come out tonight,

Buffalo gals, won't you come out tonight,

And dance by the light of the moon.

Casey Jones

Maybe you know the story of the railroad engineer Casey Jones (if you don't, you can find it in *What Your Kindergartner Needs to Know*). Casey Jones was famous for always getting his train on time. But one day, as his train was speeding along the tracks, there was a stalled train on the tracks just ahead—and that's how Casey met his end. Casey Jones has become a tall-tale legend in America, and his story lives on in song. There are many versions of the song about him; here are some verses you can sing. (You can read about some other tall-tale heroes in the Language and Literature section of this book.)

Come all you rounders if you want to hear
The story of a brave engineer.
Casey Jones was the rounder's name;
On a big eight-wheeler, boys, he won his fame.

Early one mornin' about half past four
He kissed his wife at the station door,
He mounted to the cabin with his orders in hand.
And he took his farewell trip to that Promised Land.

(chorus)
Casey Jones mounted to the cabin,
Casey Jones, with his orders in his hand,
Casey Jones mounted to the cabin,
And he took his farewell trip to that Promised Land.

Suggested Resources

Recordings of Favorite Songs for Children

Great Songs of the Old West by Roy Rogers and Dale Evans (Rockbeat Records)

The Broadway Kids Sing America by The Broadway Kids (Koch Records)

This Land Is Your Land: The Asch Recordings, Vol. 1 by Arlo Guthrie and Woody Guthrie (Smithsonian Folkways)

The Hero in You by Ellis Paul (Black Wolf Records)

Books About Music, Songs, and Instruments

Story of the Orchestra: Listen While You Learn About the Instruments, the Music and the Composers Who Wrote the Music! by Robert Levine, Robert T. Levine, and Meredith Hamilton (Black Dog & Leventhal Publishers, 2000)

Casey Jones adapted by Stephen Krensky and illustrated by Mark Schroder (First Avenue Editions, 2007)

V
Mathematics

Introduction

In school, any successful program for teaching math to young children follows these three cardinal rules: (1) practice, (2) practice, and (3) practice. Not mindless repetition, of course, but thoughtful and varied practice, in which children are given opportunities to approach problems from a variety of angles, and in which, as they proceed to learn new facts and operations, they consistently review and reinforce their earlier learning. Psychologists who specialize in the subject explain that the gaining of ability through practice is *not* opposed to mathematical understanding, but in fact is the prerequisite to thoughtful problem solving. Those who take extreme positions that polarize practice and problem solving are greatly oversimplifying the issues.

Some well-meaning people fear that practice in mathematics (for example, memorizing the addition and subtraction facts up to 18, or doing timed multiplication worksheets) leads to joyless, soul-killing drudgery. Nothing could be further from the truth. The destroyer of joy in learning mathematics is not practice but anxiety—the anxiety that comes from feeling that one is mathematically stupid or lacks any "special talent" for math.

The most effective school math programs that we know of incorporate the principle of incremental review. By incremental review, psychologists mean that once a concept or skill is introduced, it is consciously and regularly presented in later exercises, gradually increasing the depth and difficulty. This feature in mathematics materials helps to cultivate a child's automatic understanding of what is to be done. When children reach the point where they automatically know the basic facts—when, for example, they can instantly tell you what $9 + 8$ equals—then and only then are their minds left free to tackle more challenging problems that ask them to apply or extend the skills and concepts they have learned. School math programs that offer both incremental review and varied opportunities for problem solving tend to get the best results.

In the pages that follow, we present a brief explanatory outline of math skills and concepts that should form part of a good second-grade education. But we must emphasize that this outline is *not meant to constitute a complete math program.* These pages can provide a useful supplement for checkup and review at home, but in school children need more extensive and regular opportunities for practice and review than these pages can offer.

Suggested Resources

· ·

Family Math by Jean Kerr Stenmark, Virginia Thompson, and Ruth Cossey (University of California, Berkeley, 1986); to order call 510-642-1910
Software: *Math Blaster* (Davidson); *Math Workshop* (Broderbund)

Working with Numbers to 100

Skip-Counting

Mario: Can you count to 100 really fast?

Dana: Sure. One, two, skip a few, a hundred!

Dana's way is funny, but you know better ways to count to 100, like counting by fives or by tens. Try it now. Count out loud by fives to 100. Then count out loud by tens to 100.

When you count by fives and tens, you are skip-counting, because you skip over some numbers. You should also learn to skip-count by twos and by threes. Practice skip-counting by twos now by reading only the numbers in color in the lines below. Keep practicing until you can do it without looking at the numbers.

1, 2, 3, 4, 5, 6, 7, 8, 9, 10, 11, 12, 13, 14, 15, 16, 17, 18, 19, 20
1, 2, 3, 4, 5, 6, 7, 8, 9, 10, 11, 12, 13, 14, 15, 16, 17, 18, 19, 20

Some Special Math Words

When you add numbers together, the numbers you add are called the *addends*. The answer you get is called the *sum*.

$$\begin{matrix} 5 \\ +3 \end{matrix} \Big\} \text{ addends}$$
$$\overline{8 \text{ sum}}$$

You can have more than two addends. What are the addends here?

$$2 + 3 + 5 = 10$$

When you subtract, the number left over is called the *difference*. In $9 - 7 = 2$, the difference is 2. What is the difference here?

$$\begin{matrix} 7 \\ -4 \end{matrix}$$
$$\overline{3}$$

Even and Odd Numbers

Try this. Gather a small pile of crayons. Count how many you have. Then arrange them in pairs. After you arrange them in pairs, are there any left over? If there are none left over, then you picked up an *even* number of crayons. If there is one left over, then you picked up an *odd* number of crayons.

There are 11 crayons here. 11 is an odd number.

When you start at 0 and count by twos, you are naming the even numbers. The even numbers up to 30 are:

0, 2, 4, 6, 8, 10, 12, 14, 16, 18, 20, 22, 24, 26, 28, 30

When you start at 1 and count by twos, you are naming the odd numbers. The odd numbers up to 30 are:

1, 3, 5, 7, 9, 11, 13, 15, 17, 19, 21, 23, 25, 27, 29

Can you name the next even number after 30? Can you name the next odd number after 29?

Between, One More, and One Less

When a number comes in the middle of two other numbers, we say it is *between* them. For example, 7 is between 6 and 8. What number is between 11 and 13? (12.) What numbers are between 5 and 9? (6, 7, and 8.)

You know that 9 comes just before 10. Another way of saying that is, 9 is one less than 10. You can say that 11 comes just after 10, or that 11 is one more than 10. If I give you a number, can you tell me what is one less and one more than the number? Let's try it. The number is 8. What is one less than 8? What is one more than 8? Practice telling what is one less and one more than any number up to 100. Try these:

5   19   30   43

Counting with a Tally

Imagine you're at a basketball game. You want to keep track of how many points your favorite player scores, so you use a tally. You mark down a small straight line for each point he scores. After his first basket, which is worth two points, you make two lines like this:

||

After his next basket, you mark down two more points, for a total of four, like this:

||||

Then he makes a free throw, which is worth only one point. How many points does that make in all? Five so far. When you get to five in a tally, you make a line through the first four lines, like this:

卌

Later, when the game is over, you can quickly skip-count by fives to see how many points your favorite player scored. Can you tell from this tally how many points he scored?

卌 卌 卌 卌 卌 ||

Wow, 27 points—that's a good game!

Using Graphs

The children in Mrs. Chen's class chose their favorite kind of fruit. They put their choices on a graph, like this:

Our Favorite Fruits

bananas							
peaches							
apples							
grapes							

0   1   2   3   4   5   6   7

We call this kind of graph a bar graph, because it shows information in the form of bars. A bar graph can also look like the one on the right.

This graph shows favorite pets of the children in Mr. Levy's class. Just by looking quickly at the graph, without reading any numbers, can you tell what pet is the favorite of most children? Now read the graph and tell how many children liked dogs best, how many liked cats best, how many liked birds best, and how many liked fish best.

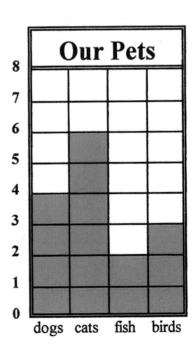

Our Pets

8
7
6
5
4
3
2
1
0

dogs   cats   fish   birds

Writing Numbers as Words

Can you write the words for the numbers from 1 to 10? You should also learn to write the words for the numbers from 11 to 20.

11 eleven	16 sixteen
12 twelve	17 seventeen
13 thirteen	18 eighteen
14 fourteen	19 nineteen
15 fifteen	20 twenty

Practice writing those words until you can do it easily. Also, practice writing the words for the tens up to 100:

10 ten	60 sixty
20 twenty	70 seventy
30 thirty	80 eighty
40 forty	90 ninety
50 fifty	100 one hundred

Be careful with "forty." It doesn't have a *u* in it, as "four" and "fourteen" do.

Once you know these words, you can write the words for any number up to 100. Here are some examples:

21 twenty-one   45 forty-five   83 eighty-three

Can you write the words for these numbers?

14   33   42   59   76

Reading a Number Line

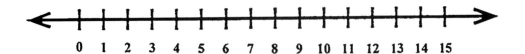

This is a number line. It shows the numbers in order. A number line has arrows because the numbers keep on going forever. All the numbers you've learned, and a whole lot more, can be shown on a number line.

You can use a number line to practice addition and subtraction. For example, to find the sum of 7 + 4 on a number line, first go forward to 7. Then go forward four more numbers. Where do you end? On 11. So 7 + 4 = 11.

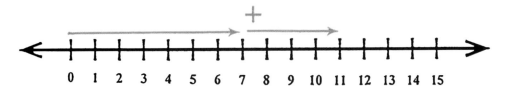

You can also use a number line to practice subtraction. For example, to find the difference of 32 – 7, first go forward on the number line to 32.

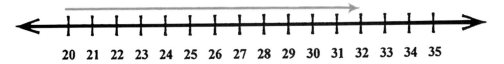

Then go backward seven numbers.

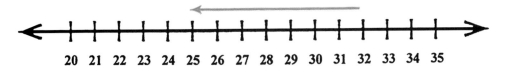

Where do you end up? At 25. So, with the help of a number line, you can figure out that 32 – 7 = 25.

Review: Addition Facts to 12

Review these addition facts with sums up to 12. Practice until you know the sums without having to stop to count.

Sum of 0	Sum of 1	Sum of 2	Sum of 3	Sum of 4
$0 + 0 = 0$	$1 + 0 = 1$	$2 + 0 = 2$	$3 + 0 = 3$	$4 + 0 = 4$
	$0 + 1 = 1$	$1 + 1 = 2$	$2 + 1 = 3$	$3 + 1 = 4$
		$0 + 2 = 2$	$1 + 2 = 3$	$2 + 2 = 4$
			$0 + 3 = 3$	$1 + 3 = 4$
				$0 + 4 = 4$

Sum of 5	Sum of 6	Sum of 7	Sum of 8
$5 + 0 = 5$	$6 + 0 = 6$	$7 + 0 = 7$	$8 + 0 = 8$
$4 + 1 = 5$	$5 + 1 = 6$	$6 + 1 = 7$	$7 + 1 = 8$
$3 + 2 = 5$	$4 + 2 = 6$	$5 + 2 = 7$	$6 + 2 = 8$
$2 + 3 = 5$	$3 + 3 = 6$	$4 + 3 = 7$	$5 + 3 = 8$
$1 + 4 = 5$	$2 + 4 = 6$	$3 + 4 = 7$	$4 + 4 = 8$
$0 + 5 = 5$	$1 + 5 = 6$	$2 + 5 = 7$	$3 + 5 = 8$
	$0 + 6 = 6$	$1 + 6 = 7$	$2 + 6 = 8$
		$0 + 7 = 7$	$1 + 7 = 8$
			$0 + 8 = 8$

Sum of 9	Sum of 10	Sum of 11	Sum of 12
$9 + 0 = 9$	$10 + 0 = 10$	$11 + 0 = 11$	$12 + 0 = 12$
$8 + 1 = 9$	$9 + 1 = 10$	$10 + 1 = 11$	$11 + 1 = 12$
$7 + 2 = 9$	$8 + 2 = 10$	$9 + 2 = 11$	$10 + 2 = 12$
$6 + 3 = 9$	$7 + 3 = 10$	$8 + 3 = 11$	$9 + 3 = 12$
$5 + 4 = 9$	$6 + 4 = 10$	$7 + 4 = 11$	$8 + 4 = 12$
$4 + 5 = 9$	$5 + 5 = 10$	$6 + 5 = 11$	$7 + 5 = 12$
$3 + 6 = 9$	$4 + 6 = 10$	$5 + 6 = 11$	$6 + 6 = 12$
$2 + 7 = 9$	$3 + 7 = 10$	$4 + 7 = 11$	$5 + 7 = 12$
$1 + 8 = 9$	$2 + 8 = 10$	$3 + 8 = 11$	$4 + 8 = 12$
$0 + 9 = 9$	$1 + 9 = 10$	$2 + 9 = 11$	$3 + 9 = 12$
	$0 + 10 = 10$	$1 + 10 = 11$	$2 + 10 = 12$
		$0 + 11 = 11$	$1 + 11 = 12$
			$0 + 12 = 12$

Review: Subtraction Facts from Numbers to 12

Review these subtraction facts from numbers up to 12. Practice until you know them by heart.

From 0	From 1	From 2	From 3	From 4
$0 - 0 = 0$	$1 - 0 = 1$	$2 - 0 = 2$	$3 - 0 = 3$	$4 - 0 = 4$
	$1 - 1 = 0$	$2 - 1 = 1$	$3 - 1 = 2$	$4 - 1 = 3$
		$2 - 2 = 0$	$3 - 2 = 1$	$4 - 2 = 2$
			$3 - 3 = 0$	$4 - 3 = 1$
				$4 - 4 = 0$

From 5	From 6	From 7	From 8
$5 - 0 = 5$	$6 - 0 = 6$	$7 - 0 = 7$	$8 - 0 = 8$
$5 - 1 = 4$	$6 - 1 = 5$	$7 - 1 = 6$	$8 - 1 = 7$
$5 - 2 = 3$	$6 - 2 = 4$	$7 - 2 = 5$	$8 - 2 = 6$
$5 - 3 = 2$	$6 - 3 = 3$	$7 - 3 = 4$	$8 - 3 = 5$
$5 - 4 = 1$	$6 - 4 = 2$	$7 - 4 = 3$	$8 - 4 = 4$
$5 - 5 = 0$	$6 - 5 = 1$	$7 - 5 = 2$	$8 - 5 = 3$
	$6 - 6 = 0$	$7 - 6 = 1$	$8 - 6 = 2$
		$7 - 7 = 0$	$8 - 7 = 1$
			$8 - 8 = 0$

From 9	From 10	From 11	From 12
$9 - 0 = 9$	$10 - 0 = 10$	$11 - 0 = 11$	$12 - 0 = 12$
$9 - 1 = 8$	$10 - 1 = 9$	$11 - 1 = 10$	$12 - 1 = 11$
$9 - 2 = 7$	$10 - 2 = 8$	$11 - 2 = 9$	$12 - 2 = 10$
$9 - 3 = 6$	$10 - 3 = 7$	$11 - 3 = 8$	$12 - 3 = 9$
$9 - 4 = 5$	$10 - 4 = 6$	$11 - 4 = 7$	$12 - 4 = 8$
$9 - 5 = 4$	$10 - 5 = 5$	$11 - 5 = 6$	$12 - 5 = 7$
$9 - 6 = 3$	$10 - 6 = 4$	$11 - 6 = 5$	$12 - 6 = 6$
$9 - 7 = 2$	$10 - 7 = 3$	$11 - 7 = 4$	$12 - 7 = 5$
$9 - 8 = 1$	$10 - 8 = 2$	$11 - 8 = 3$	$12 - 8 = 4$
$9 - 9 = 0$	$10 - 9 = 1$	$11 - 9 = 2$	$12 - 9 = 3$
	$10 - 10 = 0$	$11 - 10 = 1$	$12 - 10 = 2$
		$11 - 11 = 0$	$12 - 11 = 1$
			$12 - 12 = 0$

Addition Facts with Sums of 13, 14, 15, 16, 17, and 18

You know your addition facts with sums up to 12 very well, right? (See page 330 if you want to review or practice.) Now here are more addition facts with sums up to 18. Learn these by heart, so that you can give the sums quickly without having to stop to count.

Sum of 13	Sum of 14	Sum of 15	Sum of 16	Sum of 17	Sum of 18
$9 + 4 = 13$	$9 + 5 = 14$	$9 + 6 = 15$	$9 + 7 = 16$	$9 + 8 = 17$	$9 + 9 = 18$
$8 + 5 = 13$	$8 + 6 = 14$	$8 + 7 = 15$	$8 + 8 = 16$	$8 + 9 = 17$	
$7 + 6 = 13$	$7 + 7 = 14$	$7 + 8 = 15$	$7 + 9 = 16$		
$6 + 7 = 13$	$6 + 8 = 14$	$6 + 9 = 15$			
$5 + 8 = 13$	$5 + 9 = 14$				
$4 + 9 = 13$					

Subtraction Facts from 13, 14, 15, 16, 17, and 18

You know your subtraction facts from numbers up to 12 very well, right? (See page 331 if you want to review or practice.) Here are more subtraction facts with numbers up to 18. Learn these facts and you will be able to solve subtraction problems quickly and easily.

From 13	From 14	From 15	From 16	From 17	From 18
$13 - 4 = 9$	$14 - 5 = 9$	$15 - 6 = 9$	$16 - 7 = 9$	$17 - 8 = 9$	$18 - 9 = 9$
$13 - 5 = 8$	$14 - 6 = 8$	$15 - 7 = 8$	$16 - 8 = 8$	$17 - 9 = 8$	
$13 - 6 = 7$	$14 - 7 = 7$	$15 - 8 = 7$	$16 - 9 = 7$		
$13 - 7 = 6$	$14 - 8 = 6$	$15 - 9 = 6$			
$13 - 8 = 5$	$14 - 9 = 5$				
$13 - 9 = 4$					

Adding in Any Order, and Adding Three Numbers

It does not matter what order you add numbers in; the sum is still the same.

$$9 + 4 = 13 \quad \text{and} \quad 4 + 9 = 13$$

$$7 + 12 = 19 \quad \text{and} \quad 12 + 7 = 19$$

That's why you can check your work by adding the numbers in a different order. For example, when you are adding three numbers, first add down, like this:

$$
\begin{array}{c}
4 \\
3 \\
+5 \\
\hline
12
\end{array}
\qquad
\begin{array}{c}
7 \\
+5 \\
\hline
12
\end{array}
$$

Then check by adding up, like this:

$$
\begin{array}{c}
4 \\
3 \\
+5 \\
\hline
12
\end{array}
\qquad
\begin{array}{c}
4 \\
+8 \\
\hline
12
\end{array}
$$

Either way, no matter what order you add in, you get the same sum.

Doubles and Halves

When you add a number to itself, you are doubling the number. When you add 3 and 3, you double 3. $3 + 3 = 6$, so double 3 is 6. Another way to say that is "twice 3 is 6."

Practice doubling the numbers from 1 to 9 until you know them by heart:

$1 + 1 = 2$ $4 + 4 = 8$ $7 + 7 = 14$
$2 + 2 = 4$ $5 + 5 = 10$ $8 + 8 = 16$
$3 + 3 = 6$ $6 + 6 = 12$ $9 + 9 = 18$

Look at the sums of the doubles. Do you see a pattern? Do you see how the sums go up by twos? Did you also notice that when you double any number, the result is an even number? Even if you double an odd number, the double turns out even. Try it now. Double 3, and you get 6. Double 5 and you get 10. So all even numbers are a number doubled. What number is doubled to get 2? What number is doubled to get 6?

Doubles can help you when you're adding. If you know that $7 + 7 = 14$, then you can quickly figure what $8 + 7$ is. You know that 8 is one more than 7. So $8 + 7$ must be one more than $7 + 7$.

$7 + 8$ is the same as $7 + 7 + 1$
$7 + 8 = 14 + 1$
$7 + 8 = 15$

Try to work out some more of these "double-plus-one" problems. What is 6 + 7?

6 + 7 is the same as 6 + 6 + 1
6 + 7 = 12 + 1
6 + 7 = 13

Now try these doubles-plus-one problems on your own:

5 + 6 = __
9 + 8 = __
8 + 7 = __

If you learn your doubles up to 20, then you'll also know how to divide numbers in half. If you cut a piece of bread in two equal parts, then each part is a half. When a number is divided in two equal parts, each part is a half.

What is half of 8? You know the answer if you know what number you double to make 8. You double 4 to make 8. So 4 is half of 8.

What number do you double to get 4? To get 4, you double 2. So half of 4 is 2. What number do you double to make 12? To get 12, you double 6. So half of 12 is 6. Can you tell me what half of 6 is?

What is half of 6?

How many things make up a dozen? There are 12 in a dozen. So if I ask you to buy half a dozen eggs, how many should you buy?

Sum of 10

All of the problems below have a sum of 10. See if you can give the missing number in each problem.

$$5 + \underline{} = 10 \qquad 3 + \underline{} = 10 \qquad 4 + \underline{} = 10$$
$$6 + \underline{} = 10 \qquad 2 + \underline{} = 10 \qquad 8 + \underline{} = 10$$
$$1 + \underline{} = 10 \qquad 7 + \underline{} = 10 \qquad 9 + \underline{} = 10$$

Practice your sums of 10, because you will be able to do lots of math problems more easily if you know by heart the numbers that add up to 10.

Checking Addition and Subtraction

Addition is the opposite of subtraction. So you can always check a subtraction problem by doing addition, like this:

$$
\begin{array}{ccc}
17 & 8 & 8 \\
-9 & +9 & +9 \\
\hline
8 & & 17
\end{array}
$$

When you check, you should end up with the same number you began with. You began by subtracting from 17. When you check, you add 8 and 9 and you get 17, so you know you got the right answer.

You can also check addition by doing subtraction, like this:

Fact Families

A fact family brings together addition facts with their opposite subtraction facts. Here is a fact family you may know:

$5 + 2 = 7$ $7 - 2 = 5$
$2 + 5 = 7$ $7 - 5 = 2$

Practice forming fact families with the new addition and subtraction facts you've learned, using numbers up to 18. For example:

$9 + 4 = 13$ $13 - 4 = 9$
$4 + 9 = 13$ $13 - 9 = 4$

Do you see how making fact families is just like checking addition by subtraction and checking subtraction by addition?

Here are two more addition facts. Can you give the rest of the facts in each fact family?

$9 + 7 = 16$ $8 + 5 = 13$

_____   _____

_____   _____

_____   _____

Finding the Missing Number

Practice finding the answers to problems with a missing number, like this:

$$7 + \underline{} = 12 \quad \text{(The missing number is 5.)}$$
$$\underline{} - 6 = 7 \quad \text{(The missing number is 13.)}$$

When you know your addition and subtraction facts by heart, then you can quickly solve a problem with a missing number. Just by looking at this problem, can you tell me the missing number?

$$3 + \underline{} = 5$$

Sometimes you might need to figure out the missing number. You can do that by thinking about what you've learned from fact families, and from checking addition with subtraction, as well as checking subtraction with addition. You know that addition and subtraction are opposites. So look at this problem:

$$9 + \underline{} = 17$$

If you don't know the missing number instantly, you can figure it out by turning the addition problem into a subtraction problem.

$$17 - 9 = 8$$

So the missing number is 8.

$$9 + 8 = 17$$

To figure out the missing number in a subtraction problem, you can turn it into an addition problem. For example:

$$\underline{} - 8 = 5$$

You can find the missing number by adding 5 and 8.

$$5 + 8 = 13$$

So the missing number is 13.

$$13 - 8 = 5$$

Practice doing problems with missing numbers. Here are some to get you started.

$8 + \_\_ = 14 \qquad 3 + \_\_ = 15 \qquad 9 + \_\_ = 18 \qquad 8 + \_\_ = 17$

$\_\_ - 6 = 6 \qquad \_\_ - 7 = 8 \qquad \_\_ - 6 = 9 \qquad \_\_ - 7 = 9$

Missing Number Problems with Greater Than and Less Than

Do you remember the signs for greater than and less than? The sign > means "greater than." The sign < means "less than." When you see 10 > 8, you read that as "10 is greater than 8." Try reading the following out loud:

$9 > 7 \qquad 7 + 6 > 5 + 6 \qquad 23 < 72 \qquad 15 - 8 < 11$

You can do missing-number problems with the greater-than and less-than signs. With these problems, there may be more than one right answer, like this:

$$15 - \_\_ > 11$$

You could fill in that blank with 0, 1, 2, or 3. They're all correct.
Try these problems:

$7 + \_\_ < 12 \qquad 13 - \_\_ > 8$

Working with Equations

When you write $7 - 4 = 3$, or $5 + 3 = 8$, you are writing an *equation*. An equation compares numbers using an equals sign: $=$. As you know, the equals sign means "is the same as." All of these are equations:

$$7 + 7 = 14 \qquad 36 = 36 \qquad 4 + 1 = 9 - 4$$

Whenever you change one side of an equation, you have to make the same change to the other side so the two sides stay equal. For example, let's say that we're adding triangles. Look at the groups of triangles in this picture:

You can use an equation with numbers to stand for your groups of triangles:

$$3 + 5 = 8$$

Now, if you add 2 triangles to the side with 3 and 5 triangles, then what do you have to do to the side with 8 triangles if you want the two sides to stay equal? You have to add 2 triangles to the 8 triangles as well.

In an equation when you add 2 to one side, then to stay equal, you have to add 2 to the other side as well:

$$2 + 3 + 5 = 2 + 8$$

Tens and Ones

You know that 1 ten is the same as 10 ones.

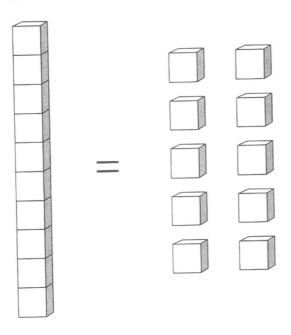

When you have 27 of something, you have 2 tens and 7 ones. You can write 27 as a sum of tens and ones:

$$27 = 20 + 7$$

How many tens are in 34? How many ones? So you can write 34 as a sum of tens and ones:

34 is the same as 30 + 4

Practice writing some numbers as a sum of tens and ones. For example, you can write 46 as 40 + 6. Following that pattern, how would you write 77? How about 32, 56, and 98?

Adding Numbers with Two Digits

Another word for any of the numbers from 0 to 9 is "digit." The number 43 has two digits, a 4 and a 3. As you know, 43 is 4 tens and 3 ones. When we look at the digits in the number 43, we say that the 4 is in the tens place and the 3 is in the ones place.

When you add two-digit numbers, first you add the ones; then you add the tens. When we write an addition problem with two-digit numbers, we say that the numbers in the ones place are in the ones column, and the numbers in the tens place are in the tens column. Let's figure out this sum:

$$\begin{array}{r} \text{tens}\ \text{ones} \\ 23 \\ +35 \\ \hline \end{array}$$

First we add the numbers in the ones column. Add 3 and 5, and you get 8. Then add the numbers in the tens column. Add 2 and 3, and you get 5. But you're really adding 2 tens and 3 tens, which makes 5 tens, or 50. So the sum is 5 tens plus 8 ones, or 50 + 8, which equals 58.

$$\begin{array}{r} \text{tens}\ \text{ones} \\ 23 \\ +35 \\ \hline 58 \end{array}$$

Sometimes when you add two-digit numbers, you have to regroup. For example, look at this problem.

$$\begin{array}{r} 48 \\ +26 \\ \hline \end{array}$$

You begin by adding the numbers in the ones column. When you add 8 + 6, you get 14 ones. You know that 14 is the same as 10 + 4. So you need to regroup 14 into 1 ten and 4 ones. You write the 4, which means 4 ones, at the bottom of the ones column.

Then you write the 1, which means 1 ten, at the top of the tens column, and add it to the other tens.

Add the ones and regroup.

$$
\begin{array}{r}
1 \\
48 \\
+26 \\
\hline
4
\end{array}
$$

Now add the tens.

$$
\begin{array}{r}
1 \\
48 \\
+26 \\
\hline
74
\end{array}
$$

Altogether you have 7 tens and 4 ones, which makes a sum of 74.

Writing a new ten at the top of the tens column is also called carrying. In the problem above, when you added the numbers in the ones column, you got 14. You wrote the 4 at the bottom of the ones column. Then you wrote a 1 (for 1 ten) at the top of the tens column, which is the same as saying that you "carried the 1" (for 1 ten) to the tens column.

Checking Addition by Changing the Order of Addends

It does not matter what order you add numbers in because the sum is still the same: $7 + 3 = 10$ and $3 + 7 = 10$. So you can check your answer to an addition problem by writing the addends in a different order and then adding again. You should get the same sum both times. For example:

$$
\begin{array}{r} 37 \\ +55 \\ \hline 92 \end{array}
\qquad
\begin{array}{r} 55 \\ +37 \\ \hline 92 \end{array}
$$

Change the order of the addends.

Adding Three Numbers

Let's try adding three numbers. First you add the numbers in the ones column. If they add up to more than 10, you need to regroup and carry.

$$
\begin{array}{r} \text{tens ones} \\ 43 \\ 28 \\ +14 \\ \hline \end{array}
$$

When you add $3 + 8 + 4$, you get 15. So you need to regroup. Write the 5 at the bottom of the ones column; then carry the 1 (for 1 ten) to the top of the tens column. Add the numbers in the tens column (don't forget to add the 1 you carried), and you'll get the sum.

$$
\begin{array}{r} 1 \\ 43 \\ 28 \\ +14 \\ \hline 85 \end{array}
$$

Subtracting Numbers with Two Digits

When you subtract from a two-digit number, first you subtract the numbers in the ones column. Here's an example:

$$\begin{array}{r} 97 \\ -55 \\ \hline \end{array}$$

You start by subtracting the ones: $7 - 5$ leaves 2. You write 2 at the bottom of the ones column. Then you subtract the tens. When you take 5 tens away from 9 tens, the difference is 4 tens. So you write 4 at the bottom of the tens column.

tens ones
$$\begin{array}{r} 97 \\ -55 \\ \hline 2 \end{array}$$
Subtract the ones.

tens ones
$$\begin{array}{r} 97 \\ -55 \\ \hline 42 \end{array}$$
Subtract the tens.

Sometimes when you subtract you will need to regroup. But instead of changing 10 ones to 1 ten, you will regroup 1 ten into 10 ones. Let's see how it works.

Pretend you have 27 pencils. You want to take away 9 pencils. How many will you have left? Let's write that as a subtraction problem.

$$\begin{array}{r} 27 \\ -9 \\ \hline \end{array}$$

Look at the numbers in the ones column. You want to take away 9, but you only have 7 ones. Remember, however, that 27 is the same as 2 tens and 7 ones.

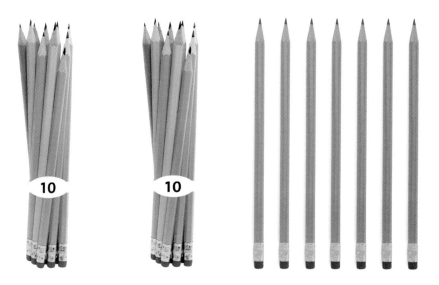

Take 1 of those tens and regroup it with the ones. That will leave you with 1 ten and 17 ones.

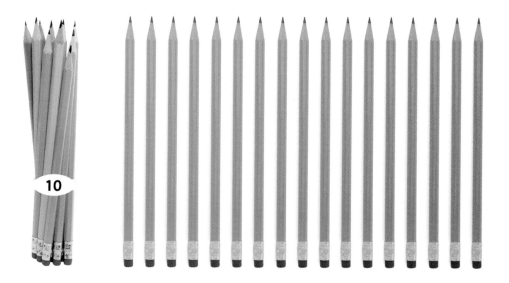

You have regrouped 2 tens and 7 ones into 1 ten and 17 ones. Some people say that you have "borrowed" 1 ten from the tens column and put it in the ones column. Now, you know how to take away 9 from 17. That leaves you with 8 ones. But don't forget you still have 1 ten left. So $27 - 9 = 18$.

Let's do some more subtraction problems with regrouping and learn a way to write the problems to keep each step clear as you go along. Look at the ones column in this problem:

$$\begin{array}{r} 65 \\ -48 \\ \hline \end{array}$$

8 is greater than 5, so you can't take away 8 from 5. You need to regroup. You know that 65 is the same as $60 + 5$, or 6 tens and 5 ones. Take 1 ten and add it to the 5 ones.

What does that leave you with? 5 tens and 15 ones. Cross out the 6 in the tens place and write 5 above it. Cross out the 5 in the ones place and write 15 above it. Now you can subtract easily. Remember, start with the ones first.

tens	ones
5	15
̶6̶	̶5̶
−4	8
	7

Subtract the ones.

tens	ones
5	15
̶6̶	̶5̶
−4	8
1	7

Now subtract the tens.

Checking Two-Digit Subtraction

Remember that addition is the opposite of subtraction, so you can check subtraction by addition. Here's a subtraction problem.

$$
\begin{array}{r}
62 \\
-35 \\
\hline
27
\end{array}
$$

You can check this by going from bottom to top and turning it into an addition problem. The sum should be the same as the number you first subtracted from, which is 62. Try it. Does it check?

$$
\begin{array}{r}
27 \\
+35 \\
\hline
\end{array}
$$

Adding and Subtracting Horizontally, Vertically, and in Your Head

You know that addition and subtraction problems can be written in two ways: across or up and down. We also say that a problem written across is written horizontally. A problem written up and down is written vertically. Either way, the answer comes out the same.

$$11 + 17 = 28 \quad \textit{is the same as} \quad \begin{array}{r} 11 \\ +17 \\ \hline 28 \end{array}$$

$$23 - 12 = 11 \quad \textit{is the same as} \quad \begin{array}{r} 23 \\ -12 \\ \hline 11 \end{array}$$

Horizontal   Vertical

When you see a two-digit addition problem written horizontally, it is sometimes easier to solve it by writing it over vertically. For example, what is the sum of 12 + 39? Rewrite the problem vertically, and make sure you keep all the ones in the ones column and the tens in the tens column.

$$\begin{array}{r} \text{\scriptsize tens}\ \text{\scriptsize ones} \\ 1\ 2 \\ +3\ 9 \\ \hline \end{array} \qquad \begin{array}{r} \text{\scriptsize tens}\ \text{\scriptsize ones} \\ 1 \\ 1\ 2 \\ +3\ 9 \\ \hline 1 \end{array} \qquad \begin{array}{r} \text{\scriptsize tens}\ \text{\scriptsize ones} \\ 1 \\ 12 \\ +39 \\ \hline 51 \end{array}$$

Rewrite the problem vertically.   Add the ones and regroup.   Add the tens.

Here is a way to solve a horizontal two-digit addition problem in your head. Try this problem: find the sum of 57 + 32. First, you break the numbers into tens and ones: 57 is the same as 50 + 7. 32 is the same as 30 + 2. In your head, add the tens: 50 + 30 is 80. Now add the ones: 7 + 2 is 9. So the sum is 80 + 9, or 89.

If you need to solve a subtraction problem written horizontally, you can re-write it vertically.

$$65 - 43 = \underline{} \qquad \textit{rewrite vertically as} \qquad \begin{array}{r} 65 \\ -43 \\ \hline \end{array}$$

You can also look at the problem as it's written horizontally and try to solve it in your head. Try to find the difference of 65 – 43. Break the numbers into tens and ones: 65 is the same as 60 + 5, and 43 is the same as 40 + 3. 60 – 40 = 20, and 5 – 3 = 2. So the difference is 22.

It's not as easy to add and subtract in your head when you have to regroup. When you have to regroup, you will probably want to rewrite the problem vertically.

But even when you need to regroup, you can learn to add and subtract in your head if you think of a math fact you already know. For example, think first of what you know to solve

$$28 + 6 = \underline{}$$

You know that $8 + 6 = 14$.
So in your head regroup 28 as $20 + 8$, like this: $20 + 8 + 6 = \underline{}$
Now add $8 + 6$, which you know is 14: $20 + 14 = \underline{}$
Now you can figure out the sum in your head: $20 + 14 = 34$

Now try a subtraction problem in your head.
$35 - 8 = \underline{}$

You know that $15 - 8 = 7$.

So in your head regroup 30 as $20 + 15$, like this: $20 + (15 - 8) =$ ___

Now subtract 8 from 15, which you know is 7. $20 + 7 =$ ___

Now you can figure out the answer in your head. $20 + 7 = 27$

So $35 - 8 = 27$.

It may be tough at first to do problems like these in your head, but keep trying. With practice, it will get easier, and then you'll be ready to tackle even harder and more interesting math problems. When you're ready for a challenge, try doing these problems in your head:

$38 + 7 =$ ___ $43 - 8 =$ ___ $25 + 8 =$ ___ $65 - 6 =$ ___

Adding and Subtracting 9 in Your Head

You can use a little trick to solve problems that ask you to add or subtract 9. For example: $25 + 9 =$ ___. Change the 9 to 10, and in your head you can quickly figure out that $25 + 10 = 35$. Now, just subtract 1 from 35 (because 10 is 1 more than 9) and you get the answer, 34. So to add 9 in your head, a shortcut is to add 10, then take away 1.

Now let's try subtracting 9. Here's the problem: $53 - 9 =$ ___. Change the 9 to 10, and in your head you can quickly figure out that $53 - 10 = 43$. Now, because you're subtracting, and you've taken away 1 more than 9, you need to add that 1 back. Add 1 to 43 and you get the answer, 44. So to subtract 9 in your head, a shortcut is to subtract 10, then add 1.

Try doing these in your head:

$37 + 9 =$ ___ $76 - 9 =$ ___ $45 + 9 =$ ___ $58 - 9 =$ ___

Estimating and Rounding to the Nearest Ten

Donny likes to collect baseball cards. When you visit him, he opens a box and pours out a pile of cards. "Wow! How many cards do you have?" you ask. "About 300," says Donny.

Sometimes it's easier to say about how many you have instead of exactly how many. When you say about how many, you are *estimating*.

Sometimes when you are adding and subtracting, you only need to know roughly what the answer is. When you don't need to know the exact answer, then you can estimate the answer—you can figure out *about* what it is. For example, how would you estimate the sum of 23 + 45? To begin, you turn the numbers into numbers that are easier to work with in your head. It's easier to work with numbers like 10, 20, 30, 40, 50, and so on. So you need to round the number to the nearest ten.

Let's see what it means to round 23 to the nearest ten. Look at this number line.

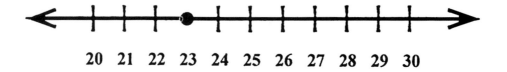

You can see that 23 is between 20 and 30, but it's closer to 20. So 23 rounded to the nearest 10 is 20.

What is 45 rounded to the nearest ten? To answer that, you need to know a special rule: when a number is exactly between two numbers, you round up to the greater number.

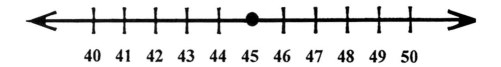

You can see on the number line that 45 is exactly between 40 and 50. So you round it up to 50.

Let's go back to our addition problem. How would you estimate the sum of 23 + 45?

$$
\begin{array}{r}
23 \quad \textit{rounds to} \quad 20 \\
+45 \quad \textit{rounds to} \quad +50 \\
\hline
70
\end{array}
$$

So 23 + 45 is about 70.

You can also use estimation when you subtract two-digit numbers and only need to know roughly what the difference is. For example:

$$
\begin{array}{r}
87 \quad \textit{rounds to} \quad 90 \\
-41 \quad \textit{rounds to} \quad -40 \\
\hline
50
\end{array}
$$

So 87 − 41 is about 50.

Fractions

A fraction is a part of something. In first grade you learned these fractions:

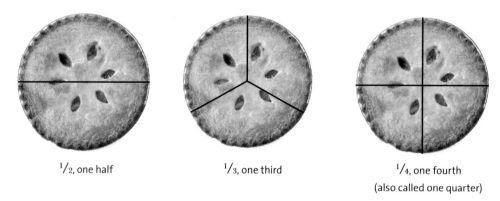

$^{1}/_{2}$, one half $\qquad$ $^{1}/_{3}$, one third $\qquad$ $^{1}/_{4}$, one fourth
(also called one quarter)

If something is divided into five equal parts, each part is one fifth, which in numbers is written as $^{1}/_{5}$. Here is a pizza divided into five equal slices. Each slice is $^{1}/_{5}$.

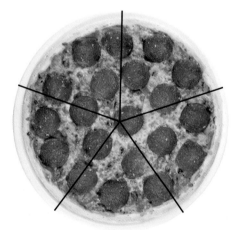

Each slice is $^{1}/_{5}$ (one fifth).

A fraction has a top number and a bottom number. The bottom number tells how many equal parts there are. The top number tells how many equal parts you are talking about. For example, look again at the pizza divided into five equal slices. If you ate two slices, what fraction of the whole pizza did you eat? You ate ²/₅ (two fifths).

Look at this circle. It is divided into four equal parts. One part is blue. What fraction of the circle is blue?

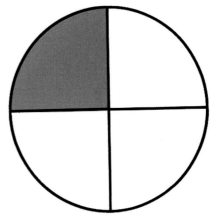

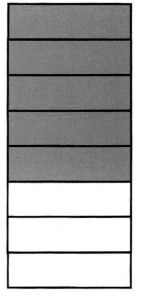

Here is a rectangle divided into six equal parts. Each part is ¹/₆ (one sixth). Four parts of the rectangle are blue. What fraction is blue? ⁴/₆ (four sixths) of the rectangle is blue.

Here is another rectangle divided into eight equal parts. Each part is ¹/₈ (one eighth). Five of the parts are blue. What fraction is blue? ⁵/₈ (five eighths) of the rectangle is blue.

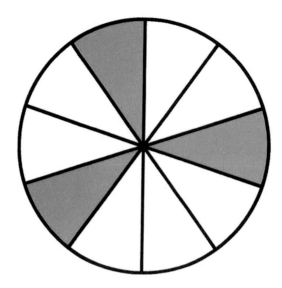

This circle has ten equal parts. What do you think each equal part is called? Each part is $\frac{1}{10}$ (one tenth). Count how many parts are blue. What fraction of the circle is blue?

You can also use fractions to talk about parts of a group. For example, there are eight girls in the class. Three of them are on the soccer team. What fraction of the girls are on the soccer team? $\frac{3}{8}$ (three eighths) of the girls are on the soccer team.

Working with Numbers to 1,000

The Hundreds

. . . .

Count out loud by tens from 10 to 100. How many tens are in 100?

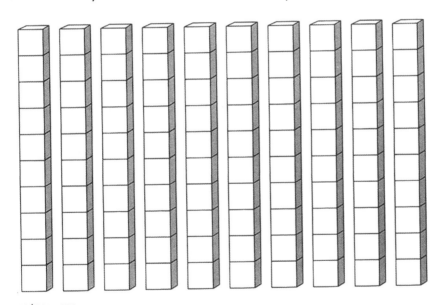

10 tens = 100

100 is the same as 10 tens. 100 is written in words as "one hundred."

Here are the numbers and words for the hundreds. Learn to write the numbers and words, and practice counting the hundreds out loud.

100	one hundred
200	two hundred
300	three hundred
400	four hundred
500	five hundred
600	six hundred
700	seven hundred
800	eight hundred
900	nine hundred

Counting Between Hundreds

Let's count out loud by ones, starting with 100. After 100 comes

101, 102, 103, 104, 105, 106, 107, 108, 109, 110, 111, 112 . . .

Okay, you can stop for now. When you read those numbers, you say "one hundred one," "one hundred two," "one hundred three," "one hundred four," "one hundred five," and so on. (Notice that you don't say "one hundred and one" or "one hundred and twelve"—there's no "and" in these numbers.)

Now, let's start at 189 and keep on counting.

189, 190, 191, 192, 193, 194, 195, 196, 197, 198, 199 . . .

What comes after 199? A new hundred, which is 200. After 200, you can keep counting in the same way:

200, 201, 202, 203, 204, 205, 206, 207, 208, 209, 210, 211, 212 . . .

What comes after 299? 300. You can keep counting until you get to 999 (nine hundred ninety-nine). What's the number after that? It's 10 hundreds, but we use a new name for it:

1,000 one thousand

Count On!

. . . .

Practice counting by hundreds from 100 to 1,000, like this:

100, 200, 300, 400, 500, 600, 700, 800, 900, 1,000

Now try counting by fifties to 1,000. The numbers below will get you started, and you finish:

50, 100, 150, 200, 250, 300, 350 . . .

Practice counting by tens and by fives from any hundred to the next hundred. For example:

by tens (from 400):
400, 410, 420, 430, 440, 450, 460, 470, 480, 490, 500

by fives (from 525):
525, 530, 535, 540, 545, 550, 555, 560 . . . (on to 600)

Now try this: count by tens from any old number. For example, start with 37. Here are some numbers to get you started. You go on a bit longer:

37, 47, 57, 67, 77, 87, 97, 107, 117, 127 . . . (go on to 227)

Count by tens from 176. Again, here are some numbers to get you started.

176, 186, 196, 206, 216, 226 . . . (go on to 326)

Practice until you can count easily by tens from any number. Also, practice counting backward by tens from any number. For example:

235, 225, 215, 205, 195, 185, 175 . . . (Can you keep going backward by tens to 25?)

> Practice writing the words for three-digit numbers. For example:
> 843   eight hundred forty-three
> 607   six hundred seven
> You try writing the words for 156, 403, and 987.

Place Value

Remember that we call numbers like 21 and 73 "two-digit" numbers. Notice that 100 has one more digit. It is a three-digit number. We say that the first digit is the hundreds place. You know where the next digits are—in the tens place and the ones place.

hundreds tens ones
1 0 0

Let's look at the number 245 (two hundred forty-five). The 2 in the hundreds place means there are 2 hundreds. The 4 in the tens place means there are 4 tens. And what does the 5 in the ones place mean?

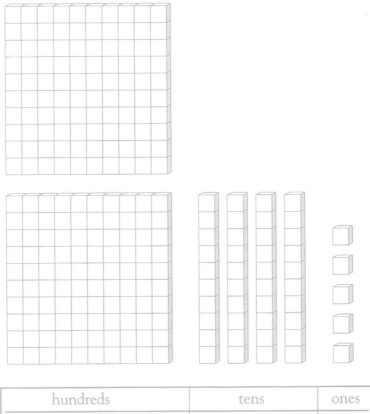

hundreds	tens	ones
2	4	5

You can use place-value blocks to help you understand what each digit in a three-digit number means, like this:

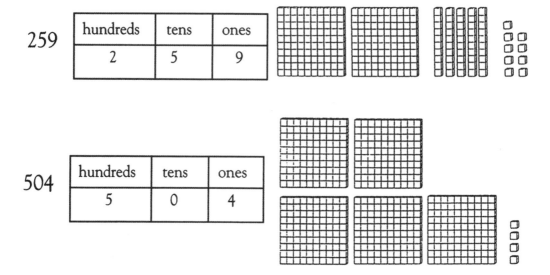

259 | hundreds | tens | ones |
|---|---|---|
| 2 | 5 | 9 |

504 | hundreds | tens | ones |
|---|---|---|
| 5 | 0 | 4 |

Only one of the following numbers has 8 tens and 4 hundreds. Can you tell which one? (You might find it helpful to write the numbers in a place-value block.)

418   884   814   148   481   448

Expanded Form

You know that 73 is 7 tens and 3 ones. You know that another way to write 73 is 70 + 3. When you write 73 as 70 + 3, you are writing the number in expanded form. ("Expanded" means "stretched out.")

You can also write three-digit numbers in expanded form. For example, in expanded form, 273 is 200 + 70 + 3. Here are other examples:

359 = 300 + 50 + 9
603 = 600 + 3 (There are no tens in this number.)
740 = 700 + 40 (There are no ones in this number.)

Try writing these numbers in expanded form:

394   571   805   630   912

Comparing Three-Digit Numbers

Which number is greater: 689 or 869? When you compare a three-digit number, look at the hundreds place first. If you look at the hundreds place in 689 and 869, you'll see that 8 is greater than 6. So you can quickly say that 869 > 689.

If the number in the hundreds place is the same, then you need to look at the tens place. For example, 371 > 359.

If the numbers in both the hundreds place and the tens place are the same, then look at the ones place. For example, 863 < 867.

Put the correct sign between the following pairs of numbers.

>   <   =

greater than   less than   equal to

876___599   348___384   765___769   252___225

Adding Three-Digit Numbers

To find the sum of three-digit numbers, first add the ones. Then add the tens, and then add the hundreds.

$$
\begin{array}{r}
253 \\
+338 \\
\hline
\end{array}
\qquad
\begin{array}{r}
^{1}\\
253 \\
+338 \\
\hline
1
\end{array}
\qquad
\begin{array}{r}
^{1}\\
253 \\
+338 \\
\hline
91
\end{array}
\qquad
\begin{array}{r}
^{1}\\
253 \\
+338 \\
\hline
591
\end{array}
$$

Find the sum.   Add the ones.   Add the tens.   Add the hundreds.

Regroup if necessary.

Regrouping Tens as Hundreds

In the addition example above, you needed to regroup ones as tens. Sometimes when you add you need to regroup tens as hundreds. It's not much different from regrouping ones as tens. Let's see by finding the sum of 80 + 40. How many tens are in 80? Yes, 8, and 40 is 4 tens.

8 tens + 4 tens = 12 tens

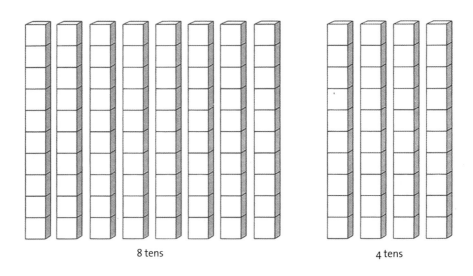

8 tens   4 tens

So now you have 12 tens. You can take 10 of the tens and group them together to make 1 hundred, with 2 tens left over. So 12 tens is the same as 1 hundred and 2 tens.

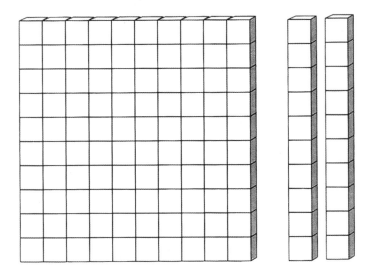

In an addition problem, when you have 10 or more tens, you need to regroup them as hundreds. Here is an example:

$$
\begin{array}{c}
276 \\
+663 \\
\hline
\end{array}
\qquad
\begin{array}{c}
276 \\
+663 \\
\hline
9
\end{array}
\qquad
\begin{array}{c}
1 \\
276 \\
+663 \\
\hline
39
\end{array}
\qquad
\begin{array}{c}
1 \\
276 \\
+663 \\
\hline
939
\end{array}
$$

Find the sum.   Add the ones.   Add the tens.   Add the hundreds.

Regroup if necessary.

When you add the tens in this problem, you add 7 tens plus 6 tens. That makes 13 tens. 13 tens is the same as 1 hundred and 3 tens. So you write 3 at the bottom of the tens column, then you carry the 1 (which stands for 1 hundred) to the top of the hundreds column.

Now let's do a problem in which you have to regroup both tens and ones.

$$
\begin{array}{r} 638 \\ +265 \\ \hline \end{array}
\qquad
\begin{array}{r} \scriptstyle 1 \\ 63\!\!\not8 \\ +265 \\ \hline 3 \end{array}
\qquad
\begin{array}{r} \scriptstyle 11 \\ 638 \\ +265 \\ \hline 03 \end{array}
\qquad
\begin{array}{r} \scriptstyle 11 \\ 638 \\ +265 \\ \hline 903 \end{array}
$$

Find the sum.   Add the ones. Regroup.   Add the tens. Regroup.   Add the hundreds.

Practice doing many three-digit addition problems until you can do them easily. Check your addition. Remember, you can check yourself by changing the order of the addends, then adding again to see if you get the same answer.

Subtracting from a Three-Digit Number

To subtract from a three-digit number, first subtract the ones. Then subtract the tens. Then subtract the hundreds.

$$
\begin{array}{r} 582 \\ -269 \\ \hline \end{array}
\qquad
\begin{array}{r} \scriptstyle 7\ 12 \\ 5\!\!\not8\!\!\not2 \\ -26\,9 \\ \hline 3 \end{array}
\qquad
\begin{array}{r} \scriptstyle 7\ 12 \\ 5\!\!\not8\!\!\not2 \\ -26\,9 \\ \hline 13 \end{array}
\qquad
\begin{array}{r} \scriptstyle 7\ 12 \\ 5\!\!\not8\!\!\not2 \\ -26\,9 \\ \hline 3\,13 \end{array}
$$

Find the difference.   Subtract the ones. Regroup if necessary.   Subtract the tens. Regroup.   Subtract the hundreds.

Remember, you can check subtraction by adding, like this:

$$
\begin{array}{r} 582 \\ -269 \\ \hline 313 \end{array}
\qquad
\begin{array}{r} 313 \\ +269 \\ \hline \end{array}
\qquad
\begin{array}{r} \scriptstyle 1 \\ 313 \\ +269 \\ \hline 582 \end{array}
$$

As you know, sometimes when you subtract you need to regroup 1 ten as 10 ones. For example, you would need to regroup 1 ten as 10 ones in this problem:

$$\begin{array}{r} 82 \\ -\ 57 \\ \hline \end{array}$$

In some problems, you may also need to regroup 1 hundred as 10 tens. Say that you have 230 pencils. They are bundled together in 2 hundreds and 3 tens.

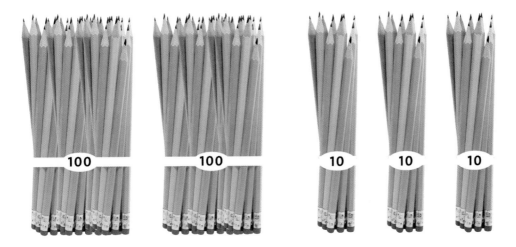

You want to give away 60 pencils. How can you do this? You only have 3 tens, but 60 is 6 tens. So you need to regroup one of the hundreds into tens.

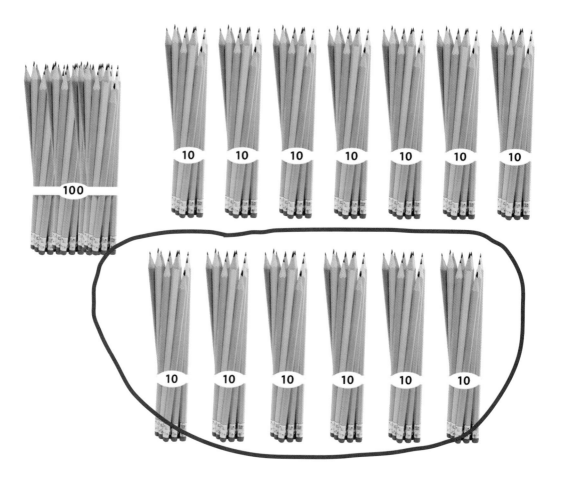

You can regroup 2 hundreds and 3 tens as 1 hundred and 13 tens. Take away 6 tens (the pencils circled in the picture), and that leaves you with 1 hundred and 7 tens, or 170 pencils. So 230 – 60 = 170.

Now let's try another subtraction problem in which you need to regroup 1 hundred as 10 tens.

$$
\begin{array}{r}
556 \\
-372 \\
\hline
\end{array}
\qquad
\begin{array}{r}
55\,6 \\
-37\,2 \\
\hline
4
\end{array}
\qquad
\begin{array}{r}
{}^{4}\,{}^{15} \\
\cancel{5}\cancel{5}6 \\
-3\,7\,2 \\
\hline
8\,4
\end{array}
\qquad
\begin{array}{r}
{}^{4}\,{}^{15} \\
\cancel{5}\cancel{5}6 \\
-3\ 72 \\
\hline
1\ 84
\end{array}
$$

Find the difference.   Subtract the ones.   Subtract the tens.   Subtract the hundreds.

Practice doing many three-digit subtraction problems until you can do them easily. Remember, you can check your subtraction by adding.

Money

Coins and Dollar Bills

Can you name these coins and tell how many cents each is worth?

Here's another coin that you may see sometimes, called a half dollar. It is worth 50 cents.

A half dollar

Here is a picture of a one-dollar bill.

Here is the way you write one dollar, using numbers and the dollar sign:

$1.00

$1.00 is worth the same as 100 pennies.

$1.00 = 100¢

You can write amounts of money using the cents sign or the dollar sign.

cents ¢   dollars $

When you write an amount of money with a dollar sign, the numbers to the right of the little dot (called a decimal point) are cents. For example, $1.50 is 1 dollar and 50 cents. $2.98 is 2 dollars and 98 cents.

You can write amounts less than a dollar with a dollar sign or a cents sign.

$$\$0.89 = 89¢$$

You read $0.89 and 89¢ in the same way—89 cents.

How much does this toy cost?

How would you write 79¢ using a dollar sign instead?

How Many Make Up a Dollar?

Let's learn how many coins of different types it takes to make up a dollar. At the same time, let's see what fraction of a dollar each coin is.

Two half dollars equal one dollar. A half dollar is $\frac{1}{2}$ of a dollar.

Four quarters equal one dollar. A quarter is $\frac{1}{4}$ of a dollar.

Ten dimes equal 1 dollar. A dime is $\frac{1}{10}$ of a dollar.

Quarters and Counting by 25

Henry wants to buy an ice cream at the school cafeteria. It costs 50¢. His mother gives him quarters to pay for the ice cream. How many quarters does she give him?

Mr. Jones buys a newspaper. It costs 25¢. He gives the man a dollar bill. The man gives him quarters for change. How many quarters does he give Mr. Jones?

Remember: 2 quarters make 50¢, and 3 quarters make 75¢, and 4 quarters make $1.00. When you count quarters, you count by 25s. Practice counting by 25s to 200:

25, 50, 75, 100, 125, 150, 175, 200

Counting Money

When you count coins, start with the coins that are worth most. For example, from left to right, how much is this?

| 25¢ | 50¢ | 60¢ | 70¢ | 75¢ | 76¢ | 77¢ |

Those coins add up to 77¢. What is another way of writing 77¢, using the dollar sign?

Now let's count the money on the next page. Count the dollars before you count the coins.

Starting with the dollar bills, you have $2.00. Three quarters make 75¢ more, or $2.75 in all so far. Two dimes make $2.85, $2.95. Now, for the three nickels. The first nickel makes $3.00 even. Then you get $3.05, $3.10. At last, the pennies. You count $3.11, $3.12, $3.13, $3.14. Altogether you have $3.14.

Practice counting money until you can do it quickly without making mistakes.

Adding and Subtracting Money

When you write down amounts of money, you add and subtract the amounts in the same way you add and subtract other numbers. For example:

$$
\begin{array}{r}
1 \\
67¢ \\
+18¢ \\
\hline
85¢
\end{array}
\qquad
\begin{array}{r}
1 \\
\$1.85 \\
+3.64 \\
\hline
\$5.49
\end{array}
\qquad
\begin{array}{r}
6\ 12 \\
\$6.7\cancel{2} \\
-4.2\ 6 \\
\hline
\$2.46
\end{array}
$$

Notice that when you need to regroup in a money problem, you do the same as you would in a regular addition or subtraction problem. In a money problem, don't forget to write the $ or ¢ sign in your answer, and remember to bring down the decimal point, too.

Word Problems

As you practice math, you will do many word problems. The trick is figuring out what the word problem is asking you to do. Is it asking you to add? Or maybe to subtract?

What is this word problem asking you to do? The second-grade classes at Brownsville Elementary collected cans for recycling. Ms. Johnson's class collected 345 cans. Mr. Franklin's class collected 275 cans. How many cans did they collect in all?

This is an addition problem. To solve it,

You write:

345
+275

You add:

11
345
+275
620

You check:

11
275
+345
620

The second-grade classes collected 620 cans in all. Now, try another word problem:

Margaret brings $3.65 to a movie. The movie ticket costs $2.75. After she buys her ticket, how much money does she have left?

This is a subtraction problem. To solve it,

You write:

$3.65
− 2.75

You subtract:

2 16
$3̶.6̶5
− 2.75
$0.90

You check:

1
$0.90
+2.75
$3.65

How would you solve this problem?

At the museum gift shop, Tricia bought a poster for $6.47. Her friend Joanie bought a necklace for $4.29. How much more did Tricia spend than Joanie?

When a word problem asks you "how much more," you need to subtract, like this:

You write:

$ 6.47
− 4.29

You subtract:

317
$6.4̶7̶
− 4.29
$2.18

You check:

1
$2.18
+4.29
$6.47

So Tricia spent $2.18 more than Joanie.

Measurement

Measuring Length

When you measure how long something is, you measure its length. Length can be measured in different units, such as inches and feet.

This paper clip is 1 inch long. The leaf is 3 inches long.

Practice measuring different objects in inches using tools such as a ruler or a tape measure.

Most things are not exactly a certain number of inches long. Sometimes you just need to estimate how long something is. For example, rounding to the nearest inch, this pencil is about 6 inches long.

At home or school, you may have a ruler that is 12 inches long. 12 inches is also called a foot.

12 inches = 1 foot

Practice measuring in feet and inches. You might start by measuring how tall you or your friends are.

In the United States, we use inches and feet to measure length, but in many other countries, such as Japan, France, and Germany, they use a unit called centimeters. This toy car is 3 centimeters long.

A centimeter is shorter than an inch; it's not quite half an inch. If you have a foot ruler at home or school, check to see if it also has centimeters on one edge, then practice measuring some objects in centimeters.

When we write measurements, we often use abbreviations, like this:

inches = in.   feet = ft.   centimeters = cm

Measuring Weight

When you measure how heavy something is, you are measuring weight. We often measure weight in pounds. The abbreviation for pounds is a little strange, but you can remember it: *lb*. The book in this picture weighs 1 pound.

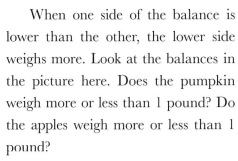

One tool for weighing is called a balance. When the balance is level, both sides weigh the same.

When one side of the balance is lower than the other, the lower side weighs more. Look at the balances in the picture here. Does the pumpkin weigh more or less than 1 pound? Do the apples weigh more or less than 1 pound?

Look again at the pictures of the balances with the book, pumpkin, and apples. Then list the objects in order from the lightest to the heaviest. (From lightest to heaviest, they are the apples, the book, the pumpkin.)

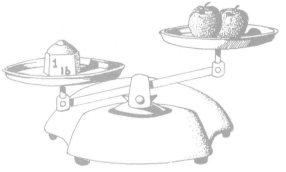

Measuring Time

The Calendar

We measure time in many units, including years, months, and days. You probably know what year it is now, and what month, too. Can you tell me what they are? Sometimes you need to check a calendar to tell what day of the month it is. Practice reading a calendar to identify what day it is, as well as what day of the week it is.

On this calendar, the day marked in color is October 15th. What day of the week is it? You know it's a Tuesday, because the number is in the column under Tuesday. One day on this calendar is circled. Can you say the date that's circled, and what day of the week it is? (The circled day is October 25th, and it's a Friday.)

OCTOBER

SUNDAY	MONDAY	TUESDAY	WEDNESDAY	THURSDAY	FRIDAY	SATURDAY
		1	2	3	4	5
6	7	8	9	10	11	12
13	14	15	16	17	18	19
20	21	22	23	24	(25)	26
27	28	29	30	31		

You may have noticed that to say what day of the month it is, we use the ordinal numbers, which are numbers that tell what number something is in an order. Instead of saying, "Today is October five," we usually say, "Today is October fifth" or "Today is the fifth of October."

The months of the year have anywhere from 28 to 31 days. Practice saying and writing the ordinal numbers up to 31st. Here they are, written as numbers and words.

1st	first	17th	seventeenth
2nd	second	18th	eighteenth
3rd	third	19th	nineteenth
4th	fourth	20th	twentieth
5th	fifth	21st	twenty-first
6th	sixth	22nd	twenty-second
7th	seventh	23rd	twenty-third
8th	eighth	24th	twenty-fourth
9th	ninth	25th	twenty-fifth
10th	tenth	26th	twenty-sixth
11th	eleventh	27th	twenty-seventh
12th	twelfth	28th	twenty-eighth
13th	thirteenth	29th	twenty-ninth
14th	fourteenth	30th	thirtieth
15th	fifteenth	31st	thirty-first
16th	sixteenth		

Can you say and write the names of the twelve months of the year in order, starting with January? Do you know how many days are in each month? (Do you remember the poem that begins, "Thirty days hath September"?) Can you write the names of the days of the week?

Clock Time to 5 Minutes

How many minutes does it take for the minute hand to go once all the way around the clock? Another way of asking that question is, how many minutes are in an hour?

There are 60 minutes in 1 hour. One hour (or 60 minutes) is how long it takes for the hour hand on a clock to move from one number to the next number. (The hour hand is the short hand.)

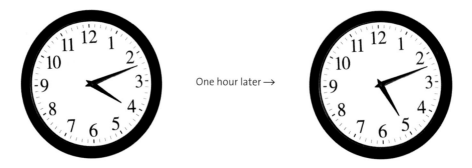

One hour later →

On a clock, when the minute hand (the long hand) moves from one number to the next, 5 minutes have passed. For example, the time on this clock is 5 minutes after 4.

When the minute hand moves from the 1 to the 2, that means 5 more minutes have gone by. What time will it be then? It will be 10 minutes after 4.

You can count by fives for each new number on a clock face to find out how many minutes have passed since the hour. For example, look at this clock. The minute hand is on the 7. How many minutes have passed since the hour? Count by fives, starting with the 1 on the clock (touch each number on the clock face as you count aloud): 5, 10, 15, 20, 25, 30, 35.

So when the minute hand is on the 7, 35 minutes have passed since the hour. Now look at the hour hand (the short hand). It is between the 5 and the 6. That means the time is after 5 o'clock, but it is not yet 6 o'clock. It is 35 minutes after 5.

There's a short way to write 35 minutes after 5. It looks like this:

5:35

The two little dots are called a colon. The number to the left of the colon tells the hour. The number to the right of the colon tells the minutes. The quick way to say this time is just to say "five thirty-five" instead of "35 minutes after 5."

Half and Quarter Hours

There are 30 minutes in half an hour. On this clock, the time is 30 minutes after 2, which is also called "half past two."

When it is more than 30 minutes past the hour, we sometimes count backward around the clock and say how many minutes it is until the next hour. For example, look at this clock.

What time does the clock show? If you count by fives, you'll see that it's 40 minutes past 5. You can also say that it's 20 minutes before 6. This makes sense because, as you know, there are 60 minutes in an hour, and 20 + 40 = 60. For 20 minutes before 6, people also say "it's 20 to 6" or "20 of 6" or "20 till 6"—they all mean the same thing.

Can you tell the time on this clock by saying how many minutes before the hour it is?

When you learned about fractions, you learned that another word for one fourth is "one quarter." Fifteen minutes is one quarter of an hour. That is why when the time is 4:15, people often say that it's "quarter past 4" or "quarter after 4."

4:15, or quarter past 4

Do you remember what A.M. and P.M. mean? The A.M. hours are the hours before noon. The A.M. hours are between 12 midnight and 12 noon. Time after noon is called P.M. The P.M. hours are between 12 noon and 12 midnight.

So in each day there are 12 A.M. hours and 12 P.M. hours, which makes how many hours in a whole day? (12 + 12 = 24 hours in a day.)

Do you go to bed closer to 9:00 A.M. or 9:00 P.M.? Does the sun rise closer to 6:00 A.M. or 6:00 P.M.?

Here's a clock that shows 2:45, which is the same as 15 minutes before 3. You can also say 2:45 as "quarter to 3."

So "quarter past" means 15 minutes after the hour, and "quarter to" means 15 minutes before the hour.

2:45, or quarter to 3

How Much Time Has Passed?

Sometimes we need to know how much time has passed. Billy leaves his house at 2:00 to go play with Carlos. Billy's mother tells him to be back home in 3 hours. So when does Billy have to be back home? At 5:00. From 2:00 to 5:00 is 3 hours.

At 10:00 in the morning Andrea's stomach starts to growl. She knows that she must wait until 1:00 before lunch will be served in the school cafeteria. How many hours will pass before she can eat lunch? To figure this out, you can't just subtract 10 from 1. Instead, first you think that from 10:00 to 12:00 is 2 hours, and from 12:00 to 1:00 is 1 hour. So 1 + 2 = 3 hours before Andrea can eat lunch. Poor Andrea!

When Christie left school

Christie gets out of school at 2:45. She goes to the library and then to soccer practice. When she gets home, it is 5:45 P.M. How many hours have passed since she got out of school? To help you figure that out, look at these two clocks.

You can see that the minutes are the same on both clocks. When the minutes are the same, the change in hours tells you how much time has gone by. Three hours passed between the time Christie left school and the time she got home.

When she got home

Geometry

Plane Figures

You know the names of these flat shapes:

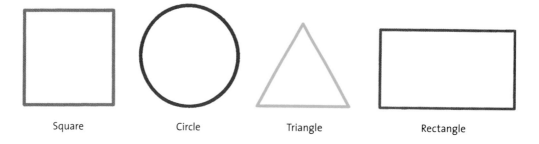

Square   Circle   Triangle   Rectangle

Flat shapes are also called *plane* shapes or plane figures. Can you answer these questions about some plane shapes?

- All rectangles and squares have the same number of sides—how many? (Four sides.) What's the difference between a rectangle and a square? (All the sides of a square are the same length.)
- How many sides does a triangle have? (Three.)
- What do we call figures that are the same size and shape? (We call them congruent.)

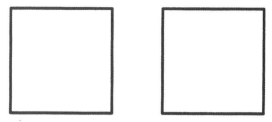

These two squares have the same shape and the same size. They are congruent.

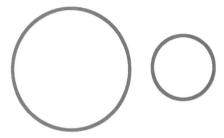

These two circles have the same shape but not the same size. They are not congruent.

interior

exterior

The inside of a shape is called the interior. The outside of a shape is called the exterior.

You can measure the length of the sides of a square or rectangle. When you add up the length of all four sides of a square or rectangle, you get the perimeter, which is the distance around a plane figure. Look at this rectangle.

Add the length of each side: 1 + 1 + 2 + 2 = 6 inches. The perimeter is 6 inches.

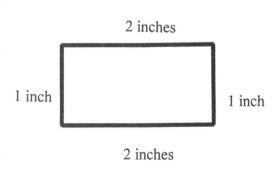

2 inches

1 inch

1 inch

2 inches

Solid Figures

Trace this pattern on a piece of paper. Cut it out, then fold at the dotted lines and tape the edges.

You have made a solid figure called a cube.

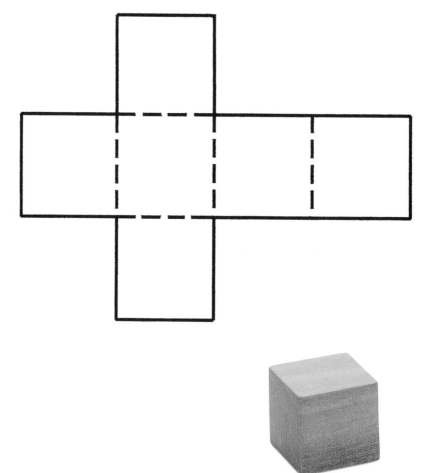

cube

Do you see how each side of the cube is a square?

Here are the names and shapes of other solid figures:

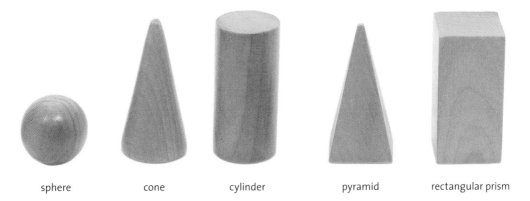

sphere   cone   cylinder   pyramid   rectangular prism

What plane shape is each side of the pyramid? (A triangle.)

Imagine that you were to cut a sphere-shaped object, like an orange, down the middle. What plane shape would you see? (A circle.)

Here are some things you might see at home or school. Each one has the shape of a solid figure. Can you name the solid figure for each object?

Points, Lines, and Segments

In math, a point is an exact spot. You show a point with a dot like this: •

You can give the point a name, to make sure that we can tell it from other points. In math, to name a point we use the letters of the alphabet. So we'll call it point A, like this:

•

A

If you put two points on a paper and then connect them, you will have a line. Here is a line going through point A and point B:

A   B

A line is straight and goes on forever. The arrows show that the line continues forever in both directions. The line goes through points A and B, so we call it line AB or line BA. A short way to write line AB is $\overleftrightarrow{AB}$.

A segment is a part of something. A line segment is a part of a line. A line goes on forever, but a line segment has two endpoints.

C   D

We name a line segment by its endpoints. What do you think this line segment is called?

It can be called either line segment CD or line segment DC. A short way to write line segment DC is $\overline{DC}$.

A line that goes across is called a *horizontal* line. A line that goes up and down is called a *vertical* line.

Have you ever seen the piece of equipment used by a gymnast called the parallel bars? If lines run side by side and never meet, they are called *parallel* lines. Here are some pairs of parallel lines:

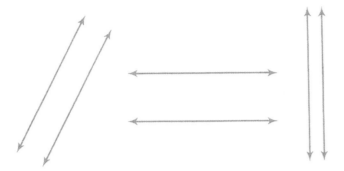

Parallel lines always stay the same distance apart. They never cross each other. When two lines meet and form an exact L (either a forward or backward L), then those lines are called *perpendicular*. Here are two pairs of perpendicular lines:

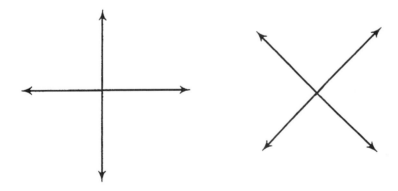

These two lines meet but are not perpendicular:

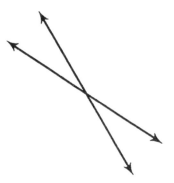

You can find perpendicular lines in any square or rectangle. Use your finger to trace the perpendicular lines in these figures:

Lines of Symmetry

Take a piece of blank paper and fold it exactly in half so the two parts match. Now open the paper. Do you see the line down the middle, formed by the crease where you folded the paper? That is called a line of symmetry. A line of symmetry divides a shape into two parts that match.

A line of symmetry

If a shape can be divided into two parts that match, we say it is symmetric. These two figures are symmetric:

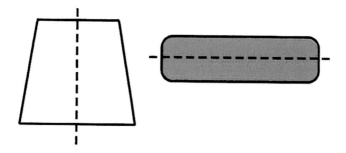

These two figures are not symmetric.

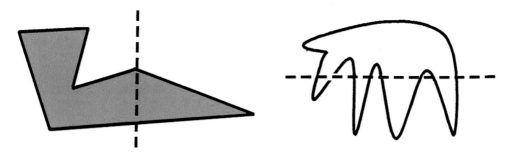

Multiplication

What Is Multiplication?

Multiplication is a quick way of adding the same number over and over again. Here's an example. There are five groups of two turtles. How many are there in all?

You could add 2 five times: $2 + 2 + 2 + 2 + 2 = 10$.

You could also say that 5 twos = 10. You can write that as a multiplication problem:

$5 \times 2 = 10$

We read that as "five times two equals ten." The sign × means "times," and it shows that you are multiplying. You can also write that problem as

$$\begin{array}{r} 5 \\ \times\ 2 \\ \hline 10 \end{array}$$

The numbers in a multiplication problem have special names. The numbers that are being multiplied are called factors. The answer is called the product. In $4 \times 3 = 12$, 4 and 3 are factors, and 12 is the product.

$$4 \qquad \times \qquad 3 \qquad = \qquad 12$$

factor   factor   product

What are the factors and what is the product in this multiplication problem?

$5 \times 2 = 10$

Practicing Multiplication

When you are learning to multiply, it can help to practice with things you can count, such as pennies, dried beans, or buttons.

For example, to figure out 6×4, you can make 6 groups of 4, like this:

Count how many you have altogether. You should get 24. So $6 \times 4 = 24$.

You can also practice by turning a multiplication problem into an addition problem. For example, what is 4×2? You can change that to $2 + 2 + 2 + 2$, which equals 8. So $4 \times 2 = 8$.

What is 5×3? You can change that to $3 + 3 + 3 + 3 + 3$, which equals 15. So $5 \times 3 = 15$.

Adding 3 over and over again is the same thing as counting by threes: 3, 6, 9, 12, 15. When you count by threes, you get the products of multiplying by 3, like this:

$1 \times 3 = 3$
$2 \times 3 = 6$
$3 \times 3 = 9$
$4 \times 3 = 12$
$5 \times 3 = 15$

Practice counting by twos, threes, fours, and fives. This will help you learn your multiplication tables for 2, 3, 4, and 5.

Two as a factor	Three as a factor	Four as a factor	Five as a factor
$2 \times 0 = 0$	$3 \times 0 = 0$	$4 \times 0 = 0$	$5 \times 0 = 0$
$2 \times 1 = 2$	$3 \times 1 = 3$	$4 \times 1 = 4$	$5 \times 1 = 5$
$2 \times 2 = 4$	$3 \times 2 = 6$	$4 \times 2 = 8$	$5 \times 2 = 10$
$2 \times 3 = 6$	$3 \times 3 = 9$	$4 \times 3 = 12$	$5 \times 3 = 15$
$2 \times 4 = 8$	$3 \times 4 = 12$	$4 \times 4 = 16$	$5 \times 4 = 20$
$2 \times 5 = 10$	$3 \times 5 = 15$	$4 \times 5 = 20$	$5 \times 5 = 25$
$2 \times 6 = 12$	$3 \times 6 = 18$	$4 \times 6 = 24$	$5 \times 6 = 30$
$2 \times 7 = 14$	$3 \times 7 = 21$	$4 \times 7 = 28$	$5 \times 7 = 35$
$2 \times 8 = 16$	$3 \times 8 = 24$	$4 \times 8 = 32$	$5 \times 8 = 40$
$2 \times 9 = 18$	$3 \times 9 = 27$	$4 \times 9 = 36$	$5 \times 9 = 45$

Practice the multiplication tables for 2, 3, 4, and 5 often. In third grade you will learn the rest of the multiplication tables.

Multiplying by 10

Here are 5 groups of beans, with 10 beans in each group:

How many beans are there in all? To find the answer, you could add 10 five times. Or you could count by tens. Try it. Put your finger on each group of beans as you count by tens: 10, 20, 30, 40, 50. There are 50 beans in all.

So 5 groups of 10 equals 50. You can also say that as a multiplication problem:

$$5 \times 10 = 50$$

In the picture above, cover one group of beans with your hand. Now, how many beans are in four groups of 10? You could add 10 four times, or count by tens: 10, 20, 30, 40. The quick way is to multiply.

$$10 \times 4 = 40$$

So four groups of 10 equals 40. $4 \times 10 = 40$, and, as you learned earlier, $5 \times 10 = 50$. Do you see a pattern here? Can you figure out how many are in two groups of ten? How many are in three groups of 10?

You are learning to multiply by 10. See if you can give the products for these problems that ask you to multiply by 10. (Later, practice these problems until you know the answers quickly.)

$$\begin{array}{cccccccccc} 10 & 10 & 10 & 10 & 10 & 10 & 10 & 10 & 10 & 10 \\ \times 1 & \times 2 & \times 3 & \times 4 & \times 5 & \times 6 & \times 7 & \times 8 & \times 9 & \times 10 \end{array}$$

Three Rules for Multiplication

Rule 1. *No matter what order you multiply numbers in, the product is always the same.* For example, look at the groups of crayons in the picture. Three groups of 2 equal the same as two groups of 3.

3 x 2 = 6

2 x 3 = 6

Rule 2. *When you multiply a number by 1, the product is always that number.*

$1 \times 7 = 7$ $5 \times 1 = 5$ $6 \times 1 = 6$ $75 \times 1 = 75$

Rule 3. *When you multiply a number by 0, the product is always 0.*

$0 \times 9 = 0$ $6 \times 0 = 0$ $0 \times 3 = 0$ $89 \times 0 = 0$

Word Problems and Missing Factors

You will need to use multiplication to solve some word problems, like this one: Nine children went to the store. Each child bought 2 pencils. How many pencils did they buy in all?

You could add 2 nine times, but it's easier to multiply: $9 \times 2 = 18$. They bought 18 pencils in all.

Lisa has four boxes. In each box she can fit five bottles of orange juice. How many bottles of orange juice does she have in all if she fills the boxes?

Lisa has the same number of bottles of orange juice in each box. So you could add 5 four times, but it's much quicker to multiply. You write: $4 \times 5 = 20$. Lisa has 20 bottles of orange juice.

Here's another word problem. The librarian asked Robert to help her move books to some new shelves across the room. Robert can carry five books at a time. He makes six trips across the room. How many books does he carry in all?

Robert carries the same number of books each time. So you multiply: 5 × 6 = 30. Robert carried 30 books in all.

Here's a different kind of problem. It gives you the product but asks you to figure out one of the factors.

Mrs. Johnson wants to buy cupcakes for her class. There are 16 children in the class. The cupcakes come in packages of four. How many packages does she need to buy?

You can put that in the form of a multiplication problem: 4 × __ = 16. Four times what equals 16? If you know your multiplication tables well, then you know the answer is 4 because 4 × 4 = 16. So Mrs. Johnson needs to buy four packages of cupcakes.

You can practice your multiplication facts by solving problems with missing factors, like these:

$$3 \times \underline{} = 18$$
$$5 \times \underline{} = 35$$
$$4 \times \underline{} = 28$$
$$2 \times \underline{} = 14$$
$$3 \times \underline{} = 30$$

Another way to solve multiplication problems with missing factors is to use division—which you will learn about in third grade.

VI
Science

Introduction

Children gain knowledge about the world around them in part from observation and experience. To understand magnetism, insect life cycles, or human body systems, children need opportunities to observe and experiment. *Benchmarks for Science Literacy* (a 2013 report from the American Association for the Advancement of Science) notes: "For students in the early grades, the emphasis should overwhelmingly be on gaining experience with natural and social phenomena and on enjoying science."

While experience counts for much, knowledge building is also important, for it helps bring order to a child's curiosity and coherence to a child's scientific knowledge. Only when topics are presented systematically and clearly can children make steady and secure progress in their scientific learning. The child's development of scientific knowledge and understanding is in some ways a very disorderly and complex process, different for each child. But a systematic approach to the exploration of science, one that combines experience with knowledge building, can help provide essential foundation for deeper understanding at a later time. It can also provide the kind of knowledge that one is not likely to gain from observation alone. Consider, for example, how people long ago believed that the earth stood still while the sun orbited around it, a misconception that "direct experience" presented as fact.

In this section we introduce second graders to a variety of topics consistent with the early study of science in countries that have had outstanding results in teaching science at the elementary level. Along the way we suggest some resources to take you beyond these pages. Reading this section and other recommended books will be important, but always remember that your child needs imaginative help from adults providing opportunities for observation and hands-on experience of the natural world.

Life Cycles

Have you ever heard the question "Which comes first, the chicken or the egg?" Think about it. How would you answer? You need a chicken to lay the egg. So the chicken comes first. But you need an egg to hatch the chicken. So the egg comes first. Around and around—there is really not one answer to the question, is there? It is a cycle, like a wheel or a circle, something that goes around and around and around, without a beginning or an end.

We can think of many different cycles in nature. All living things, plants and animals, are born, grow, and eventually die. To keep life going, living things reproduce, which means they have babies or make more young, just like themselves. It is a cycle.

The life cycle of a chicken

The life cycle of a butterfly

Parents and their babies

Let's go back to thinking about chickens. Imagine a farmyard with lots of chickens. One of the chickens lays an egg, and out of the egg hatches a little baby chick. The chick grows up to be a hen. The hen mates with a rooster, then soon the hen reproduces by laying an egg. Out of the egg hatches a chick, a baby chicken. Even if the rooster and the mother hen die, that chick grows up and becomes a hen or a rooster. The cycle continues.

A baby chicken grows inside an egg.

Cycles of Life: Frogs and Flowers

Animals and plants both go through stages in their life cycle including birth, growth, reproduction, and death.

First let's look at the life cycle of a frog.

Imagine a little pond. At the edge of the pond you see something floating on the greenish-brown water. It's a bunch of frog eggs. They look like little balls of almost-clear jelly, all clumped together.

If you look closely, you see a dark speck inside each little ball. Over time, the speck grows and begins to take shape. When it hatches, it has a broad face and a swishy little tail. It's a baby frog, called a tadpole. It lives in water and swims around in the pond. It doesn't look that much like a frog . . . yet.

As the tadpole grows, two little legs begin to sprout from the back of its body. Soon, two more little legs begin to grow in front. At the same time, the tadpole's tail gets smaller and its body gets bigger. It starts to look like a frog.

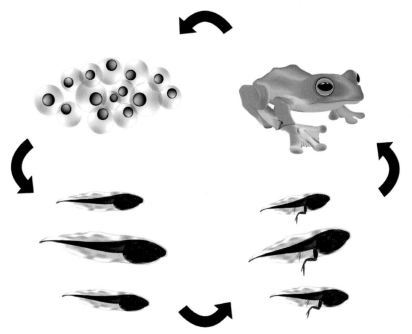

The life cycle of a frog

When its legs are big and strong and its tail has disappeared altogether, the frog hops out of the water. It can still swim, but mostly it lives on the land now. When the frog gets old enough, it is ready to reproduce, or have babies.

The female frog lays eggs. Remember those little jelly balls in the pond? She lays a lot—about one thousand eggs at a time—but not all of them hatch into tadpoles because many other creatures in the pond, such as fish or snakes, like to eat frog eggs.

The female frog lays the eggs, and the male frog fertilizes them, and then the fertilized eggs float in the water, little tadpoles growing inside. The life cycle of the frog keeps on going.

Plants also go through life cycles of birth, growth, reproduction, and death. When you plant a seed in the ground, with the right combination of rain and sunshine, the seed sprouts and a plant starts growing. Roots grow down and leaves grow up. The plant grows bigger, until it is mature. A mature plant may have flowers and seeds, like in the sunflower.

Flowers help the plant reproduce. The male part of the flower makes pollen. Then the wind blows, or maybe a bee lands on the flower and carries the male pollen to the female part of the flower. Now the flower has been pollinated, and it keeps growing until it makes seeds. Those seeds fall onto the ground to sprout, starting the cycle of plant life all over again.

Seeds develop in the middle of the sunflower.

On the flower above, the pistil and stamen, the male and female parts of the plant, are the long tendrils sticking out from the center.

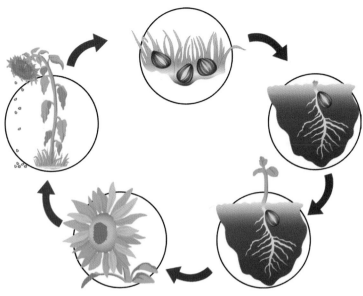

The life cycle of a plant

The Cycle of the Seasons

For many living things, the life cycle follows the cycle of the year's four seasons: spring, summer, fall, and winter.

For example, a sunflower seed sprouts from the ground in the spring. The plant grows tall and makes flowers in the summer. In the fall, once the plant is fully grown, the seeds ripen and fall to the ground. In the winter, the plant dies.

Some of the seeds that fell to the ground will start the sunflower's cycle all over. The very next spring, seeds will sprout and new plants will begin to grow.

Spring, summer, fall, winter: it's another cycle of nature. The four seasons happen over and over again from year to year. Let's look at how the lives of some plants and animals in one typical region of North America change with the different seasons.

> **What About You?**
> Has your child ever planted a seed to watch it sprout and grow? Does she remember what the seed needs to sprout?

Spring

After the cold winter, nature seems to wake up and come alive. In spring, as the earth grows warmer, the seeds of plants begin to sprout. A sunflower seed sends roots down into the warm soil, while a little green seedling pushes up through the dirt to become a new sunflower plant. Maple and oak trees send sap up from their roots to their branches to help new leaves sprout and grow. Sap is a sugary liquid that carries nutrients inside trees. You can eat the sap of some trees—that's where maple syrup comes from!

In spring, many animals wake up from a long winter nap. Squirrels scurry about, and young bears born during the winter join their mothers to search for food. Birds that flew south during the winter to stay warm now return and build nests to lay their eggs. Insect eggs that lay quietly all winter now begin to hatch. From some, out come tiny grasshoppers that feed on the just-budding leaves of the plants.

Talk and Think

Depending on where you live, the changing seasons will look and feel different. These descriptions fit much of North America, but you may live in an area where there are other signs of the season. As you read, stop to talk about how the seasons change in your own environment.

Summer

In summer, when the weather is warm and there's plenty of sunshine, many plants and animals grow larger. The little sunflower's seedling grows into a mature, adult plant and begins to make seeds. Fruits (such as apples) and vegetables (such as pumpkins) grow bigger and begin to ripen. Trees add inches to their branches.

Baby animals that were born in the spring grow bigger and stronger during the summer. Tadpoles grow into adult frogs. Young insects like grasshoppers become adults. The baby birds that hatched out of their eggs in the spring grow up, learn to fly, and look for their own food.

Fall

In the fall (or autumn), many plants become mature, which means fully grown. On an apple tree, the apples grow heavy on the branches, and if you don't pick them, they fall to the ground. Acorns fall from the oak trees. From a vine on the ground, a pumpkin grows big and turns orange all over. In the fields, stalks of wheat turn brown and bend over, weighed down by plump heads of grain. On

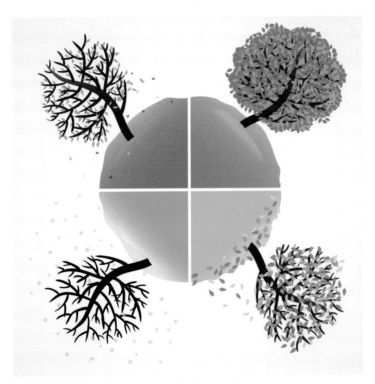

Each year, the cycle continues around and around.

many trees, the leaves turn from green to red, gold, yellow, and brown, and then fall to the ground.

As the weather gets cooler, many animals prepare for the coming changes. Squirrels scurry about gathering nuts and storing them for the cold months ahead. Bears eat as much as they can to build up extra fat, and they look for a den to protect them from the cold. Some birds, like the Canada goose and the robin, fly far away, or *migrate*, before the winter. They fly south to warmer weather, and they will fly back north when spring comes returns. In the oceans, big whales also migrate to warmer waters. Some gray whales swim for thousands of miles to find warmer water.

Winter

In winter, the world of living things grows more quiet and still. Many small green plants have shriveled up and died, leaving their seeds in the ground. The seeds will sit quietly through the winter; they will be ready to sprout when warm weather arrives again. Trees that have dropped their leaves may look dead, but they're alive. They're just *dormant*, not actively growing but, in a way, sleeping through the winter.

Some animals sleep through the winter, or **hibernate**. For example, chipmunks sleep in their holes through most of the winter. They don't eat, but they are able to stay warm because their bodies use up all the fat they built up by eating during summer and fall. Frogs hibernate, too. They burrow into the cold mud at the bottom of a pond and wait for spring to come again.

Did you know? Bears also hibernate in the winter.

Birds that migrated south in the fall spend the winter resting and eating. They need to build up their strength for the long trip back north in the spring. Then, as surely as the earth moves along in its orbit around the sun, spring comes again. The weather warms up, sap rises, seeds sprout, animals awaken from hibernation, and the cycle of life on earth begins again.

The Water Cycle

There are cycles of life among plants and animals. There are cycles of the seasons. Now let's talk about another cycle in nature called the water cycle.

We can find water in the three different states of matter: as a solid, a liquid, or a gas. The water you drink is a liquid. Frozen water—an ice cube—is a solid. When a pot of water boils on the stove, the steam rising from it is a gas. Another name for it is water vapor. You can't see or touch it, but there is always water vapor in the air around you.

Did you know? Steam is made up of very tiny drops of liquid water that are held up in the air. When water is a gas, you cannot see the water vapor!

No matter whether it is solid, liquid, or gas—ice, water, or water vapor—it's always water. That's an important idea to remember as we talk about the water cycle in nature.

Evaporation

Think of some places on the earth where you can find water. Did you think of rivers, lakes, and, most of all, oceans? There is lots of water on this planet; in fact, water covers almost two thirds of the surface of the earth!

You can do this evaporation experiment with a glass of water.

The water in rivers, lakes, and oceans is liquid, but every day some of this liquid turns to gas. Every day, as the sun shines down, some of the water *evaporates:* that means it turns into water vapor and mixes with the air. Do you see the word "vapor" inside that big green word "evaporation" at the top of this page?

Here's a question to think about: where do you think most of the water vapor in the air comes from? Hint: Where is most of the water on the earth? That's right, the oceans.

There's water vapor in the air around you right now! Try this: Put a few inches of water in a glass. With a piece of tape or a washable marker, mark where the water comes up to. Then put the glass where it won't be disturbed. Every day come back and check how much water is in the glass. What has happened to the water? Every day the glass holds a little less water. The water has evaporated. It has turned into water vapor and become part of the air around you. Maybe you're breathing it in right now!

At different times, there are different amounts of water vapor in the air. When we talk about the amount of water vapor in the air, we talk about humidity. A day with a lot of moisture in the air has high **humidity**. A day with very little water in the air has low humidity. On a hot, humid summer day, have you ever heard someone complain, "It's not the heat, it's the humidity"? That means that what makes us feel sticky and uncomfortable on such a day isn't so much the high temperature but instead the high amount of water vapor in the air.

New Word

"Humidity" is moisture in the air. Some days, when there is a lot of moisture in the air—days with high humidity—the air feels heavier when you are outside, and you tend to feel sticky. That's the water vapor in the air touching your skin!

Going Up, Going Down

When it rains hard, puddles of water form on the ground. When it stops raining and the sun starts to shine, what happens to the puddles? Slowly they get smaller, and then they go away. Where does the puddle water go? Some of it evaporates. It turns to water vapor and goes up into the air, just as steam rises from a pot of water that you heat on the stove. Sometimes, when the light and temperature are just right, you can even see the water vapor coming off a puddle.

After it rains, what happens to the puddles?

The water that doesn't go up into the air soaks down into the earth. It becomes groundwater, which is the name for water found under the ground. When people drill a well, they are drilling down to find the groundwater. Once they dig deep enough to find this underground water, they can put long pipes into the hole and then pump the water up to use in their homes, schools, or other places.

Condensation and Precipitation

What happens to the water vapor in the air? Some of it mixes with the air near the ground and some of it rises high into the sky, way up where the air is cooler. In this coolness, the water vapor turns back into little droplets of liquid water. When water vapor turns from a gas back into a liquid, we say it *condenses*.

It's hard to see condensation happen, but here is an experiment you can try. Fill a glass with ice and water. Make sure the outside of the glass stays good and dry. Let it sit for a little while, maybe five or ten minutes. Pretty soon you can see and feel water on the outside of the glass. Where did that water come from? Your glass didn't leak. The water came from the air. The ice water made the glass colder than the air around it, which made the air around the glass cool. Then the water vapor in the air condensed—it turned back into liquid—on the outside of your glass.

The same thing happens high in the sky. When water vapor condenses into droplets of liquid, it forms clouds. Even though they may look like cotton candy, clouds are made of billions of water droplets (or sometimes, if the air is very cold, billions of tiny ice particles). In the clouds, the water droplets bump against each other, but instead of saying "excuse me" and getting out of each other's way, they join and turn into bigger drops.

When the drops get heavy enough, they fall from the clouds—it's raining! Or, if it's cold enough, instead of rain, snow will fall. Snow is water frozen into tiny crystals that fall as snowflakes.

This picture shows three different types of clouds. On the left are wispy, feathery cirrus [SIHR-us] clouds. They form high in the sky and are made of tiny ice crystals. In the middle are big, puffy cumulus [KYOOM-yuh-lus] clouds. They are usually signs of fair weather. On the right are stratus clouds, which look like flat gray sheets. When a dark layer of stratus clouds covers the sky, it often means rain is on the way.

Talk and Think
With your child, take a look at your local forecast. Is there a chance of precipitation? What kind? Is it warm or cold outside?

Rain and snow are both forms of *precipitation*, which means that the water vapor is condensing and falling from the sky. Weather reporters on television or the radio sometimes say, "There's a chance of precipitation." That means there's a chance that water, in some form, is going to fall from the sky. It could be snow, rain, hail, or sleet. They are all forms of precipitation.

Putting It All Together: The Water Cycle

Every day, all the time, the water on the earth is going up and down, evaporating and condensing. Liquid water evaporates and turns into a gas up in the air. Then it condenses into liquid or solid forms and falls back to earth as rain, snow, or ice—refilling rivers, lakes, and oceans. We can draw all these movements of water as a cycle. This is called the water cycle.

The water cycle

Every day, water evaporates from the earth, especially from the oceans. As it rises into the sky, the water vapor condenses into little droplets that form clouds. When the droplets get big enough, then the water falls back to the earth as some form of precipitation. It fills rivers, lakes, and oceans, and some of it soaks into the earth's groundwater. From the rivers, lakes, and oceans, water evaporates and rises into the sky, and—well, you know what happens next. That's the never-ending water cycle: on and on it goes, over and over.

The Human Body

There are many things you learn about in science that you can't see for yourself. You can't see your stomach. You can't see your bones. Those are all inside your body.

There are also things that are too small for our eyes to see, but we still know they exist. Why? We know because people have seen them by using special tools, like magnifying glasses. Have you ever looked through a magnifying glass? You look through the *lens*, or the special glass, and things are magnified, or made to look bigger.

If you have a magnifying glass, look at the back of your hand through it. The hairs look thicker and your skin looks like it has little hills and valleys. Now imagine that you have a super-powerful magnifying glass, and you use it to look at just one hair on your body. It makes the hair look almost like a telephone pole sticking up out of the ground. And when you look even closer, you see that the hair is made up of many, many little pieces.

These are blood cells as seen under a microscope.

Many scientists and doctors use a super-powerful magnifying glass to study the human body. It's called a microscope. Microscopes can be made of glass lenses, just like a magnifying glass. Other microscopes are made differently, but they all do the same thing. They make tiny things look bigger, so we can see and study them.

Anton van Leeuwenhoek

Anton van Leeuwenhoek, the man who looked through lenses

One of the first people to explore the world of tiny things through magnifying lenses was a man named Anton van Leeuwenhoek [LAY-wun-hook]. He was born in Holland in 1632. Leeuwenhoek made his living as a merchant, buying and selling cloth. He was a curious and inventive man. He made his own magnifying lenses out of pieces of glass and looked through them just to see what he could find.

One day Leeuwenhoek tried something new. He brought a bottle of water from a nearby lake. The water in that lake always looked sort of dirty, and he wanted to look at that dirt more closely.

He put a drop of lake water under the magnifying lens and looked with wonder at what he saw. There, inside the drop of water, was a bunch of tiny, squirming, squiggly shapes—living creatures in the water, too tiny to see with your eyes but clear enough through his microscope.

Then Leeuwenhoek scraped some brown stain from his teeth. (People didn't do a very good job brushing their teeth back then.) He put what he scraped from his teeth under the magnifying lens, and what do you think he saw? More tiny, squirmy, squiggly shapes! There were tiny creatures living inside his own mouth!

Now, some people might be grossed out by what Leeuwenhoek saw, but he was a true scientist. He was fascinated, and he wanted to learn more. He called the little creatures that he saw under the lens *animalcules*, which was his word for "little tiny animals." Today we call them **microorganisms,** a word that means "tiny living things."

> ### Make a Connection
> Help your child find Holland on a world map or globe, explaining that it is a country in Europe that is also called the Netherlands today. People who come from Holland, or the Netherlands, are called Dutch people.

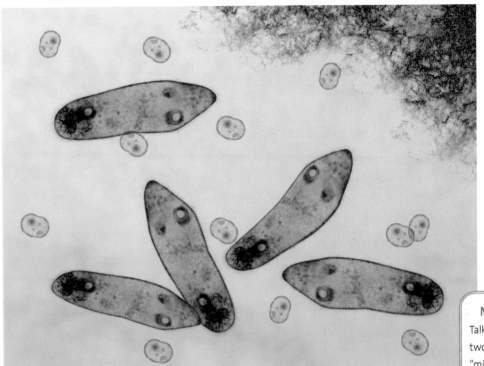

These are microorganisms, like those observed by Anton van Leeuwenhoek in a drop of water.

New Word
Talk about the two words "microorganism" and "microscope" with your child. "Micro" means small, and an organism is a living thing, so a microorganism is a small living thing. The same prefix, "micro," attached to the word "scope," meaning something you look through, makes the word "microscope," which is something you look through to see small things.

Leeuwenhoek built more and more **microscopes**—more than two hundred of them. He also collected all sorts of interesting things to look at through his microscopes: blood, meat, ants, fleas, leaves, flowers. Many people, scientists and others, heard about the amazing things that could be seen through Leeuwenhoek's lenses. Even the queen of England and the czar of Russia came to see.

Leeuwenhoek had two very important new ideas: the idea that there are tiny living things everywhere, and the idea that we can make lenses that magnify those things and help us see them. His work and ideas were very important to other scientists in his time and afterward.

The Microscope

by Maxine Kumin

Anton Leeuwenhoek was Dutch.
He sold pincushions, cloth, and such.
The waiting townsfolk fumed and fussed,
as Anton's dry goods gathered dust.
He worked, instead of tending store,
at grinding special lenses for
a microscope.

Some of the things he looked at were:
mosquitoes' wings, the hairs of sheep, the legs of lice,
the skin of people, dogs, and mice;
ox eyes, spiders' spinning gear,
fishes' scales, a little smear
of his own blood,
and best of all,
the unknown, busy, very small
bugs that swim and bump and hop
inside a simple water drop.

Impossible! most Dutchmen said.
This Anton's crazy in the head.
He says he's seen a horsefly's brain.
We ought to ship him off to Spain.
He says the water that we drink
is full of bugs. He's mad, we think!

They called him domkop, which means dope.

That's how we got the microscope.

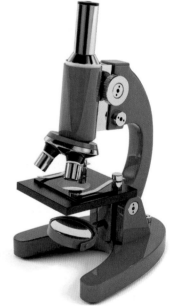

A microscope

Cells and Tissues, Organs and Systems

Thanks to Anton van Leeuwenhoek and other smart people hundreds of years ago, we know that all living things are made up of cells, even if we can't see the cells by looking with just our eyes. *Cells* are the building blocks of all plants and animals. Every living thing—a flower petal, a maple leaf, a blade of grass, a worm, your body—is made up of cells.

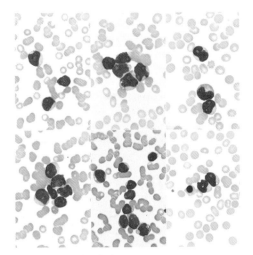

These are blood cells from a person.

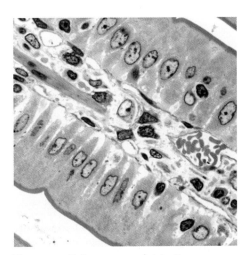

These are cells from a person's intestines.

Cells can grow and change, just as you do. Cells can grow into different shapes, depending on what part of a living thing they make up and what job they perform. In your body, there are many different kinds of cells. Your brain cells are very different from your stomach cells, and both of those are different from your skin cells or your bone cells.

A lot of cells of the same kind join together to form a *tissue*. No, this isn't the kind of tissue you blow your nose in! This kind of tissue is a group of the same kinds of cells that work together. These different tissues work together to form *organs*. Some of the most important organs in your body are your brain, your heart, and your lungs.

Some tissues and organs in your body work together like the members of a team. The parts that work together are called a system. For example, your mouth, teeth, tongue, stomach, and intestines all work together to help you chew and digest your food. They're all important players on the team called the digestive system.

You have already learned about some of the most important systems in your body: the skeletal system, the muscular system, the circulatory system, the nervous system, and the digestive system. There is always more to learn! Let's learn more about the digestive system.

What Happens to the Food You Eat?

Have you heard the saying "An apple a day keeps the doctor away"? By eating apples and other healthy foods, you stay strong and healthy. How does that happen?

To get what it needs from an apple, your body needs to digest the apple. *Digesting* means breaking food down into little pieces—so little you can't see them with just your eyes—so that your body can take those pieces and use them for energy and for building its own cells, tissues, and organs.

You take a bite of apple and you chew it up and swallow it, right? You know how to eat. But have you ever thought about what is happening when you are eating?

The digestive process begins even before you take a bite. Pretend you're holding a big, juicy apple.

Your eyes, your nose, and your fingertips send signals to your brain, and your brain sends a message to your mouth and stomach: "Get ready, food is coming!"

When you take a bite of the apple, your tongue tastes the sweetness and tells your brain, "Mmm, here's something good and sweet." Then your brain sends an order to the parts of your mouth called the salivary [SAL-ih-VEH-ry] glands: "Get to work!"

The salivary glands start making a watery liquid called saliva. Maybe you call it spit. Believe it or not, it's really important. The saliva in your mouth helps make the food you eat wet and soft, so you can swallow it. It has chemicals that help you digest your food.

Your teeth are important players on the digestive team as well. They cut, munch, and crunch the food into smaller and smaller pieces. Your front eight teeth, four on the top and four on the bottom, are called your *incisors*. To "incise" means to "cut," and these teeth cut into your food as you bite it.

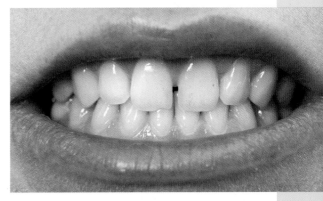

Right next to your incisors are four pointy teeth called *canines* [KAY-nines]. They tear the food into pieces.

After your incisors and canines bite and tear the apple, your tongue pushes the pieces of food to the teeth in the back of your mouth, which have flat tops for grinding the food into pieces small and soft enough to swallow.

Gulp!—you swallow. Down that bite goes. But where does it go? It goes down your throat, through a tube called the esophagus [eh-SOFF-ah-gus], and into your stomach.

Do you know where your stomach is? Put your right hand to the left of the center of your body. Feel your ribs. Your stomach is inside there. Your stomach is made of muscles that mix and stir up the food you have eaten, adding special juices that help digest the food. In your stomach, the bite of apple you took no longer looks anything like an apple. All the grinding, stirring, and added juices make it look like soup. The food has been broken down into pieces almost small enough that your body can use.

From your stomach the soupy stuff moves to the intestines. Your intestines are a long, coiled-up tube that winds around inside your belly. If you could take

> ### New Word
> By the way, "canine" is an old Latin word for dog! Why do you think your sharp, pointy teeth are called canines? Can you point to the canine teeth in the image?

your intestines out of your body and stretch them out straight, they would be longer than you are tall! First your food goes through a narrow part of the wound-up tube, called the small intestine, and then it moves into a wider part, called the large intestine.

In your small intestine, the soupy food is mixed with more liquids and chemicals that break down the food into bits too small to see. The good particles, called the *nutrients* [NOO-tree-ents], get absorbed into your blood. Your heart pumps your blood through your body, and your blood carries the nutrients to all your cells. That's how the good nutrients in food get to every part of your body.

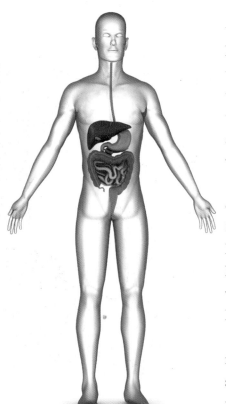

As your blood passes through your body, it goes through another organ in the digestive system, the liver. Take your left hand and feel the lowest rib on the right side of your body. Your liver is just under there, and it's about as big as your shoe. One job of the liver is to clean your blood. It also sends liquids and chemicals to the small intestine to help digest what you eat.

Not every bit of the food you eat becomes nutrients sent through the blood to the cells in your body. Some is left over and cannot be digested. That stuff keeps moving through your intestines. Whatever is left after your body takes what it needs becomes solid waste and comes out of your body through the little hole called the anus when you go to the bathroom.

You go to the bathroom to get rid of liquid waste from inside your body, too. How does this happen? It starts with your blood. The blood in your body has two jobs. It carries good, healthy nutrients through your body, and it carries waste away from the cells of your body. As your blood flows, it goes through two organs called the kidneys. The kidneys clean your blood, and what is left over is watery liquid waste called urine. The kidneys send the urine into a little bag in your body called the bladder. When you go to the bathroom, you push the urine out of the bladder through a little tube called the urethra [yoo-REE-thra].

Daniel Hale Williams, a Brave Doctor

When people decide to become doctors and nurses, they need to be ready to be brave. Sometimes they will see things that are scary, because they have to help people when they are very sick or badly hurt. Sometimes they will have to make quick decisions and do things that are very hard. Here is a story about a man whose decision to be a doctor showed that he was brave in many different ways.

His name was Daniel Hale Williams. He was born in 1856, at a time when many African Americans were enslaved. Daniel's parents had never been slaves, though. His father ran a barbershop. Black men came to his shop for haircuts and shaves. Daniel enjoyed his time in his father's barbershop, listening to the men talk about the day when the slaves would be free and when black and white people would live equally together.

Daniel Hale Williams

Daniel wanted to go to school. He read every book he could get his hands on. He saved his money and paid his way through private school, and he still wanted to learn more. He convinced the town doctor to hire him as an assistant, and he read many books about the human body and medicine. He attended Chicago Medical College and became an M.D.—a doctor of medicine.

In the entire city of Chicago, there were only four African American doctors.

But there were many African American people living there, and Daniel Hale Williams worried that they needed better health care. As far as Dr. Williams was concerned, it did not matter whether his patients were black or white, but for some people then, it still mattered. He got upset when he saw that black patients did not receive the same medical care as whites and when he saw that smart young African American women could not study to be nurses just because of the color of their skin. To right these wrongs, Dr. Williams built Provident Hospital in Chicago in 1891, the first hospital in the United States where black and white nurses and doctors cared for black and white patients all together.

Founding Provident Hospital took courage, but so did many of the operations Dr. Williams performed there. One man came in bleeding badly. He had been stabbed in the chest with a knife, and it looked as if he might die. In those days, there was no such thing as an X-ray machine that let doctors see what was happening inside a patient's body. But Dr. Williams knew he had to find out what was happening inside the man's chest. Yes, it was dangerous, but unless he took the chance, the man might die. The most important thing, Dr. Williams understood, was to *sterilize* all his medical equipment—to clean all his surgical tools extra carefully, so no germs or bacteria touched the body of the patient.

Six other doctors assisted as Dr. Williams carefully cut open the man's chest so that he could see what the knife had done. Williams found that it had cut into the man's heart. He carefully stitched the tissue around the man's heart and then stitched the man's chest back together. "SEWED UP HIS HEART!" read newspaper headlines around the world. Daniel Hale Williams had successfully performed the world's first heart surgery.

Daniel Hale Williams was brave enough to try new surgical techniques, and careful enough that he succeeded in them. He never stopped believing that everyone deserved quality health care and education.

A Healthy Plate of Food

Your digestive system breaks down food so that your body can use the nutrients to keep you strong and healthy, but for your digestive system to do a good job, you need to give it good food to work with.

To be sure you're eating enough of the food that's good for you, take a look at the picture of a plate of food on the next page. People who study good food, called nutritionists, made this picture to help us remember what foods are best for us to eat. If the food you eat in one day could fit like this on your plate, you are making good choices. You are eating a *balanced diet*.

This plate is divided into four sections. Each section is a different color. There is also a glass by the side of the plate. These five areas stand for the five kinds of foods our bodies need to grow and stay healthy and strong.

Red stands for fruits. Let's name some fruits: apples, oranges, bananas, plums, cherries, peaches.

Green stands for vegetables. Let's name some vegetables: broccoli, green peas, green beans, lettuce, carrots.

The red and green section together cover half of the plate. That means that half of the food you eat every day should be fruits and vegetables. Do you eat that way?

Let's look at the other half of the plate.

Orange stands for grains. Here are the names of some grains: wheat, oats, rice, corn. Another word for grains is "cereal," which tells you one of the ways you eat grains. Bread is made of grains that have been ground up into flour, mixed with other ingredients, and baked in the oven. It's best to eat whole grains, which means you are getting the most nutrients in that grain. Whole-wheat bread and brown rice give you whole grains. White bread and white rice don't.

Purple stands for protein. Protein comes from meat or fish, nuts or dried beans like pinto beans or kidney beans. Chicken, eggs, and tofu give your body protein as well.

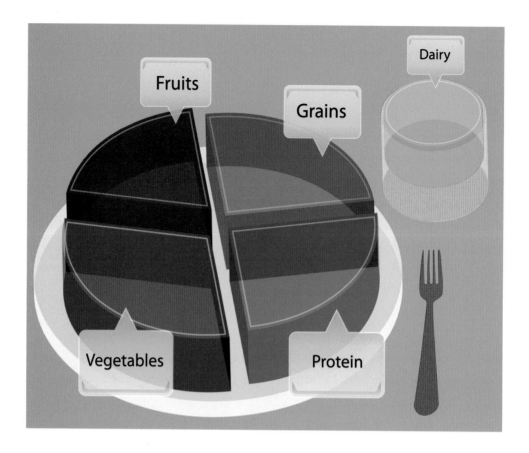

The blue glass stands for dairy products. Do you know what comes from a dairy? Milk—and all the things we make from milk, such as cheese and yogurt.

If you filled your plate to match this picture, what kind of food would you eat the most of? You'd eat lots of vegetables and plenty of grains. Not just one bowl of cereal in the morning, but good whole-wheat bread at lunch and good brown rice at dinner, for example.

Can you think of foods that you like to eat that aren't on this plate or in the glass? Where is the candy? Where is the soda? They aren't there because nutritionists tell us we would be stronger and healthier if we didn't eat so much sugar.

Soda, candy, cookies, cakes, and ice cream—these foods are all made with a lot of sugar. Your body does need sugar for energy, but good foods, such as vegetables, fruit, grains, and protein, already give your body the sugar it needs. You'll stay strong and grow healthy if you try not to eat too many sweets or drink too much soda.

Vitamins and Minerals

By eating lots of fruits and vegetables, your body gets the vitamins and minerals it needs. The broccoli and carrots this family is eating both have lots of vitamin A, for example. Among other things, vitamin A helps you to see.

Here's something else you can't see that science has shown us to be important—the vitamins and minerals that your body gets by eating healthy food, like fruit and vegetables. If you don't eat enough vitamins and minerals, you could get very sick.

There are a lot of different vitamins. They are named with letters of the alphabet.

- Vitamin A helps the skin, tissues, and eyes grow strong. You can get plenty of vitamin A by eating carrots, sweet potatoes, and other orange vegetables, and by drinking milk.
- There are eight different vitamins called B vitamins. In many ways, they help keep your body healthy. Most come in meat, and many come in vegetables as well.

- Vitamin C helps cells grow strong, and it helps your body fight against disease. You get plenty of vitamin C by eating oranges, tomatoes, and broccoli.
- Vitamin D is important because it helps your teeth and bones grow strong. Your skin makes some vitamin D from sunshine, and you also get vitamin D from tuna, egg yolks, and milk.

Your body needs a lot of different minerals, too. Some important minerals your body needs are calcium, magnesium, potassium, and iron. Yes, iron—the same iron that we use to make the steel that goes into cars and bicycles. But don't worry. You don't have to bite down on a piece of metal. Your body only needs tiny amounts of all these minerals, and they come naturally in the good food you eat.

Florence Nightingale

Florence Nightingale, a brave nurse

Florence Nightingale was born in 1820 into a wealthy English family. Her family expected her to marry a rich gentleman and raise a wealthy English family when she grew up.

But Florence had different plans. She loved to use her mind. She was fascinated by mathematics. When a young man asked her to marry him, she thought long and hard, and then said no. She believed that she was destined to lead another sort of life.

When she told her family that she wanted to work as a nurse in a hospital, they were shocked. In those days, hospitals were dirty, dreary places. Wealthy people paid doctors to come to their homes to take care of anyone who got sick. Only people with little money stayed in hospitals, since most hospitals were so filthy that diseases spread faster there than anywhere else.

But Florence Nightingale understood that hospitals could, and should, be kept clean. She had visited a hospital in Germany where women took excellent care of patients. The place was clean, and people often got well there. Florence Nightingale believed that the hospitals in England could become that *sanitary,* or clean, and she devoted her life to making that happen.

In 1854, England entered into war in Crimea. The English government asked Florence Nightingale and about forty other nurses to travel to the Crimea and run a hospital. The British soldiers in the war really needed help. Many of them were badly wounded and many were very sick. The hospital they had was dirty. People got sick simply by being in the hospital. Wounded soldiers were cold and starving. It was not a place where many would be able to get well.

Talk and Think

Ask your child to think of the ways she stays clean in order to stay healthy. Does she wash her hands before dinner? Take baths? What else?

Florence Nightingale did everything she could to keep the British soldiers from dying. She cleaned their beds and cooked them good food. She worked late into the night, carrying a lamp so she could see. Soldiers called her "the lady with the lamp." She gave them hope as well as medical care. Florence Nightingale became famous around the world for the good work she was doing.

After the war, Florence Nightingale continued to work for better medical care. She wrote many reports with careful facts and figures to show that fewer people would die if hospitals were cleaner. She also helped start a nursing school in London. She spoke out for the poor, saying that they deserved good, clean medical care. She showed everyone how much nurses can contribute to helping people stay alive and healthy.

Thanks to Florence Nightingale's work and ideas, nursing is a respected profession. Many people in hospitals get better today, thanks to the special care that nurses give them.

Insects Everywhere!

Insects! They are everywhere! How many insects can you name?

There's the fly that buzzes around the room. There's the bee that sips nectar from the flowers to make into honey. There are butterflies with beautiful, colorful wings. And don't forget the mosquito that lands on your skin and leaves you with an itchy bite.

In the United States and Canada alone, there are more than 100,000 different kinds of insects, but that's just the beginning. Around the world, there are almost a million kinds of insects.

Most insects are smaller than one of your fingernails. Some are so small you have to use a microscope to see them, but some can grow as big as your hand. Some are black or gray, and some have many colors. Some crawl. Many fly. With so many kinds of insects, you can find them in all sorts of sizes and colors, but every one of those insects' bodies follows certain important rules. Let's meet some different kinds of insects.

Meet a Fly

Hi there. I'm a fly. I'll bet you have seen lots and lots of flies, haven't you? I'm told that you find us flies rather annoying, so I'm guessing that you've swatted at one of my billions of cousins at least once in your life!

I have a few things I'm proud of that I want you to know about us flies. For example, did you know that I could walk straight up a wall and across the ceiling? I have thousands of tiny hairs on my feet that act like suckers and help me hold on.

I am a housefly, the most common type of fly, but there are many other kinds of flies. Scientists divide all the insects of the world into families. Just like you, an insect shares certain special traits with the other insects in its family. All flies, for instance, have just two wings. Horseflies, deerflies, robber flies, fruit flies, gnats, and mosquitoes all belong to the same insect family that I do.

Some insects with the word "fly" in them don't belong in our family. Dragonflies have four wings, for instance. They are part of another insect family.

Insect Legs and Body Parts

One way to tell if a creature is an insect is to count the legs. All insects have six legs, three on each side. That means worms aren't insects, because they have no legs at all, and spiders aren't insects, because they have eight legs. It means that flies and ladybugs, mosquitoes and butterflies are insects—all of them have six legs.

Another way to tell if a creature is an insect is to count its body parts. Every insect has three parts to its body: the head, the thorax, and the abdomen.

This insect has six legs and two antennae, or feelers. Can you point them out?

An insect head has eyes for seeing and a mouth for eating. It also has antennae, or feelers, for feeling, tasting, and smelling the things around it.

The middle part of an insect's body is called the thorax. *Thorax* is a word that comes from the Greek word for "chest." Many insects have wings attached to the thorax.

The hind part of an insect's body is called the abdomen. *Abdomen* is a word often used for people, too, to refer to the belly. In most insects, the abdomen is the largest of their three body parts.

Meet a Beetle

I'll bet you already know what kind of insect I am. Yes, I'm a ladybug. People love ladybugs. I am part of the biggest insect family on earth: beetles. There are more than 400,000 kinds of beetles around the world. You know some already. For instance, fireflies are beetles.

Maybe I should tell you what makes a beetle a beetle. First of all, because beetles are insects, we have two antennae and six legs. Our bodies are divided into three parts: head, thorax, and abdomen.

We have two pairs of wings, but our front wings are not for flying. They are thick, hard, protective coverings that make it difficult for animals to bite or crush us. Our bodies are usually hard and shiny, as if we are wearing heavy armor that protects us.

The Insect Exoskeleton

Where's your skeleton? It's inside your body. You have skin, and under the skin you have muscle, and that muscle wraps around the bones that hold up your body. You might even say your body is soft on the outside and hard on the inside.

Insects are different. Insect bodies are hard on the outside and soft on the inside. They have *exoskeletons*, which means they have skeletons outside their bodies. While your skeleton is made of hard bones, insect skeletons are made of a material called "chitin" [KITE-un]. The exoskeleton is a hard outer layer, like a knight's suit of armor, that protects their soft insides.

Meet a Cockroach

Hi there. I hear you already met a fly. I am another insect that loves to live in houses and apartments where humans live. I especially like it underneath kitchen sinks and inside kitchen cupboards. My cousins and I often hide during the day, so you may not even notice us, but if you sneak in at night and quickly turn on the light, you might see me, but I'll run and hide as fast as I can!

I am a cockroach, another kind of insect. Do you think I look anything like a fly? Not much, but there are important ways fly and cockroach bodies are built the same. That's why we are both considered insects.

Are They Insects?

Insects are one of the largest groups of animals in the animal kingdom. What distinguishes insects from other members of the animal kingdom? First, to be an insect, you must have six legs—not two, not eight, only six. Second, to be an insect, you must also have three body sections. Do you remember what they are? Finally, to be an insect, you must have an exoskeleton. You can use these three rules (six legs, three body sections, and exoskeleton) to figure out if an animal is an insect or not. Take a look at the examples on the next page to see if you can tell which are insects, which are not insects, and why.

Is this an insect? No, it has many more than six legs. It's not an insect. It's a millipede.

Is this an insect? It seems to have three body parts, but how many legs can you count? Eight! It's not an insect. It's a spider.

Is this an insect? At first you might say no, but this is a caterpillar on its way to becoming a butterfly. Only six of those things it walks on are true legs, and its body does have three sections.

Insect Life Cycles

Just as chickens, frogs, and flowers go through life cycles, so do insects. In fact, the life cycle of insects is so interesting, there is a special word for it. The word is "metamorphosis" [MET-uh-MORE-fuh-sis]. It comes from a Greek word for "changing shape." Let's see why.

A female butterfly lays eggs. They look like tiny beads attached to the bark of a tree or the underside of a leaf. When the eggs hatch, out comes—no, not a butterfly, not yet—a caterpillar. The caterpillar is the *larva* [LAHR-vuh], which is another word for baby insect.

The life cycle of a butterfly

The caterpillar crawls up and down the stalks of plants, finding fresh green leaves to chew on. The caterpillar eats and eats and grows longer and fatter. Finally the caterpillar attaches itself to a leaf or twig and makes a tough, shiny covering, called a cocoon. The caterpillar wraps itself inside the cocoon. Now the larva has become a *pupa* [PYOO-puh].

From the outside, the pupa looks asleep. It looks as if nothing is happening. But inside, the insect is still growing and changing shape. When the pupa finally opens, the adult insect comes out, and it's a butterfly!

When it first comes out, the butterfly is wet and all folded up. Slowly it spreads its wings to dry. Now the butterfly is fully grown, ready to fly from flower to flower to look for food.

That's a lot of changing shapes—a true metamorphosis. This insect goes through four different stages in its life cycle:

egg → larva → pupa → adult

Meet a Praying Mantis

Hello. Let me introduce myself. People tell me I'm one of the most fascinating insects on earth, but you probably won't find me in your home, the way you can find flies and cockroaches. I like it better out-of-doors.

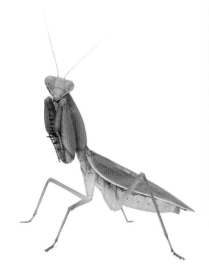

I'm a praying mantis. Do you see where I got my name? I was named for the way I hold my two front legs together in front of me, as though I am praying. I might look like I am praying, but in fact, I'm hunting for my next meal. I eat other insects, and my incredibly fast front legs are designed to reach out and grab my food in the blink of an eye.

A Simpler Kind of Metamorphosis

Different insects go through different kinds of metamorphosis. For some insects, like butterflies and ants, the baby, or larva, doesn't look like the adult. As it grows it goes through a complete change of shape. For other insects, the larva looks like a little adult.

For example, when a baby grasshopper hatches from an egg, it looks like a little tiny grasshopper. It eats and eats, and it grows so big that it outgrows its baby exoskeleton. That splits open and drops off, just like an old coat that doesn't fit anymore.

Out climbs a bigger grasshopper. When this happens, we say the grasshopper has molted, which means that it has shed an old exoskeleton and is developing a new one. A grasshopper molts about five times during its life cycle, growing from a newly hatched larva to an adult.

A praying mantis also sheds its exoskeleton like this. It molts just like a grasshopper!

Meet an Ant

Hello there. I'm one of the most common insects on the planet. I'm pretty sure you have seen insects that look just like me. Do you know what I am? I'm an ant.

There are many different kinds of ants that look a bit different, live in different places, and behave differently, but there's one thing we all share: like honeybees, we are social insects. We live in colonies, and we raise and care for our young together.

We ants make underground tunnels—miles and miles of tunnels, full of little chambers, or rooms, where we work and eat. A colony of ants can be small, with only twelve ants, or huge, with a million ants or more.

An Ant Colony

Ants live and work together in communities called colonies. If you ever find a few ants in your house or at your school, it means there's an ant colony close by.

Sometimes the ants will show you the directions to their colony. Here is an experiment you can try.

When you find ants at home or at school, put a spoonful of syrup near them. You may have to wait an hour, or even a day, but after a while, you will see a parade of ants walking to the syrup and another line of ants walking away, each one carrying a tiny droplet of syrup back to the colony.

How do the ants tell each other where the syrup is? They don't use language like we do, but their bodies communicate with chemicals. When the first ant found the syrup, it got very excited. That excitement made its body lay down a tiny chemical trail to the food. Other ants sensed that chemical signal, and they followed the trail to the syrup.

Ants cooperate in many other ways, too. They build complicated nests. They share the work of taking care of the babies and young ants. When a special ant, called the queen, lays the eggs, other ants called workers dig tunnels and help keep the eggs clean and warm. When the eggs hatch, the worker ants gather food and help feed the larvae [LAHR-vee: plural of "larva"]. In some colonies, other ants, called soldiers, protect the colony against insect enemies.

Worker ants, larvae, and cocoons. The ant cocoons are also known as pupae [PYU-pee].

Meet a Honeybee

Buzzzzz! Buzzzzz! I'll bet you know what kind of insect I am. I am a honeybee, and yes, that's right, I'm the kind of insect that makes honey. Yum!

Some insects like to stay by themselves, but we honeybees are social. Humans are social, too, which means that they live and work together in a group or community. It is the same with us honeybees.

We live together in a hive. We all have special jobs. We depend on one another, solving problems as a team. We gather and share food. We build our homes together. We cooperate to raise our young, and we help protect one another from enemies. To do all this, we even have special ways we communicate with each other. We don't use words, but we do have ways to tell each other where we have been or where there are sweet flowers blooming.

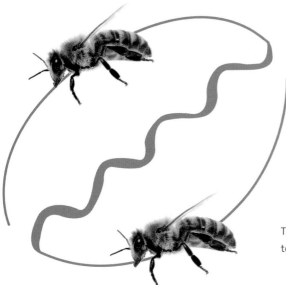

These lines show the pattern of a bee "dancing" to communicate with other bees.

In a Beehive

Have you ever tasted sweet, golden honey? Do you know where honey comes from? From the hives of honeybees! Bees make honey from sweet liquid called nectar that they gather from the insides of flowers. They make the honey to feed their babies, the honeybee larvae.

People work as beekeepers. They wear special clothing so they don't get stung. They build special beehives for the honeybees. They can open the hives and take out some honey for people to eat, but they always leave some honey behind, so the larvae will grow into adult honeybees.

Some people, called beekeepers, raise bees in boxes. Beekeepers collect the honey and beeswax from the hives.

In a honeybee hive, there are three different kinds of bees:

- Queen
- Workers
- Drones

All of these bees have their special jobs dedicated to making baby bees called larvae.

Every hive has only one queen bee. She is female, and she grows bigger than the rest. Her job is to lay all the eggs in the beehive. She is the mother of every bee in the hive. In the spring and summer, she will lay hundreds or even thousands of eggs in a single day!

In any hive, most of the bees are workers. They are female, but they do not lay eggs. They keep busy, taking care of the queen by feeding and cleaning her.

A queen bee surrounded by workers

The worker bees also build the inside of the beehive. Their bodies can make wax, and they shape it into little six-sided compartments where they store the honey. Sometimes when you buy a jar of honey, you get some of the beehive wax as well.

The workers do other work as well. They are babysitters and grocery shoppers, which, in the honeybee world, means they take care of the growing larvae and they fly out to find flowers with sweet nectar out of which they make the honey.

A honeybee hive has many drone bees as well. The drones are male. Their only job is to mate with the queen to help her make more bees. They are the fathers of every bee in the hive.

Meet an Entomologist

Hi there. I'm the last one to introduce myself in this section on insects. But I'm no insect, am I? I have two legs, not six. I don't have any antennae. My skeleton is inside my body. So you might ask: What am I doing here?

I am an *entomologist* [EN-tuh-MOLL-uh-jist]. Studying insects is my job.

I have some good news and some bad news about insects.

First, the bad news: There are some things insects do that cause problems. They can damage the plants we grow for food. Leafcutter ants can strip the leaves from a whole grove of orange trees in one night, and without leaves, the trees can't make oranges. The Colorado potato beetle is another example. They can eat all the leaves in a big potato field, so none of the plants can make potatoes.

There is another way insects can cause problems. Some insects can be dirty. They can spread germs. When flies, ants, and cockroaches walk across our kitchen countertops with the same feet they use to crawl through dirt, they can contaminate our food and make us sick.

That's the bad news. Now for the good news—there's plenty of it! We count on honeybees and other insects to carry pollen from one plant to another. We call them pollinators, and without them, there would be no beautiful flowers or sweet fruit.

We also use products that insects make. Thanks to the honeybees, we have delicious honey. From honeybees we also get beeswax, which is used to make candles and lip balm.

From silk moths, another insect, we get the beautiful cloth called silk. The silk moth lays its eggs on the leaves of mulberry trees. Caterpillars hatch out of the eggs and eat and grow until they are ready to make a cocoon. Just like a spider spinning a web, the caterpillars make thin strands of silk and wrap them around and around to form a cocoon. Then people gather and unwind those strands and weave them into the cloth we call silk.

This is a silkworm with two silk cocoons. Silk cocoons are collected by people to spin silk thread for weaving.

Now you know how important insects are to our world. Think twice before squashing the next bug you see. Look at it closely. Maybe even ask an adult to help you use a book to identify it and learn its name. As someone who works every day studying insects, I promise you—insects are interesting. And they are everywhere, part of this amazing world of nature that we share with them.

Magnetism

Put some paper clips on a table. Bring a magnet near them. What happens? The clips really like that magnet, don't they? One of them might have looked like it jumped off the table in order to stick to the magnet. Or it may cling when the magnet touches it. Lift the magnet, and the paper clip stays stuck. Pull the clip off, and you can feel it still clinging.

What you're feeling is the magnet's force of attraction. It pulls on the paper clip. It's strong enough to pull a paper clip up off the table once the magnet moves close enough. It's strong enough to hold a paper clip and keep it from falling onto the floor. You can't see the magnetic force, but it's there.

What Do Magnets Attract?

Will the magnet attract everything? Let's try to see. For example, will it pull a shoelace, a tissue, or a plastic comb toward it?

No. The magnet attracts the paper clips, but it does not attract a shoelace, a tissue, or a comb. What's the difference? The paper clip is made of steel and has the metal called iron in it. Shoelaces, tissues, and combs do not.

Magnets attract things made of iron. But magnets won't attract copper or aluminum. Bring a magnet close to a copper penny or an aluminum soda can and you'll see. Bring a magnet close to a metal refrigerator door made of steel with iron in it. The magnet sticks to the door because of magnetic attraction.

Many magnets that we use today have been manufactured out of metals containing iron. Some magnets are made by people, but other magnets occur in nature. They can be found in stones in the earth called lodestones. Lodestones are special pieces of iron ore that act just like the magnets we make. Lodestones are the first magnets that people ever knew about, thousands of years ago.

Magnetism is a force all around us. You can't see it, but you can see the way it acts in the world. People use magnetic force every day, whether it's to attach a note to the refrigerator or lift an old wrecked car at a junkyard. Once you start looking, you will see magnets at work all around you.

Magnetic Poles

Here's an experiment you can do. You need two bar magnets to do it.

Put the two bar magnets on a table. Bring an end of one of the magnets toward an end of the other. What happens? Do they pull together or push apart?

Now turn just *one* of the magnets around, and bring the ends together. What happens now? If your magnets pulled together the first time, then this time they will push apart. If your magnets pushed apart the first time, then this time they will pull together.

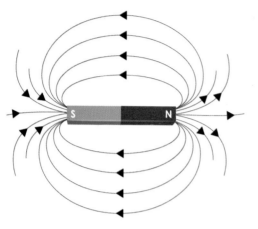

This picture uses lines and arrows to show the invisible magnetic field around a bar magnet.

Why? To find out why, let's look at a picture of a bar magnet. Even though you can't see the forces coming from that magnet, we will use little lines to show them in this picture. The lines show what's called the magnetic field. The magnetic field is present in the space around the magnet where the magnetic force is strong. If you put a paper clip inside the magnetic field, the magnet will attract the clip.

In the picture, can you see where the magnetic force is strongest? It's strongest at the two ends of the magnet where the lines of force all come together. We call those two ends where the magnetic force is strongest the magnetic poles.

Even though the poles of a magnet may look the same, they are different. We need names for these two poles so we can tell them apart. We call one the north pole and the other the south pole.

Why are the poles called north and south? For the answer, try this. Take a bar magnet and tie a string around its middle so it balances when you hold it by the string. Tie the other end of the string so that the magnet can hang and move freely. Watch what it does when you let it go.

The bar magnet will turn around until it settles in one direction. Notice something in the room that one pole (one end of the magnet) is pointing to, for example, a nearby lamp or picture. Put a little sticker on the end pointing

You can try this experiment with a bar magnet.

to the lamp or whatever you've chosen. Then gently twirl the magnet. When it stops again, what happens? The pole with the sticker is pointing in exactly the same direction, isn't it?

If you kept doing this experiment with every bar magnet you could find, every one of them would point to the same direction. That's because your magnets are finding the forces of magnetic attraction in your house and in the world around you.

To understand these ideas better, think of our planet, the Earth, as a great big magnet! The magnetic fields surrounding the Earth are strongest near the North Pole and the South Pole. So one end of your magnet is pointing north and the other is pointing south, and that's why the poles of your magnet are called north and south.

These lines represent the invisible magnetic field of our planet, the Earth.

Ask an adult to help you figure out if the sticker end of your magnet is pointing north or south. Once you know that, you can label one end of your magnet *north* and the other end *south*.

Now that you know that magnets have two different poles, let's go back and think about what happened when you brought the ends of two bar magnets together. Once they pulled toward each other, but once they pushed apart. They were following a rule of magnetic force that says, "Unlike poles attract, and like poles repel."

When the south pole of one magnet comes close to the north pole of another, they attract, or pull on, each other. That's what it means to say "opposites attract."

When the south pole of one magnet comes close to the south pole of another (or north comes close to north), they repel or push away from each other. So now you know what it means to say "Like poles repel."

These small pieces of iron between two south poles of the magnets help to show the two magnetic fields as they push away from each other.

Using a Compass

Magnets help us in many ways. One of the most useful things a magnet can do is tell us what direction we're going—north, south, east, or west. When a magnet is used in this way, we call it a compass.

Compasses help sailors find their way at sea. They help hikers find their way through forests. They can help you find your way.

If you did the experiment of tying a bar magnet to a string, you made a kind of compass. The north pole of your magnet pointed north. No matter where you carried that bar magnet, once you let it swing on the string, the north pole would always point toward north. That is how magnets inside compasses help you find your way.

Can you point to the magnet on this old compass? Which direction would it point if you held this compass in your hand?

Most compasses have a small arrow that always points north. No matter how you hold it, no matter what direction you turn, the compass arrow will always point the same way—north. If you are in the woods and you want to walk north, you hold your compass and walk in the same direction the arrow points.

But what if you want to use the compass to walk east?

First, face in the direction of the needle—north. If you are facing north, what direction is behind you? South. If you are facing north, which way is east? Is it to your right or your left? East is to your right. If you are facing north, which way is west? West is to your left.

Compasses and maps work the same way. The top is north, the bottom is south, the right is east, the left is west.

Simple Machines

Tools can help us build, dig, cut, and lift.

Every day, we depend on tools to get work done and to make work easier. With tools, we build and dig, we lift and cut, we grip and carry.

We have tools to build and dig. Can you name some of them? Hammers help us build. Shovels help us dig.

We have tools to cut and lift. Can you name some of them? Scissors help us cut. So do knives and saws. Ropes and pulleys can help us lift things bigger and heavier than we could lift using just our arms.

We use tools to grip and carry. Can you name some of them? Gloves help us grip. Baskets help us carry. There are a lot of big machines that help us carry, too, like dump trucks and boxcars.

Tools and machines help us do things. When you hear the word "machine," you may think of something like a sewing machine, a washing machine, or a bull-dozer, but there are also things we call simple machines. They make work easier. It's good to know how they do that. Let's learn about some of the simple machines that help people every day.

Levers

You probably have seen people using levers, and you didn't even know it. They are important tools that help us every day.

You use a lever when you pry open the lid of a can of paint. You use a lever when you use the claw of a hammer to pull a nail out of a board.

Levers can help you lift things. Try this. Put a stack of three or four books on a table. Line up the books with the edge of the table. Now slide one end of a ruler under the bottom of the books. Push down on the other end of the ruler. What happens? The ruler acts as a lever and helps you lift the books.

As this girl was taking a walk, she found a big rock. She wanted to see what was under it, but it was much too big and heavy for her to lift. So she found a strong stick and a little rock nearby. She pushed one end of the stick under the big rock. Then she supported the stick on the little rock. Smart! She's using the stick as a lever. When she pushes down, then the big rock moves up. With a lever, she can lift something that she could not lift with just her hands.

The big stick acts as a lever and helps the girl lift the rock.

Wheels

There's something missing in this orange drawing. You'd have a very hard time pulling your friends in this wagon because the wheels are missing!

The wheel is a simple machine that makes work easier. Wheels turn, and they help us move things. If you have a wagon or a toy car or truck, take a look at the center of one of its wheels. You can see that the wheel turns around on something.

A wheel turns around on an *axle*, which is like a stick stuck through the middle of a wheel. Sometimes one axle joins two wheels together.

A gear is a wheel with teeth. The teeth on gears fit together so that one gear can turn another. You can find gears in many machines, such as clocks and bicycles. Gears are important in big machines as well, including cars and boats and airplanes.

Talk and Think

Walk around your home or neighborhood together to find simple machines at work. Kitchen tools, garden tools, heavy construction equipment—there are many kinds of tools and machines that your child already uses. Talk together about each one.

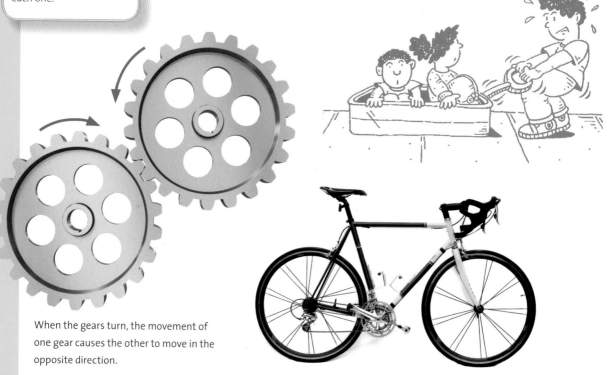

When the gears turn, the movement of one gear causes the other to move in the opposite direction.

The Force of Friction

Imagine that you're riding a bike. You're pedaling hard and the wheels are turning fast. You see a stop sign ahead, so you put on the brakes. The brakes press against the wheels and stop them from turning. That's how you stop your bike.

When the brakes press against the wheels, they cause friction. When two surfaces rub against each other, they cause friction. You can feel friction. Quickly rub the palms of your hands together, back and forth. Keep rubbing, and your hands start feeling hot. This heat is produced by the friction caused when the surfaces of your hands rub against each other.

Sometimes friction can be a good thing, such as when you use your brakes to stop a bike, or when you rub an eraser on paper to take away a mistake, but sometimes you don't want friction. For example, have you ever started riding a bike and heard a squeaking sound? That squeaking can happen when there's too much friction. It can keep wheels from turning smoothly and keep machines from working well.

When you hear the squeak from your bicycle, what do you do? You may put a few drops of oil between the chain and the gears. The oil is slippery and slidy. The oil *lubricates* the surfaces and cuts down the friction between them.

You can feel how lubrication works. First rub your hands together. Now put a few drops of liquid soap or vegetable oil in your hands; then rub them together again. Do you feel how the soap or oil lubricated your hands and cut down the friction between them?

When you put oil on the gears of your bicycle, it cuts down on friction and makes the wheels turn more smoothly.

Elijah McCoy, a Great Inventor

Elijah McCoy

Make a Connection

Talking about steam-powered locomotives gives you an opportunity to review the three states of matter: solid, liquid, and gas. Steam is water in a gaseous state.

Elijah McCoy was a man who thought a lot about friction. When he was a little boy, almost two hundred years ago, railroad trains had just been invented. Back then, locomotives ran by steam power, which means that inside every engine, a big fire heated up a tank of water. Hot steam rose up from the boiling water. The pressure of the steam pushed on iron rods and got gears moving, which made the wheels of the engine turn.

Engines fascinated young Elijah McCoy. His parents saw his interest, and even though they were a big family—Elijah had twelve brothers and sisters!—they saved enough money to send Elijah across the Atlantic Ocean to Scotland, where he studied how steam engines operated. He came back home to the United States knowing a lot about machines and engines.

Elijah McCoy was an African American man. His parents had been slaves many years before. Although he and his family were now free, there were still many people who held the mistaken belief that an African American couldn't possibly know much about engines. They didn't pay attention to the fact that Elijah had studied engineering in Scotland for years. A train company hired him, but they gave him the job of oiling the machinery.

The steam locomotives of those days needed constant oiling. All that hot metal moving together caused a great deal of friction. The engine parts got hot, made noise, and didn't work very well. The trains would have to stop often so that Elijah and others could climb all over the huge locomotives to oil them. It was a dangerous job, and all the stopping slowed down the trains.

Elijah McCoy started thinking there must be a better way to oil locomotives. What if he could build a machine that would squirt oil into the locomotive's moving parts while the train was moving? After two years of building models and doing experiments, he attached the first automatic lubricator onto a big locomotive. It squirted oil in just the right places, and the train could keep moving. All the train engineers and owners thought it was a great invention.

Make a Connection
To learn more about the impact of oil and steam locomotives, check out the History and Geography section.

In only a few years, steam locomotives throughout the United States, Canada, and Europe were using McCoy's automatic lubricators. Often Elijah McCoy himself would install the lubricator and explain to engineers how to use it. As the years passed, when people took a close look at a machine and its parts, they would ask, "Is it the real McCoy?" Other people by then were making automatic lubricators, but they thought Elijah McCoy's was the best.

Elijah McCoy started the McCoy Manufacturing Company and came up with more than fifty new inventions. He made one of the first lawn sprinklers and one of the first folding ironing boards, but he is most famous for the invention that made locomotives run longer, smoother, and more safely: the automatic engine lubricator.

Pulleys

A pulley helps you lift.

Put wheels and ropes together, and you can make another simple machine called a pulley. A pulley does what it says: it pulls. If you've ever pulled on a cord to raise the blinds or open the curtains on a window, then you've used a pulley. When you pull the cord down, the blind goes up. That's because a pulley changes the direction of a pull.

Pulleys work for us every day. Pulleys help people lift heavy things. Tow trucks use pulleys when they lift cars. Cranes use pulleys when they lift huge beams up to build a city's skyscrapers. Elevators use pulleys to lift people up and bring them down.

This crane uses many pulleys to lift large structures, such as pieces of wind turbines and oil rigs, as they are built.

Take a Look
If there is a flagpole at your school, take a close look at it. Does it use pulleys to help you raise and lower the flag?

Inclined Planes

Imagine you're pulling a heavy load in a wagon—maybe your brother or sister, or a pile of rocks you've collected. You come to a curb, and you have to go up the curb. You can see that it's going to be hard to pull your heavily loaded wagon up a curb. How can you make it easier?

Luckily, you see two boards nearby. You lean them from where you are up to the top of the curb. Now your wagon can roll up the boards and over the curb. Those boards made it a lot easier.

When you used those boards, you made a simple machine called an inclined plane. A plane is a flat surface. "Inclined" means "slanted" or "leaning." When you pulled your wagon up the curb, you turned two flat boards into an inclined plane.

People in wheelchairs use inclined planes all the time. They're called ramps. Ramps make it possible for people in wheelchairs to get in and out of buildings, and to roll smoothly on or off a sidewalk. Look for these inclined planes at the buildings in your town.

Wedges

Have you ever used a V-shaped simple machine called a wedge? You can use a wedge to hold something tight. If you slide a wedge under a door, it will hold the door tightly in place.

A wedge can also be used to split things apart. To split a log, you can use a wedge made of metal. As you hammer the wedge in from the top of the log, it splits the wood into two pieces.

If you took a metal wedge and sharpened the edge and put a handle on it, what would you have? You'd have an ax,

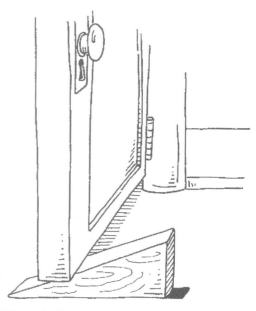

This wedge holds the door in place.

or hatchet. Thousands of years ago, people made hatchets out of sticks and stones. They chipped the edge of a stone to make it as sharp as they could, and they used leather and grass to attach the stone to a stick handle.

Today, we make ax and hatchet blades out of steel. Whether it's an ancient hatchet made of stone or a brand-new ax made of steel, the basic tool is the same: a wedge on a handle.

An ax uses a wedge to help split wood.

Screws

The last simple machine we're going to learn about is the screw. Maybe you have seen a screw before. But have you thought of it as a machine? Think about how many ways the screw helps us get work done.

How do screws work? Take a look at the kind of screw you can use to hold pieces of wood together. Do you see the slanted ridges going up and down it? Those ridges, which are called the threads, are really one long inclined plane.

To see how a screw is an inclined plane, try this. On a sheet of paper, draw a triangle like the one below. Make the bottom about 6 inches long and the short side about 3 inches high. Use a colored pencil or marker to draw the long slanted side.

You have drawn an inclined plane. Now, cut it out and wrap it around a pencil. Do you see how the colored line you drew looks like the threads of a screw? This shows how an inclined plane curves up and up on a screw.

6 inches

3 inches

Little screws hold pieces of wood together. Big screws drill deep down into the ground. When people drill wells, they use big screws called augers. As the big screw goes around and around, it pulls dirt up and makes a hole.

This big machine is an example of an auger that uses a screw to drill holes.

Suggested Resources

Cycles of Life

A Nest Full of Eggs by Priscilla Belz Jenkins (HarperCollins, 1995)

Butterfly (How Does It Grow?) by Jinny Johnson (Smart Apple Media, 2010)

From Seed to Sunflower by Gerald Legg (Franklin Watts, 1998)

The Reason for a Flower by Ruth Heller (Penguin Putnam Books for Young Readers, 1999)

Weather: The Water Cycle and More

Down Comes the Rain (Let's-Read-and-Find-Out-Science) by Franklyn M. Branley (HarperCollins, 1997)

The Snowflake: A Water Cycle Story by Neil Waldman (Milbrook Press, 2003)

Where Do Puddles Go? by Fay Robinson (Children's Press, 1995)

The Human Body

Cells, Tissues, and Organs by Richard Spilsbury (Heinemann Library, 2008)

Where Does Your Food Go? by Wiley Blevins (Scholastic, 2003)

Insects

About Insects by Cathryn Sill and illustrated by John Sill (Peachtree Publishers Ltd., 2003)

Bugs Are Insects by Anne Rockwell and illustrated by Steve Jenkins (HarperCollins, 2001)

Children's Guide to Insects and Spiders by Jinny Johnson (Simon & Schuster, 1996)

Magnetism

All About Magnets by Stephen Krensky (Scholastic, 1993)

Experiments with Magnets by Helen J. Challand (Childrens Press, 1986)

Simple Machines

Simple Machines by Ann Horvatic (Dutton, 1998)

Illustration and Photo Credits

Song (New York: published by William Dressler), Library of Congress, Prints & Photographs Division, LC-DIG-ppmsca-31279

Page 196: The Original "Star-Spangled Banner" (color litho), American School, (nineteenth century)/Private Collection/Peter Newark American Pictures/The Bridgeman Art Library

Page 197: *Gl. Jackson—At the Battle of New Orleans*, Charles Severin (New York: Published by C. Seweryn [sic], c. 1856) Library of Congress, Prints & Photographs Division, LC-USZC4-6221

Page 198: Bob Kirchman

Page 199: Mary Terriberry/Shutterstock

Page 200: *Steamer Clermont, first steamboat*, Library of Congress, Prints & Photographs Division, Detroit Publishing Company Collection, LC-D4-22603

Page 201: Bob Kirchman

Page 202: *Erie Canal, Rochester, N.Y.*, Library of Congress, Prints & Photographs Division, Detroit Publishing Company Collection, LC-D4-17931

Page 203: Lilac Mountain/Shutterstock

Page 205: Neil Webster/Shutterstock

Page 206: Everett Collection/Shutterstock

Page 209: Antonio Abrignani/Shutterstock

Page 210: Bob Kirchman

Page 212: *The overland pony express* (1867, photographed by Savage, Salt Lake City; from a painting by George M. Ottinger), Library of Congress, Prints & Photographs Division, LC-USZ62-127508

Page 214: Bob Kirchman

Page 215: *Andrew Jackson* (c. 1896), Library of Congress, Prints & Photographs Division, LC-USZC4-6466

Page 216: Jacob Wyatt

Page 217: *Se-Quo-Yah*, John T. Bowen, Library of Congress, Prints & Photographs Division, LC-USZC4-2566

Page 218: Antonio Abrignani/Shutterstock

Page 220: *A slave-coffle passing the Capitol*, Library of Congress, Prints & Photographs Division, LC-USZ62-2574

Page 222: Gail McIntosh

Page 224: *Abraham Lincoln, five dollar bill portrait*, Anthony Berger, Library of Congress, Prints & Photographs Division, LC-DIG-ppmsca-19305

Page 225(a): *Gen. Robert E. Lee*, photographed by Brady, N.Y., engraved by J. C. McRae, N.Y., Library of Congress, Prints & Photographs Division, Civil War Photographs, LC-DIG-pga-02157

Page 225(b): *Ulysses S. Grant*, C. Schussele, engraved by William Sartain, Phila., Library of Congress, Prints & Photographs Division, Civil War Photographs, LC-DIG-pga-02645

Page 226(a): *Unidentified soldier in Union uniform with bayoneted musket* (1861–1865), Library of Congress, Prints & Photographs Division, Civil War Photographs, LC-DIG-ppmsca-36882

Page 226(b): *Two unidentified soldiers in Confederate uniforms with rifle and sword*, G. F. Maitland, Library of Congress, Prints & Photographs Division, LC-DIG-ppmsca-35625

Page 227: *Clara Barton*, Library of Congress, Prints & Photographs Division, LC-USZ62-19319

Page 228: *Storming Fort Wagner* (Chicago: Kurz & Allizon Art Publishers, c. 1890), Library of Congress, Prints & Photographs Division, LC-DIG-pga-01949

Page 229: *A Polish emigrant boarding ship—he carries trunk on his shoulders* (1907), Library of Congress, Prints & Photographs Division, LC-USZ62-23711

Page 230: Jakub Krechowicz/Shutterstock

Page 232: *Children of high class, Chinatown, San Francisco* (1896–1906), Arnold Genthe, Library of Congress, Prints & Photographs Division, Arnold Genthe Collection: Negatives and Transparencies, LC-USZ62-136179

Page 233(a): *Awaiting examination, Ellis Island* (ca. 1907–1921), Library of Congress, Prints & Photographs Division, LC-B201-5202-13

Page 233(b): Joshua Haviv/Shutterstock

Page 233(c): *Sweatshop of Mr. Goldstein 30 Suffolk St.* (1908), Lewis Wickes Hine, Library of Congress, Prints & Photographs Division, National Child Labor Committee Collection, LC-DIG-nclc-04455

Page 234: *Irving Berlin* (1948), Library of Congress, Prints & Photographs Division, LC-USZ62-37541

Page 236: Blend Images/Shutterstock

Page 238: *Susan B. Anthony* (ca. 1870), Matthew B. Brady, Library of Congress, Prints & Photographs Division, LC-USZ62-30742

Page 239: *Mrs. Franklin Delano Roosevelt* (c. 1933), Library of Congress, Prints & Photographs Division, LC-USZ62-25812

Page 240: Everett Collection/SuperStock

Page 241: *Daytona Beach, Florida. Bethune-Cookman College. Dr. Mary McLeod Bethune, founder and former president and director of the NYA Negro Relations* (1943), Gordon Parks, Library of Congress, Prints & Photographs Division, FSA/OWI Collection, LC-USW3-014843-C

Page 242: *Jackie Robinson of the Brooklyn Dodgers, posed and ready to swing* (1954), Bob Sandberg, Library of Congress, Prints & Photographs Division, LC-DIG-ppmsc-00048

Page 243: Underwood Photo Archives/SuperStock

Page 246: *Dr. Martin Luther King, Jr. at a St. Augustine, Florida press conference* (1964), Library of Congress, Prints & Photographs Division, LC-USZ62-122982

Page 248: *Cesar Chavez* (1966), Library of Congress, Prints & Photographs Division, LC-USZ62-111017

Page 249: Creative Jen Designs/Shutterstock

Page 251: Bob Kirchman

Page 252: Bob Kirchman

Page 253: Yury Timoschuk/Shutterstock

Page 254: Dr. Morley Read/Shutterstock

Page 259: Gail McIntosh

Page 262: Sara Holdren

Page 263: Pablo Picasso (Spanish, 1881–1973), *Mother and Child*, 1922. Oil on canvas. 39½ x 32¹⁄₁₆ in. (100.3 x 81.4 cm). The Baltimore Museum of Art: The Cone Collection, formed by Dr. Claribel Cone and Miss Etta Cone of Baltimore, Maryland, BMA 1950.279. Photography By: Mitro Hood

Page 265: *The Great Wave of Kanagawa* from the series *"36 Views of Mt. Fuji"* (hand-colored woodblock print), Hokusai, Katsushika (1760–1849)/Private Collection/The Stapleton Collection/The Bridgeman Art Library

Page 266: *The Discobolus (Discus Thrower)*, Roman copy of Greek original (c. 450 BCE), Myron of Athens, Scala/Art Resource, NY

Page 267(a): *Galloping horse with one Hoof Resting on a Swallow, from the tomb of Wu-wei, Kansu, Eastern Han Dynasty* (bronze), Chinese School, (second century)/People's Republic of China/Giraudon/The Bridgeman Art Library

Page 267(b): Rafael Ramirez Lee/Shutterstock

Page 268: *The Oxbow (the Connecticut River near Northampton)* 1836 (oil on canvas), Cole, Thomas (1801–48)/Metropolitan Museum of Art, New York, USA/Photo © Boltin Picture Library/The Bridgeman Art Library

Page 270: *View of Toledo*, c.1597–99 (oil on canvas), Greco, El (Domenico Theotocopuli)/Metropolitan Museum of Art, New York, USA/The Bridgeman Art Library

Page 271: *Black man attacked by a jaguar (Virgin forest with setting sun)*, c. 1910, Henri

Rousseau, Bridgeman-Giraudon/Art Resource, NY

Page 272: *The Starry Night*, June 1889 (oil on canvas), Gogh, Vincent van (1853–90)/Museum of Modern Art, New York, USA/The Bridgeman Art Library

Page 273: *Passenger Pigeon*, from *"Birds of America,"* Audubon, John James/Victoria & Albert Museum, London, UK/The Bridgeman Art Library

Page 274: *Cat and Bird*.1928. Oil and ink on gessoed canvas, mounted on wood, 15 x 21" (38.1 x 53.2 cm). Klee, Paul/Digital Image © The Museum of Modern Art/Licensed by SCALA/Art Resource, NY

Page 275: *The Snail*. 1953. Gouache on cut-and-pasted paper. Matisse, Henri/Tate, London/Art Resource, NY. © 2014 Succession H. Matisse/Artists Rights Society (ARS), New York

Page 276: *I and the Village*, 1911 (oil on canvas), Chagall, Marc (1887–1985)/Museum of Modern Art, New York, USA/The Bridgeman Art Library

Page 277: *The Bird in Space*, 1940 (bronze), Brancusi, Constantin/Musee National d'Art Moderne, Centre Pompidou, Paris, France/Giraudon/The Bridgeman Art Library

Page 278: Sergii Korshun/Shutterstock

Page 279(a): *Exterior of the Parthenon at Athens in the Time of Its Builders* (engraving), English School, (nineteenth century)/Private Collection/© Look and Learn/The Bridgeman Art Library

Page 279(b): Bob Kirchman

Page 280: Shutterstock

Page 281: Kaetana/Shutterstock

Page 282: Petra B. Zaugg/Shutterstock

Page 283: Stuart Monk/Shutterstock

Page 284: Adriano Castelli/Shutterstock

Page 287: Gail McIntosh

Page 290: bikeriderlondon/Shutterstock

Page 291: *Woody Guthrie* (1943), Al Aumuller, Library of Congress, Prints &

Photographs Division, LC-USZ62-113276

Page 292: CRM/Shutterstock

Page 293: *Mozart*, Library of Congress, Prints & Photographs Division, LC-DIG-pga-00129

Page 294: Pavel L Photo and Video/Shutterstock

Page 295(a): *Portrait of Antonio Vivaldi* (oil on canvas), Italian School, (eighteenth century)/Civico Museo Bibliografico Musicale, Bologna, Italy/The Bridgeman Art Library

Page 295(b): *Johann Sebastian Bach* (1685–1750) c.1715 (oil on canvas), Rentsch, Johann Ernst (fl.early eighteenth century)/Stadtische Museum, Erfurt, Germany/The Bridgeman Art Library

Page 296: Art Archive, The/SuperStock

Page 297(a): lalito/Shutterstock

Page 297(b): Verdateo/Shutterstock

Page 297(c): Saskin/Shutterstock

Page 297(d): fotomanX/Shutterstock

Page 298: Alexander Image/Shutterstock

Page 299: Nicholas Sutcliffe/Shutterstock

Page 300(a): Juergen Faelchle/Shutterstock

Page 300(b): Elena Schweitzer/Shutterstock

Page 301(a): Venus Angel/Shutterstock

Page 301(b): Cindy Shebley/Shutterstock

Page 302: pixbox77/Shutterstock

Page 303(a): silvano audisio/Shutterstock

Page 303(b): Linda Bucklin/Shutterstock

Page 304: Linda Bucklin/ Shutterstock

Page 306: SoleilC/Shutterstock

Page 309(a): SoleilC/Shutterstock

Page 309(b): khemawattana/Shutterstock

Page 310: Luis Carlos Torres/Shutterstock

Page 311: Rodgers and Hammerstein

Page 312: 2xSamara.com/Shutterstock

Page 313: Steve Henry

Page 314: Steve Henry

Page 315: Steve Henry

Page 316: Andy Erekson

Page 319: Gail McIntosh

Page 324: Alhovik/Shutterstock

Page 335: Agorohov/Shutterstock

Page 346(a): HomeStudio/Shutterstock
Page 346(b): Julia Ivantsova/Shutterstock
Page 354(a): Svetlana Foote/Shutterstock
Page 354(b): Makushin Alexey/Shutterstock
Page 367: HomeStudio/ Shutterstock
Page 370: Vladimir Wrangel/Shutterstock
Page 371(a): Roman Sigaev/Shutterstock
Page 371(b): Steve Collender/Shutterstock
Page 371(c): aodaodaodaod/Shutterstock
Page 372: graja/Shutterstock, KIM
    NGUYEN/Shutterstock
Page 373(a): Steve Collender/ Shutterstock
Page 373(b): aodaodaodaod/Shutterstock
Page 373(c): Vladimir Wrangel/Shutterstock
Page 373(d): Vladimir Wrangel/ Shutterstock
Page 374(a): michaeljung/Shutterstock
Page 374(b): Vladimir Wrangel/Shutterstock
Page 375(a): aodaodaodaod/Shutterstock
Page 375(b): Vladimir Wrangel/Shutterstock
Page 377: Reece with a C/Shutterstock
Page 378: DVARG/Shutterstock
Page 379(a): Elnur/Shutterstock
Page 379(b): Lightspring/Shutterstock
Page 380(a): karen roach/Shutterstock
Page 380(b): Zdorov Kirill Vladimirovich/
    Shutterstock
Page 380(c): Julia Ivantsova/Shutterstock
Page 380(d): karen roach/Shutterstock
Page 380(e): lkphotographers/Shutterstock
Page 382: Gail McIntosh
Page 384: Yuriy Kulik/Shutterstock
Page 385: Yuriy Kulik/Shutterstock
Page 386: Yuriy Kulik/Shutterstock
Page 387: Yuriy Kulik/Shutterstock
Page 390: hshii/Shutterstock
Page 391(a): hshii/Shutterstock
Page 391(b): ultimathule/Shutterstock
Page 391(c): Sergio Stakhnyk/Shutterstock
Page 391(d): Fotoksa/Shutterstock
Page 391(e): Aaron Amat/Shutterstock
Page 391(f): Gjermund/Shutterstock
Page 391(g): Lana Langlois/Shutterstock
Page 396: Oleg Kozlov/Shutterstock
Page 397: art-Tayga/Shutterstock
Page 399: KIM NGUYEN/Shutterstock
Page 400: Alhovik/Shutterstock

Page 401: Evgeny Karandaev/Shutterstock
Page 402(a): racorn/Shutterstock
Page 402(b): Denisa V/Shutterstock
Page 405: Gail McIntosh
Page 408: Kerstiny/Shutterstock
Page 409(a): jps/Shutterstock
Page 409(b): Jean-Edourard Rozey/
    Shutterstock
Page 409(c): Kjuuurs/Shutterstock
Page 409(d): aaron belford/Shutterstock
Page 410: Shutterstock
Page 411: Matthew Cole/Shutterstock
Page 412(a): Steve Morrison
Page 412(b): Evgeny Karandaev/Shutterstock
Page 413: Shutterstock
Page 415: Shutterstock
Page 416: Shaber/Shutterstock
Page 417(a): Andrey_Kuzmin/Shutterstock
Page 417(b): Irafael/Shutterstock
Page 417(c): Alexander Kondratenko/
    Shutterstock
Page 418: Patrick Foto/Shutterstock
Page 419: Steve Henry
Page 420(a): CRWPitman/Shutterstock
Page 420(b): CRWPitman/Shutterstock
Page 420(c): paul prescott/Shutterstock
Page 421(a): edg/Shutterstock
Page 421(b): Andrey Jitkov/Shutterstock
Page 421(c): S. Borisov/Shutterstock
Page 422: wawritto/Shutterstock
Page 423: Jeron/Shutterstock
Page 425: Nixx Photography/Shutterstock
Page 426: Sashkin/Shutterstock
Page 427(a): Suthep/Shutterstock
Page 427(b): Jose Luis Calvo/Shutterstock
Page 428: Shutterstock
Page 429: Ocskay Bence/Shutterstock
Page 430: 3drenderings/Shutterstock
Page 431: Anonymous, Daniel Hale Williams,
    M.D., L.L.D. *Simm's Bue Book and National
    Negro Business and Professional Directory*; by
    James M. Simms, compiler and
    publisher. 1923. 104 Halftone
    photomechanical print. Science, Industry
    & Business Library, The New York
    Public Library, Astor Lenox, and Tilden

Foundations. Schomburg Center for Research in Black Culture, The New York Public Library.

Page 434: John T Takai/Shutterstock

Page 435: Monkey Business Images/Shutterstock

Page 436: *Florence Nightingale* (ca. 1910), Library of Congress, Prints & Photographs Division, LC-USZ62-5877

Page 438(a): Peter Waters/Shutterstock

Page 438(b): Henrik Larsson/Shutterstock

Page 438(c): IbajaUsap/Shutterstock

Page 438(d): skynetphoto/Shutterstock

Page 439: Kunfy Nomyek/Shutterstock

Page 440: paulrommer/Shutterstock

Page 441(a): Konstantin Sutyagin/Shutterstock

Page 441(b): Cosmin Manci/Shutterstock

Page 442: seeyou/Shutterstock

Page 443(a): Smit/Shutterstock

Page 443(b): Mr. Green/Shutterstock

Page 443(c): Cameramannz/Shutterstock

Page 444: Shutterstock

Page 445: Eric Isselee/Shutterstock

Page 446: Evgeniy Ayupov/Shutterstock

Page 447(a): Henrik Larsson/Shutterstock

Page 447(b): SweetCrisis/Shutterstock

Page 448: Beneda Miroslav/Shutterstock

Page 449(a): Klagyivik Viktor/Shutterstock

Page 449(b): Shutterstock

Page 450: l i g h t p o e t/Shutterstock

Page 451(a): l i g h t p o e t/Shutterstock

Page 451(b): Geoffrey Kuchera/Shutterstock

Page 452: JSseng/Shutterstock

Page 453(a): Ljupco Smokovski/Shutterstock

Page 453(b): Africa Studio/Shutterstock

Page 454: auremar/Shutterstock

Page 455(a): Sofaworld/Shutterstock

Page 455(b): Daniel Gale/Shutterstock

Page 456: takasu/Shutterstock

Page 458(a): snapgalleria/Shutterstock

Page 458(b): Steve Henry

Page 459: Andrea Danti/Shutterstock

Page 460: MilanB/Shutterstock

Page 461: Alex Staroseltsev/Shutterstock

Page 462: Dim Dimich/Shutterstock

Page 463: Bob Kirchman

Page 464(a): cherezoff/Shutterstock

Page 464(b): Steve Henry

Page 464(c): Anthony Hall/Shutterstock

Page 465: gielmichal/Shutterstock

Page 466: *Elijah J. McCoy.* ca. 1927, gelatin silver print. Photographs and Prints Division, Schomburg Center for Research in Black Culture, The New York Public Library, Astor, Lenox and Tilden Foundations.

Page 468: DJ Mattaar/Shutterstock

Page 469: Grandpa/Shutterstock

Page 470(a): Steve Henry

Page 470(b): Wiktor Bubniak/Shutterstock

Page 471(a): Boris Toshev/Shutterstock

Page 471(b): Steve Henry

Page 472: DyziO/Shutterstock

Text Credits and Sources

Poems

. . . .

"Buffalo Dusk," from *Smoke and Steel* by Carl Sandburg. Copyright 1920 by Harcourt Brace & Company.

"Lincoln," by Nancy Byrd Turner, courtesy of the Estate of Beverley T. Thomas.

"The Microscope," by Maxine Kumin © 1968. Reprinted with permission of the Maxine W. Kumin Trust.

"Discovery," from *Crickets and Bullfrogs and Whispers of Thunder* by Harry Behn. Edited by Lee Bennett Hopkins. Copyright 1949, 1953. Copyright © renewed 1956, 1957, 1966, 1968 by Harry Behn. Copyright © renewed 1971, 1981 by Alice Behn Goebel, Pamela Behn Adam, Prescott Behn, and Peter Behn. Used by permission of Marian Reiner.

"Harriet Tubman," from *Honey, I Love and Other Poems* by Eloise Greenfield. Text copyright © 1978 by Eloise Greenfield. Selection reprinted by permission of HarperCollins Publishers.

"Something Told the Wild Geese," from *Poems* by Rachel Field, 1934. Reprinted with the permission of Atheneum Books for Young Readers, an imprint of Simon & Schuster Children's Publishing Division, from *Poems* by Rachel Field. Copyright 1934 Macmillan Publishing Company; copyright renewed © 1962 Arthur S. Pederson. Reprinted by permission of President and Fellows of Harvard College.

"Rudolph Is Tired of the City," from *Bronzeville Boys and Girls* by Gwendolyn Brooks, 1956. Reprinted by consent of Brooks Permissions.

"Smart," from *Where the Sidewalk Ends* by Shel Silverstein. Copyright © 1974, renewed 2002 by Evil Eye Music, Inc. Selection reprinted with permission from the Estate of Shel Silverstein and HarperCollins Children's Books.

"Caterpillars," from *Cricket in a Thicket* by Aileen Fisher. Copyright © 1963, 1991 by Aileen Fisher. Used by permission of Marian Reiner on behalf of the Boulder Public Library Foundation, Inc.

Stories and Myths

. . . .

"The Blind Men and the Elephant," retold by John Godfrey Saxe (1872).

"The Fisherman and His Wife," a retelling created by the Core Knowledge Foundation from multiple sources.

"Talk," from *The Cow-Tail Switch and Other West African Stories*, © 1957 by Harold Courlander. Illustrations © 1957 by George Herzog. Reprinted with permission of Henry Holt and Company, LLC. All Rights Reserved.

"The Emperor's New Clothes," a retelling created by the Core Knowledge Foundation from multiple sources.

"How Iktomi Lost His Eyes," retold by Lindley Shutz.

"The Magic Paintbrush," retold by John Holdren.

A Christmas Carol, adapted from the original Charles Dickens story by Andrea Rowland and John Holdren.

"Before Breakfast," from *Charlotte's Web* by E. B. White. Copyright © 1952 by E. B. White. Text copyright renewed © 1980 by E. B. White. Used by permission of HarperCollins Publishers.

"El Pajaro Cu," retold by Lindley Shutz.

"Beauty and the Beast," a retelling created by the Core Knowledge Foundation from multiple sources.

"The Tongue-Cut Sparrow," adapted from the retelling by Yei Theodara Ozaki in *The Children's Hour: Folk Stories and Fables,* selected by Eva March Tappan (1907).

"The Tiger, the Brahman, and the Jackal," a retelling created by the Core Knowledge Foundation from multiple sources.

"How Wendy Met Peter Pan," adapted from J. M. Barrie's *Peter Pan and Wendy* (1911).

"John Henry," a retelling created by the Core Knowledge Foundation from multiple sources.

"Paul Bunyan," a retelling created by the Core Knowledge Foundation from multiple sources.

"Pecos Bill," a retelling created by the Core Knowledge Foundation from multiple sources.

Myths from Ancient Greece, retold by John Holdren, based on multiple sources, including *Old Greek Stories* retold by James Baldwin (1895), *Thirty More Famous Stories* retold by James Baldwin (1905), *The Children's Own Readers: Book Four* edited by Mary Pennell and A. Cusack (1929), *The Merrill Readers: Third Reader* edited by F. Dyer and M. Brady (n.d.), *Everyday Classics Sixth Reader* edited by F. Baker and A. Thorndike (1921), and *Mythology* by Edith Hamilton (1942).

"Moving West," a story created by the Core Knowledge Foundation.

Lyrics

"Do-Re-Mi," by Richard Rodgers and Oscar Hammerstein II. Copyright © 1959 by Richard Rodgers and Oscar Hammerstein II. Copyright renewed. Williamson Music (ASCAP), an Imagem Company, owner of publication and allied rights throughout the World International. Copyright Secured. All rights reserved. Used by permission.

"This Land Is Your Land," words and music by Woody Guthrie. TRO Copyright © 1956. Copyright © renewed 1958, 1970 by Ludlow Music, Inc., New York, New York. Used by permission.

Index

musical alphabet, 308–9
notation, 305–7
patriotic music, 290–91
resources, 317
scales, 310–11
singing, 289
songs, 312–17
spirituals, 221, 223
myths, 5

N
names, 119–21
Native Americans, 213–19, 229, 237
    reservations, 217–19
    stories, 33–34, 214
    "Trail of Tears," 215–16
    writing systems, 217
"The Night Before Christmas" (Moore), 12–13
Nightingale, Florence, 436–37
North America, 198–203, 210–11, 249–50
    See also American history
North Pole, 134
nouns, 110–12
number lines, 329
numbers
    comparing (greater and less than), 339, 363
    even and odd numbers, 324–25
    hundreds, 357–60
    ones and tens, 341
    place value, 360–63
    skip-counting, 323, 359–60
    three-digit numbers, 360–63
    two-digit numbers, 342–51

words for numbers, 328
    See also mathematics
nutrition, 433–34

O
oceans, 133–34
"Oedipus and the Sphinx," 95
"Old Dan Tucker," 314
Old Ironsides, 191
Olympic Games, 163–64
orchestras, 293–94
Oregon Trail, 210–11
organs, 427
origami, 161–62
The Oxbow (Cole), 268–69

P
Pan, 92
parallel lines, 393
Parks, Rosa, 242–44
Parthenon, 84–85, 278–80
parts of speech. *See* grammar
Pastoral Symphony (Beethoven), 296
past tense verbs, 113–15
patriotic music, 290–91
"Paul Bunyan," 80–83
"Pecos Bill," 72–75
percussion instruments, 300–302
Pericles, 167, 174
periods, 109
perpendicular lines, 393–94
Persian Wars, 169–72
"Peter Pan" (Barrie), 67
philosophy, 174–76
phonics, 3
Picasso, Pablo, 263–64
pioneers, 204–11
pitch, 308–9
Plains Indians, 214, 217–19
plane figures, 388–89

plant life cycles, 411–16
Plato, 174–75
plural nouns, 111–12
poetry, 5, 7–21
points, lines, and segments, 392–94
poles, 134
Pony Express, 211–12
Poseidon, 86, 90
present tense verbs, 113–15
problem solving, xxviii–xxix, xxxii
"Prometheus Brings Fire, Pandora Brings Woe," 93–94
proverbs, 122–27
Pueblo Indians, 213
pulleys, 467–68
punctuation marks, 3, 109–10, 118, 121

Q
Qin Shihuangdi, 153–55
question marks, 110

R
railroads, 204, 212, 232, 466–67
rain forest, 254
Ramayana, 144–46
ramps, 469
read-alouds, 5
reading, 3–4
    comprehension, xxxii
    resources, 4
    standardized test scores, xxvii
    See also literature
religions, 132
    Buddhism, 146–49
    Confucianism, 151–53
    festivals and celebrations, 145–46
    Hinduism, 141–46

religions (*cont.*)

    religious freedom, 229–30

    sacred books, 144–45

Revolutionary War, 182–83

rhythm, 306–7

Rig Veda, 144

Robinson, Jackie, 241–42

Rodin, Auguste, 267–68

Roman gods, 90

Roosevelt, Eleanor, 238–40

Roosevelt, Franklin D., 238, 241

rounding, 352–53

Rousseau, Henri, 271

"Rudolph Is Tired of the City" (Brooks), 15

S

Saint-Saëns, Camille, 299

sayings, 122–27

scales, 310–11

science, 407–73

    doctors and nurses, 431–32, 436–37

    human body, 423–37

    insects, 438–55

    inventions, 466–67

    life cycles, 408–12

    magnetism, 456–61

    microscopes, 423–26

    resources, 473

    seasons, 413–16

    simple machines and tools, 462–72

    water cycle, 417–22

screws, 471–72

sculpture, 266–68, 277

seasons, 413–16

sentences, 108–10

Sequoyah, 217

shapes

    balls, 282

    plane figures, 388–89

    solid figures, 390–91

Siddhartha Guatama, 146–48

singular nouns, 111–12

skills, xxviii–xxx, xxxii

skip-counting, 323, 359–60

slavery, 220–23

    Emancipation Proclamation, 227–28

    Underground Railroad, 222–23

"Smart" (Silverstein), 16

The Snail (Matisse), 274–75

social studies, 131

Socrates, 174

solid figures, 390–91

"Something Told the Wild Geese" (Field), 14

songs, 312–17

South America, 252–54

South pole, 134

Sparta (Greece), 165–66, 168

spelling, 3

spirituals, 221, 223

standardized test scores, xxvii

The Starry Night (van Gogh), 272

"The Star-Spangled Banner" (Key), 192–95, 290

Statue of Liberty, 231, 233

steamboats, 200

stories, 5–6, 22–71

    American tall tales, 72–83, 316–17

    Ancient Greek myths, 84–107

stringed instruments, 298–99

subtraction, 329–39

    checking differences, 336–37

    facts to 12, 331

facts from 13 to 18, 332

fact families, 337–39

halving, 334–35

money, 376

three-digit numbers, 366–69

two-digit numbers, 345–51

in your head, 349–51

"Swift-Footed Atalanta," 101–2

"Swing Low, Sweet Chariot," 221

symmetry, 279–80, 394–95

symphonies, 293

synonyms, 117

T

"The Tale of Rama and Sita," 144–45

tallies, 326

telling time, 384–87

Thebes, 165–66

"There Was an Old Lady Whose Nose" (Lear), 19

"There Was an Old Man with a Beard" (Lear), 18

"Theseus and the Minotaur," 96–97

The Thinker (Rodin), 267–68

"This Land Is Your Land" (Guthrie), 291

Thoreau, Henry David, 204

three-digit numbers, 360–69

"The Tiger, the Brahman, and the Jackal," 63–66, 147

time concepts

    A.M. and P.M., 386

    chronological sense, 131–32

About the Editors

E. D. HIRSCH, Jr., is the founder and chairman of the Core Knowledge Foundation and professor emeritus of education and humanities at the University of Virginia. He is the author of several acclaimed books on education issues including the bestseller *Cultural Literacy*. With his subsequent books *The Schools We Need and Why We Don't Have Them*, *The Knowledge Deficit*, and *The Making of Americans*, Dr. Hirsch solidified his reputation as one of the most influential education reformers of our time. He and his wife, Polly, live in Charlottesville, Virginia, where they raised their three children.

JOHN HOLDREN is senior vice president of content and curriculum at K12 Inc., America's largest provider of online education for grades K–12. He lives with his wife and two daughters in Greenwood, Virginia.